Gender and
Peacebuilding

GENDER AND PEACEBUILDING

Claire Duncanson

polity

First published in 2016 by Polity Press

Polity Press
65 Bridge Street
Cambridge CB2 1UR, UK

Polity Press
350 Main Street
Malden, MA 02148, USA

ISBN-13: 978-0-7456-8251-8
ISBN-13: 978-0-7456-8252-5 (pb)

A catalogue record for this book is available from the British Library.

Library of Congress Cataloging-in-Publication Data

Names: Duncanson, Claire, 1974– author.
Title: Gender and peacebuilding / Claire Duncanson.
Description: Cambridge, UK ; Malden, MA : Polity Press, [2016] | Series:
    Gender and global politics | Includes bibliographical references and index.
Identifiers: LCCN 2015027163 | ISBN 9780745682518 (hardcover : alk.
    paper) | ISBN 0745682510 (hardcover : alk. paper) | ISBN
    9780745682525 (pbk. : alk. paper) | ISBN 0745682529 (pbk. : alk.
    paper)
Subjects: LCSH: Women and peace. | Women and human security. |
    Peace-building. | Sex role and globalization. | United Nations. Security
    Council. Resolution 1325.
Classification: LCC JZ5578 .D86 2016 | DDC 327.1/72082–dc23 LC
    record available at http://lccn.loc.gov/2015027163

Typeset in 10.5 on 12pt Sabon
by Toppan Best-set Premedia Limited
Printed and bound in the UK by CPI Group (UK) Ltd, Croydon

For further information on Polity, visit our website: politybooks.com

Contents

Abbreviations

7-PAP	Seven-Point Action Plan of the United Nations Secretary-General on Women, Peace and Security
CEDAW	Convention on the Elimination of Discrimination Against Women
CSOs	civil society organizations
DAW	Division for the Advancement of Women
DCAF	Democratic Control of Armed Forces
DDR	Disarmament, Demobilization and Reintegration
DPKO	Department of Peacekeeping Operations
DRC	Democratic Republic of Congo
EIA	environmental impact assessment
FDI	foreign direct investment
FRY	Federal Republic of Yugoslavia
GBI	gender budget initiative
GDP	gross domestic product
GIA	gender impact assessment
GNWP	Global Network of Women Peacebuilders
GSDRC	Governance and Social Development Resource Centre
ICAN	International Civil Society Action Network
ICTJ	International Centre for Transitional Justice
IDPs	internally displaced persons
IFIs	international financial institutions (IMF, World Bank, etc.)
IMF	International Monetary Fund
INSTRAW	International Research and Training Institute for the Advancement of Women

IPE	international political economy
LGBTQ	lesbian, gay, bisexual, transgender and queer
LNP	Liberian National Police
LRA	Lord's Resistance Army
MONUSCO	United Nations Organization Stabilization Mission in the DRC
NAPs	National Action Plans
NGOs	non-governmental organizations
OECD-DAC	Organization for Economic Cooperation and Development – Development Assistance Committee
OHCHR	Office of the High Commissioner for Human Rights
OSAGI	Office of the Special Adviser on Gender Issues and Advancement of Women
PRDP	Peace, Recovery and Development Plan
PRSPs	Poverty Reduction Strategy Papers
SAPs	Structural Adjustment Programmes
SOEs	state-owned enterprises
SRSG-SVC	Special Representative of the Secretary-General on Sexual Violence in Conflict
SSJ	Social Services Justice
SSR	security sector reform
UN	United Nations
UNDP	United Nations Development Programme
UNIFEM	United Nations Development Fund for Women
UNPBC	United Nations Peacebuilding Commission
UNPFA	United Nations Population Fund
UNSC	United Nations Security Council
UNSCR	United Nations Security Council Resolution
UNSG	United Nations Secretary-General
UNTAC	United Nations Transitional Authority in Cambodia
WACPU	Women and Children Protection Unit (of the LNP in Liberia)
WIB	Women in Black
WILPF	Women's International League for Peace and Freedom
WIPNET	Women in Peacebuilding Network (in Liberia)
WPAs	Women's Protection Advisers
WPS	Women, Peace and Security

Acknowledgements

My sincere thanks go to Louise Knight, Pascal Pocheron, Nekane Tanaka Galdos and Justin Dyer at Polity Press. From the initial conversations about the idea for the book to the meticulous copy-editing, the team at Polity have been fantastic. I also have to thank the two anonymous reviewers, who provided such helpful feedback.

The University of Edinburgh provided a wonderful institutional setting in which to write this book, providing me with a semester sabbatical in 2014 to get the first draft of the manuscript together, and supportive colleagues with whom to share the pleasures and pains of a project of this kind. It is impossible to single out members of Politics and International Relations here at Edinburgh because so many provided encouragement and support.

I have presented some of the material in this book at various conferences, including the United Nations Association of Edinburgh's International Peace conference in October 2014, and the International Studies Association (ISA) Annual Convention in 2015 in New Orleans. I would like to thank the audiences at these events for their excellent questions, and, in particular, Soumita Basu, for her incisive comments on my ISA presentation. Friends and colleagues from the ISA's Feminist Theory and Gender Studies section continue to be a great source of inspiration and insight, and it has been a real pleasure showcasing their work in this book. Two in particular, Synne Lastaad Dyvik and Lauren Greenwood, deserve a huge thank you for reading the entire draft in its early stages, and providing invaluable feedback.

I am lucky to have friends who are not just wonderful but supremely talented. Some have skills that were directly helpful, and here I have to thank in particular Ailsa Bathgate and Megan Bastick, who each read a chapter and provided incredibly useful feedback. Others contributed in ways which were less obvious, but no less important – sustaining me with great food, good chat and long runs – when the writing of this book threatened to overwhelm. Alan, CJ and Martha put up with the stress and the late nights with great forbearance, and I dedicate this book to them.

Introduction

Decades of feminist scholarship have demonstrated that war is gendered in its causes and consequences. From the language and policies of state leaders to the strategies and tactics of armed groups in conflict zones, a gendered ideology is at work privileging confrontational and combative approaches to conflicts of interest. War is also experienced differently by different people depending on their gender, ethnic, sexual and class identities. At the start of 2014, humanitarian organizations appealed for aid to help 52 million people in conflict zones in urgent need of assistance and protection. By the end of the year, the number had gone up by almost 50 per cent to 76 million (UN 2015). Overwhelmingly, these people are civilians, and the majority are women and girls. Wars wrench civilians from their 'everyday productive activities, rites and celebrations and pitch them into states of violent turmoil, confused movement, precarious existence and deep grief unrelieved by the normal symbols of mourning' (Turshen 2015). An increasingly common feature of wars is sexual violence, both that perpetrated by armed groups as a deliberate strategy and as part of a more generalized trend in the context of a conflict-ridden society undergoing socioeconomic stress (True 2012: 126). Sexual violence is more commonly inflicted upon women and girls (Cohen and Nordås 2014: 421). Women are also affected by war in particular ways because of their designated role in nearly all societies as the main carers of the young, the old and the vulnerable – a job made particularly challenging in wartime (Sjoberg 2014: 34–8).

As such, feminists have argued, it is crucial to include women and gendered analyses within attempts to build peace. Peace processes are underway in many conflict-affected areas today, but women and gender analyses are rarely central to these processes. This is despite the extensive architecture that has been built up at the United Nations (UN) to tackle the challenges that women in conflict-affected areas face in building peace, from their exclusion from formal 'Track 1'[1] negotiations to the ongoing insecurities – physical violence and lack of access to basic needs – which undermine their peace-building potential. In October 2000, in recognition of the impact of war on women and the role women could and should be playing to bring about sustainable peace, the United Nations Security Council (UNSC) adopted Resolution 1325 (hereafter 1325), which called for an understanding of gender to be 'mainstreamed' into peace operations. Since then, 1325 has been complemented by a series of further Security Council Resolutions, which strengthen the Women, Peace and Security (WPS) architecture around the '3 Ps': the *protection* of women and girls from gender-based violence in armed conflict, particularly rape and other forms of sexual abuse, and an end to impunity for these crimes; the *participation* of women in all aspects of peacebuilding at every level in national and regional institutions, including in significant posts at the UN itself; and the mainstreaming of gender into mechanisms for the *prevention* of armed conflict. In addition, in 2005 the UN created a Peacebuilding Commission (UNPBC) whose formative resolutions reaffirm 'the important role of women in the prevention and resolution of conflicts and in peace-building...stressing the importance of their equal participation and full involvement in all efforts for the maintenance and promotion of peace and security and the need to increase their role in decision-making with regard to conflict prevention and resolution and peacebuilding' (UNSC 2005: Article 15). More recently, and as a significant boost to the WPS agenda, the Committee on the Elimination of Discrimination Against Women adopted its general recommendation on women in conflict prevention, conflict and post-conflict situations, General Recommendation 30 (CEDAW 2013). By placing the implementation of the Security Council WPS agenda within the broader framework of the implementation of the Convention on the Elimination of Discrimination Against Women (CEDAW), this move provides the steel girders to the architecture that promotes women's rights in conflict prevention, conflict and post-conflict situations.

Fifteen years down the line from 1325, we are now at a crucial juncture from which to assess the difference made by this considerable WPS architecture. Has it enabled feminist activists and women's organizations around the world to realize their visions of peace? In preparation for the Security Council's 15-year-on High-Level Review of the implementation of 1325, the Secretary-General commissioned a Global Study to highlight examples of good practice, implementation gaps and challenges, and priorities for action. Although this book is not linked formally to the High-Level Review and Global Study, its timeliness means it serves as a useful parallel assessment of the WPS architecture, one which is more wide ranging in scope. Its focus is not restricted to *implementation* of the WPS agenda but asks a series of broader questions. Have efforts to build peace in conflict-affected areas around the world created the sort of peace envisioned by feminists? What sort of peace is that? If the WPS agenda is not succeeding, how should feminists proceed? Given that 1325 is a relatively brief document, the product of negotiation, compromise and diplomacy, it does not cover all the goals that feminists might wish for – and the same is true of the subsequent resolutions and institutions. As such, it is important to place 1325 and the WPS agenda in this wider context.

This book thus has two main aims. Firstly, it seeks to map the literature, setting out the various feminist positions on the WPS agenda in ways which should be useful for anyone seeking to understand fully the multifaceted ways gender is relevant to peacebuilding. Secondly, it aims to set the agenda for future feminist scholarship and activism in the field. It argues that there is a need for more feminist focus on the political economy of peacebuilding: specifically, naming neoliberal policies as part of the problem in post-conflict contexts and, more importantly, identifying solutions. I will come back to elaborate on these aims and the particular contributions of the book at the end of this introductory chapter. Firstly, however, as is traditional, here I set out some definitions and background to the key concepts of peacebuilding and gender.

What is peacebuilding?

Peacebuilding can be conceived of in both narrow and broad terms. It can be defined narrowly as the UN's efforts to assist countries recently emerging from conflict and refer to only those operations which the UNPBC currently has on its agenda (Burundi, Sierra Leone, Guinea, Guinea-Bissau, Liberia and the Central African Republic). Indeed, it can be defined as an exclusively post-conflict exercise, beginning only when fighting has stopped (Paris 2004: 39). Alternatively, it can be defined extremely broadly, drawing on the conceptual origins in early conflict resolution theory, as any endeavour aiming to create sustainable peace by addressing the 'root causes' of violent conflict (Galtung 1996; Lederach 1998).

This book takes something of a middle ground, not limiting itself to strictly post-conflict countries on the UNPBC's agenda but also not attempting to cover all attempts to resolve conflict at every level, from community to society to international, around the world. It focuses on cases where the international community has intervened in order to assist states on the path to peace. Along with assessing the role of the UN and the donor community, which includes international financial institutions (IFIs) and governments, it pays close attention to activities at the grassroots in these sites of intervention, and the interaction between initiatives at different levels. As such, the book discusses interventions variously described as post-conflict reconstruction, humanitarian missions, transitional justice, state building, international administrations and peacebuilding missions. International interventions may be either 'post-settlement' (e.g. Burundi) or 'post-invasion' (e.g. Afghanistan) (Paris 2004). Or, indeed, given that the 'post' is often difficult to determine, especially for women, intervention may take place while conflict is ongoing. I adopt a broad definition of the term peacebuilding, discussing all types and phases of international intervention aimed at political, legal, economic and social transformation of a war-torn state, in order to grasp the full range of challenges faced by those seeking peace and an end to gendered inequalities and oppressions.

The international community's focus on peacebuilding resulted from the recognition that one of the flaws of traditional peace*keeping* operations was that they did not address the underlying causes of conflict; nor did they do enough to assist in building the institutions, broadly conceived, which would make peace sustainable. Peace*building* can thus be seen as a more ambitious project than traditional peacekeeping. In his 1992 'Agenda for Peace', then-Secretary-General of the United Nations Boutros Boutros-Ghali insisted that, having overcome the 'immense ideological barrier' that characterized the era of Cold War, the organization must 'stand ready to assist in peacebuilding in its different contexts: rebuilding the institutions and infrastructures of nations torn by civil war and strife; and building bonds of peaceful mutual benefit among nations formerly at war' (UN 1992). That said, there is still much debate as to the extent to which peacebuilding does, and should try to, transform the root causes of conflict (Jarstad and Sisk 2008; Paris and Sisk 2009). Tackling the root causes of war is extremely challenging, especially in the era of 'new wars' (Kaldor 1999, 2012) where, rather than a contest between well-organized states that can at some point negotiate peace, war is now more often a many-sided conflict in fractured or collapsed states that no one appears to have the power to end. Recent scholarship on armed conflict has focused on the particularly challenging phenomenon of war economies, where combatants and criminals use the chaos of conflict in order to fund violence or line their own pockets (Duffield 2001; Pugh et al. 2004; Keen 2012). Meanwhile, others – predominantly women – are left in the 'coping economy', where meeting everyday needs is an ongoing challenge (Peterson 2008; Chinkin and Kaldor 2013). Indeed, given that criminality becomes one of the few avenues open to men and women for survival, the 'combat', 'criminal' and 'coping' economies are very much intertwined (Peterson 2008). These three economies have come to constitute much of the functioning economy in areas of the global South since the 1990s and are a crucial explanatory factor not only in terms of the 'causality, degree and depth of harms experienced by women in post-conflict countries' (Ní Aoláin et al. 2011: 35) but also for the failure to build sustainable peace in so many cases.

To draw on Robert Cox's terminology of 'problem-solving' and 'critical' theories, where problem-solving theories seek to improve the world as it is and critical approaches seek to transcend the existing social and political order, we can divide scholars of peacebuilding into two broad camps. Some scholars see the major challenges of peacebuilding in problem-solving terms. For them, the main obstacles to peace are intransigent individuals in the combat and criminal economies, 'spoilers' who need to be induced to the peace table. These scholars also tend to assume that the international community has benign and altruistic motives in working towards peace, and that the neoliberal reforms imposed as a condition of funding will ultimately enable post-conflict states to grow their economies and emerge as prosperous, democratic and peaceful nations (see, e.g., Chesterman et al. 2004; Marten 2004; Paris 2010).[2] Other scholars see the challenges of peacebuilding in more critical terms, in the Coxian sense. They are more sceptical about the intentions of the IFIs and donor governments who insist on neoliberal reforms as conditions for funding peacebuilding. They argue that neoliberal economic policies undermine prospects for sustainable peace by entrenching the inequalities and violence inherent in war economies (see, e.g., Duffield 2001; Pugh 2005; Kühn and Turner 2012). The assumptions that lie behind the reforms are grounded in the belief that liberalizing the market will be the best route to economic recovery and development – what Roland Paris approvingly terms 'peace-through-liberalization' (Paris 2004: 37). Critical scholars argue that neoliberal policies make multiple demands on countries in the global South to change, to cut state spending and liberalize trade, without questioning the development and trade policies of the North, such as subsidies for agriculture and protectionism, policies which perpetuate poverty and insecurity in the global South (Pugh 2005, 2006).

These critical security scholars acknowledge that the 'liberal peacebuilding' model has shifted over time. They trace in the UN approach to peacebuilding over the 1990s, in reports such as 'In Larger Freedom'[3] (UNGA 2005), which drew largely on 'Investing in Development' (UN Millennium Project 2005), and 'Breaking the Conflict Trap' (World Bank 2003a), an increasing recognition of the need to address the root causes of conflict and the requirement for more 'pro-poor' policies (Cooper 2005; Pugh 2005). Nevertheless, embedded in the texts of these documents are 'assumptions that, taken as a whole, indicate that the liberal peace project is alive and well' (Pugh 2005: 30; see also Pugh 2006). Post-conflict interventions continue to share a set of common assumptions. They largely conform to a fairly standardized model of reconstruction based on the ideology of open markets with small states practising fiscal restraint. As chapter 3 will go on to demonstrate, the 'common-sense' of the neo-liberal demand to cut the state seems always to trump 'pro-poor' development policies, even as it is recognized that post-conflict reconstruction might require higher levels of state spending and intervention. My main point here is that peacebuilding is viewed differently by different camps of scholars – as an altruistic endeavour to enable post-conflict states to provide stability, security and public services to their citizens, or as the latest form of imperialism, whereby power-ful elites maintain their position through reinforcing the hege-mony of neoliberal globalization.

What is gender?

If peacebuilding is a much-contested concept, gender is perhaps even more so. That said, as a starting point, we can usefully think of gender in two senses: as individual identity and as a symbolic system. In terms of individual identity, most feminists argue that gender is socially constructed, rather than determined by biology, and that it is best con-ceived of as a practice, a process, rather than a fixed identity. Our gender identity is formed by how we act in relation to two key things: our physical embodiment and social defini-tions of a man or woman's place in society, which we can conform to, reinforce, resist, subvert, and so on, in a variety of ways (Connell and Pearse 2015). As such, feminist scholars tend to argue that gender is fluid and shifting, although not everyone will experience it as such and many feel their gender identity to be something that is fixed. In terms of gender as a symbolic system, this is also a socially constructed system, one wherein our ideas about gender permeate and shape our ideas about many other aspects of society beyond male–female relations such that we think of certain things as masculine and feminine even when they have no relation to male and female bodies (C. Cohn 2013). We think of war as masculine, peace as feminine; toughness as masculine, weakness as feminine; confrontation as masculine, cooperation as feminine; bravery as masculine, vulnerability as feminine; and so on.

When we are talking about individuals, it is useful to remember that gender as a practice is always being enacted in relation to this symbolic realm (definitions of what is masculine and feminine) and in relation to physical embodiment. Cross-cutting both of these levels, but crucial for our understanding of gender, is the way in which gender is used to structure power relations. Of the dichotomies listed above, the masculine is nearly always privileged over the feminine side of the pairing. Feminists argue that it is as both a cause and consequence of this privileging of the masculine that men dominate as heads of households, heads of state, cultural leaders, and so on (C. Cohn 2013).

The concept of gender is further complicated by the recognition that gender is just one of the many structures of power which influence both our individual identities and the symbolic realm. Race, class and sexuality also come into play such that one's individual identity is constructed and experienced as an intersection of various axes of identity which situate us in various power dynamics, and practices and policies are constructed as superior or inferior depending on their associations with dominant races, classes and sexualities, as well as genders (Crenshaw 1989; Yuval-Davis 2006). Gender is thus a fairly complex concept. It is 'something that is constantly negotiated and renegotiated as we simultaneously engage with our own physical embodiment, participate in social practices, and take up or refuse discursive positions that are enmeshed in a network of power relations whose intricacies are peculiar to our own epoch and culture' (Hooper

2001: 38). Gender is clearly central to peacebuilding, as it is to all areas of global politics, because of the different impact of war on gendered beings, and, equally crucially, because of the way that the symbolic structure of gender influences people, practices and policies that have an impact on peace.

What have feminists had to say about gender and peacebuilding?

Before 2000, the key problem for feminists was the extent to which peace operations were gender-blind. Since the passing of 1325 in October 2000, this blindness has arguably been replaced by a wealth of research, initiatives and subsequent resolutions aiming to mainstream gender into peace operations. Rather than this putting peace operations on a linear path to more gender-sensitive peacebuilding, however, almost every initiative proposed to overcome gender blindness has proved to be fraught with challenges, risks and dilemmas – both theoretical and practical. Does emphasizing the need for protection from sexualized violence in conflict reinforce the idea that women and girls are essentially vulnerable victims? Does it reinforce the idea that sexual violence is the worst thing that can happen to women in war? Does it imply that men and boys do not need protection from the harms of war, including sexualized violence? Does emphasizing the need for women to be at the peace negotiating table reinforce ideas that they are naturally more peaceful than men, with the risk that this undermines their credibility for leadership positions in public life? Does it make women's representation seem more important than representation of peace groups or civil society more broadly? While they only scratch the surface of the issues at stake, it is these dilemmas which make the subject so fascinating, as well as being so vitally important. The journey from gender blindness to gender gaps and gender dilemmas is the subject of chapter 1, which focuses on the historical development of the WPS architecture and feminist assessments of its early years.

Feminist assessments could be said to fall into two broad camps consisting of those feminists who 'seek to understand

and reform the international community's work' and those who 'strive for a more radical reinterpretation of world structure' (Olsson and Gizelis 2013). The former group focus on strengthening the WPS agenda and making sure it is implemented to the benefit of women in conflict-affected countries. This group tends to evaluate progress in terms of the level of participation of women in peace processes (see, e.g., Anderlini 2007, 2010; R. Jenkins and Goetz 2010) and the protection of women and girls from armed conflict, assessing, for example, efforts to prosecute perpetrators of sexual violence in conflict (Nordås and Rustad 2013). Although their work might mention the importance of the economic empowerment of women as part of reconstructing society after violent conflict, it does not tend to discuss neoliberalism as the macroeconomic context of peacebuilding in explicit terms (see, e.g., Gizelis 2009; N. F. Hudson 2009; Tryggestad 2009; Olsson and Gizelis 2013).

Another broad group of feminist scholars are much more sceptical about peacebuilding. Some focus on the risks inherent in seeking to include more women in peacebuilding endeavours because of the assumption seemingly made that women are particularly peaceful or peace loving, viewing this as an essentialist conflation which is as harmful to peace as it is to women (see, e.g., Charlesworth 2008). Some see peacebuilding as a neo-imperial endeavour that is more about making the world safe for neoliberalism than it is about the human rights of people in areas of conflict (see, e.g., Orford 1999, 2003; Whitworth 2004; Richter-Montpetit 2007). For these feminists, drawing on the insights of post-colonial scholars, any inclusion of women or mainstreaming of gender within such a project merely serves to frame exploitative practices (militarism and war, neoliberal economic policies) as progressive. Peacebuilding, in this view, is a paternalist and neoimperial project, based on the assumption that more rational, stronger external countries in the West can and should be able to guide feminized countries in the global South towards peace.

This broad divide does not perfectly replicate Cox's distinction between problem-solving and critical scholars as introduced above. It would be more accurate, I think, to position all feminist scholars on the critical side of the spectrum in terms of wanting to transcend the existing social and political order. Within feminism, the divide is more about how this can be achieved – whether to work as 'insiders' or 'outsiders' (Hawkesworth 2006) in order to transform current political, economic and social structures. As such, it is not that the former group of feminists, those who seek to ensure effective implementation of the WPS agenda, are not critically informed or lack a transformatory agenda. Rather, although they might vary in the degree to which they advocate for transformatory change, they might be termed critically engaged pragmatists, seeking to strengthen the WPS architecture in ways that would further feminist visions of peace.

My position builds on both these broad camps within feminism and demonstrates the potential for synergies and increased collaboration. The latter group of feminists is, I think, right to identify the neoliberal framework as central to explaining the limitations of the WPS agenda. Yet critical feminist scholarship on international interventions has too often focused on *identifying* neoliberalism as the problem and on *detailing* the many ways in which it undermines peace-building work. There is a need for more feminist work which takes neoliberalism as the starting point and attends to how work to enhance the WPS agenda could *challenge* neoliberalism. In this book, I suggest that the most exciting feminist work on peacebuilding (see, e.g., Ní Aoláin et al. 2011; True 2014) does that, but there is room to push this area of scholarship further. Critical feminist scholarship is perhaps too pessimistic about the potential of the WPS agenda to make a difference to the quality of any resulting peace and could engage more in the sophisticated work of those who attempt to grapple with *when* and *how* measures to enhance the protection and the participation of women start to transform structures of inequality in long-lasting ways. At the same time, the feminist scholarship which aims to strengthen the WPS architecture often stops short of naming neoliberal policies as the key factor which prevents progress, and does not consider how to challenge them. What is required is more feminist scholarship on peacebuilding that engages with issues of political economy, naming neoliberal policies as part of the problem in post-conflict contexts and identifying solutions.

Sequence of chapters

One useful way of thinking about gender and peacebuilding was suggested by Jean Munro, a gender specialist at the United Nations Development Programme (UNDP), in an early report on the subject. She outlines three ways in which one might view gender in relation to peacebuilding: gender equality as a *goal*; gender as an *analytical tool* for assessing peacebuilding operations; and gender as an *approach* to peacebuilding (Munro 2000). I use Munro's schema to structure this book, but I develop and refine it in several ways.

Gender equality can be conceptualized as having both material and symbolic dimensions. As such, gender equality entails eradicating both the material disadvantages faced by many women *and* the symbolic subordination of that which is deemed feminine to that which is deemed masculine. Moreover, given the importance of understanding the way that gender intersects with other power structures, gender equality also entails eradicating the material advantages faced by those subordinated by their race, sexuality and class, whether women or men or those who identify otherwise. *Gender equality as a goal of peacebuilding*, then, as I define it in this book, is not just the liberal feminist demand for the inclusion of women in peacebuilding; it is much broader: it is the deconstruction of gendered binaries that structure oppression. Whereas Munro (2000: 4) seems to define gender equality quite narrowly as equal political participation and accepts two possible formulations such that gender equality might be a route to peace or a result of peace, my preference is to see gender equality more broadly defined as part of *what it would mean for a society to be at peace*. The second chapter (following the historical development of the WPS architecture and the feminist assessment of its early years in chapter 1) focuses on this understanding of gender equality and fleshes out how it relates to peace. Women have many insights and an impressive track record in working for peace, but linking pacifism to being a woman is a strategy fraught with risks, potentially preventing both being taken seriously. This chapter discusses this dilemma and asks whether feminist visions of peace are always 'essentialist', positioning women as 'naturally' more peaceful, and whether they exclude men as important actors for peace. It expands on feminist visions of peace, arguing that feminist peace is inclusive, expansive and transformative. Most importantly, it explores how neo-liberal economic policies are hostile to feminist visions of peace, and suggests that challenging neoliberalism must be a central and more explicit part of the WPS agenda.

When considering *gender as an analytical tool*, Munro (2000: 3) suggests that 'Gender analysis can bring to light the experiences of men and women during conflict and peace, assess needs, and show how gender relations change during and due to conflict and peace.' It thus means enquiring as to the extent to which conflict impacts differently on men and women, and to the different needs of men and women in conflict and post-conflict situations. In this book, however, I do not just consider how conflict or peacebuilding operations *impact on men and women*, but also pay attention to how gender structures both war and the peacebuilding project. In this way, gender can be an even more useful tool, one which enables us to see how the world is 'pervasively shaped by gender meanings' (Peterson 1992: 8–9). The third chapter demonstrates what gender as an analytical tool can bring to our understanding of peacebuilding. As outlined above, many feminists share with other critical security scholars concerns about the in-built assumptions of the donor community regarding the necessity of neoliberal economic reforms as part of the peacebuilding package. Feminist scholars shed light in particular on the gendered nature of these assumptions and their gendered consequences. Neoliberal economic models, for example, tend to involve cuts to the very services that women are particularly reliant upon because of their desig-nated caring role in society. This chapter thus engages in more detail with the feminist critique of peacebuilding outlined in previous chapters, which argues that even with – or, for some, particularly as a result of – the WPS agenda, peacebuilding constitutes a form of neo-imperialism, not necessarily entail-ing the conquering of new lands or extraction of resources, but primarily focused on making the world safe for the spread of neoliberal markets. The chapter illustrates the arguments with three peacebuilding interventions: Mozambique, Bosnia-Herzegovina and Afghanistan.

For Munro, *gender as an approach to peacebuilding* incorporates 'gender equality concerns in programming and policy-making as well as supporting initiatives for men and women to participate in decision making at different levels' (Munro 2000: 2). This definition is useful but could be extended to consider not just how men and women participate in decision-making but also how people of various intersecting identities can participate in peacebuilding more broadly. The fourth chapter considers this question, and in so doing assesses the extent to which current peacebuilding efforts have overcome the problems, dilemmas and obstacles outlined in previous chapters. More specifically, it asks if current efforts to engender peacebuilding are taking us towards the feminist vision of peace outlined in chapter 2, and, crucially, if they are addressing the neoliberal underpinnings of mainstream peacebuilding outlined in chapter 3 in any significant way. Most feminists have long argued that the project of engendering something is about more than *adding women* to previously male-dominated institutions. It is about recognizing gendered inequalities and trying to challenge them. It involves reconstructing masculinities (and femininities) and transforming the unequal relations between elite men and women and other subordinated groups. This chapter considers how the extant WPS architecture is achieving this more thoroughgoing and transformative understanding of engendering peacebuilding as a feminist project. Taking protection, participation and prevention in turn, it considers peacebuilding in the Democratic Republic of Congo (DRC), Syria, Burundi, Liberia and beyond, in order to assess the extent to which current peacebuilding efforts have overcome the gaps and dilemmas outlined in previous chapters.

The fifth chapter focuses on what is required in order to capitalize on the gains and overcome the obstacles discussed in the previous two chapters and to realize the peace discussed in chapter 2. It builds on the work of scholars such as Jacqui True (2013, 2014) and Fionnuala Ní Aoláin, Dina Francesca Haynes and Naomi Cahn (2011), who advocate a new approach to peacebuilding which places women's economic empowerment at its centre. The chapter details the way in which the most recent developments in the UN WPS agenda pay more attention to the importance of the economic and social rights of women in peacebuilding. It draws on the example of peacebuilding in Uganda in order to highlight both the potential and the missed opportunities of an economic empowerment approach. The chapter concludes by suggesting areas for future feminist research and advocacy which could inform a challenge to the neoliberal model of post-conflict reconstruction.

This structure, based on three different ways in which gender is relevant to peacebuilding, is a useful way of mapping the extensive feminist literature on the subject. It enables us to consider a variety of different issues and debates, from more theoretical discussions about the definition of peace to more practical concerns about achieving it. It is also useful because it enables me to pursue the main argument of this book, which is that a new approach to the challenge of engendering peacebuilding is required. Many feminist discussions of gender and peacebuilding follow a similar format. They consider the UN's good intentions and the potential gains to be made by including women in peace processes and post-conflict parliaments but conclude by making the argument that these gains are undermined by the neoliberal structures of the global economy (see, e.g., Whitworth 2004; Enloe 2007; C. Cohn 2008; L. J. Shepherd 2008; Pratt and Richter-Devroe 2011; H. Hudson 2012b; Nesiah 2013). I argue that feminist theorizing needs to start from where these arguments conclude: the neoliberal structure of the global economy. A useful feminist starting point would be: given that the neoliberal prescriptions of the donor community undermine peace and security especially for women and other marginalized groups, how can efforts to engender peacebuilding start to challenge neoliberalism? The WPS agenda could usefully address how a focus on women's social and economic rights can go beyond income generation to alter power relations within society. Strategies to achieve this would involve more lobbying of the UNSC to move away from a conception of the WPS agenda as being about women and 'women's issues' and to recognize that the WPS agenda is about assessing every post-conflict reconstruction and development project in terms of its impact on local and global gendered power relations. With this requirement in mind, this book deals with the feminist critique of neoliberalism from the outset and moves in chapters 4 and 5 to considering how feminist efforts to engender peacebuilding can begin to challenge it.

The book's main contributions, then, are, firstly, a mapping of the field, a delineation of the various feminist positions on the WPS agenda and peacebuilding more broadly. It provides this in a way that is attentive to the chronological development of the WPS architecture, so as to assess progress in the field and progression in the debates. It draws on up-to-the-minute evidence of the efforts to build peace from conflict-affected countries around the world and feminist assessments of them. As such, it provides a useful critical summary of the state of the field for established scholars and feminist peace activists and newcomers alike. Secondly, by considering how efforts to engender peacebuilding can amount to a challenge to the current global political-economic framework, it aims to set the agenda for future feminist scholarship and activism in the field of gender and peacebuilding.

Questions for discussion

1   What is peacebuilding? What are the differences between problem-solving approaches and critical approaches to peacebuilding?

2   What is gender? In what ways is gender relevant to peacebuilding? What is an intersectional approach and what difference does adopting one make to what we consider when we study peacebuilding?

3   What are the aims of 1325? What are the '3 Ps'?

Suggestions for further reading

Saram Naraghi Anderlini, 2007. *Women Building Peace: What They Do, Why It Matters.* Boulder, CO: Lynne Rienner *Drawing upon wide-ranging work in conflict zones and at policy-making institutions, Anderlini provides a rich and detailed account of women striving to engage in peace processes, presenting a compelling picture of the need for women's inclusion if there is to be genuine peace.*

Cynthia Cockburn and Dubravka Zarkov, eds. 2002. *The Postwar Moment: Militaries, Masculinities and International Peacekeeping.* London: Lawrence and Wishart.
An early work on post-conflict peacebuilding, focused on the Balkans, but still relevant, with excellent contributions from a variety of feminist scholars and activists.

Carol Cohn, ed. 2013. *Women and Wars.* Cambridge: Polity.
Provides clear evidence of the need for feminist lenses when studying war and peace. Covers all the ways that women experience war: as fighters, as refugees, as peace activists, as civilians. Includes an introduction by Cohn which conveys brilliantly the complex and multidimensional concept of gender and how it is relevant to war and peace, and an excellent chapter by Malathi de Alwis, Julie Mertus, and Tazreena Sajjad on women and peace processes.

Raewyn Connell and Rebecca Pearse. 2015. *Gender: In World Perspective.* Third edition. Cambridge: Polity.
One of the best introductions to gender around. Clear and accessible, but still sophisticated, it offers a compelling synthesis of social constructivist and poststructuralist accounts of gender. Though not addressing peacebuilding directly, this book conveys the multidimensional and dynamic character of gender relations.

Hudson, Natalie Florea. 2009. *Gender, Human Security and the United Nations: Security Language as a Political Framework for Women.* New York: Routledge.
In this book, Hudson offers a useful account of women's activism in the UN system and their efforts to achieve 1325. It subjects the goals and strategies of the global women's movement to critical scrutiny, and considers how women have both come to embrace and been impacted by the dominant security framework of the UN.

Web resources

The Global Network of Women Peacebuilders (GNWP: *http://www.gnwp.org/*)
The GNWP, a programme of the International Civil Society Action Network (ICAN), is an important women's organization monitoring the WPS agenda. It is a coalition of women's groups and other civil society organizations from around the world – mostly in conflict-affected countries – that are involved in advocacy for and action in support of the full and effective implementation of the WPS agenda.

The Institute for Inclusive Security (*http://www.inclusivesecu rity.org/*)
The Institute for Inclusive Security supports policy-makers by providing expert advice grounded in research that demonstrates women's contributions to peacebuilding. It works all round the world but focuses on five countries (Afghanistan, Pakistan, South Sudan, Sudan and Syria); the website is full of in-depth knowledge and expertise on women, peace and security in these contexts.

PeaceWomen (*http://www.peacewomen.org/*)
PeaceWomen is a programme of the Women's International League for Peace and Freedom (WILPF), the longest-standing women's peace organization in the world. Founded in 2000, PeaceWomen monitors, informs and advocates for women's rights and participation in conflict situations and promotes gender analysis in conflict prevention. It focuses in particular on monitoring the WPS agenda, and thus this site provides a wealth of important information on the effectiveness of the WPS resolutions, building in views from civil society and women's organizations around the world.

UN Women (*http://www.unwomen.org/en/what-we-do/peace-and-security*)
UN Women is the United Nations Entity for Gender Equality and the Empowerment of Women, created in 2010 by merging four previously distinct parts of the UN system: the Division for the Advancement of Women (DAW), International

Research and Training Institute for the Advancement of Women (INSTRAW), Office of the Special Adviser on Gender Issues and Advancement of Women (OSAGI) and the United Nations Development Fund for Women (UNIFEM). As part of its broad agenda for women's empowerment, it focuses on peace and security issues so it is the key UN entity pushing the WPS agenda. This page introduces UN Women's Peace and Security work, and also links to the six WPS United Nation Security Resolutions (UNSCRs).

UN Women Sourcebook on Women Peace and Security (*http://www.unwomen.org/en/digital-library/publications/2012/10/un-women-sourcebook-on-women-peace-and-security*)
This online 'sourcebook' is a collection of papers which aim to support improved implementation of the five WPS resolutions. It is a very useful starting point for up-to-date analysis of the WPS architecture and its impact. Made up of topic-specific expert contributions, it explains gender issues in a number of peace and security areas, and also acts as guidance material to support operational work.

1
Peacebuilding: From Gender Blindness to Gender Dilemmas

This chapter outlines the historical development of gender issues in peacebuilding. It makes the argument that peace operations were to a large extent gender-blind throughout the post-Cold War period and through the 1990s, but that this is arguably no longer the case. Since the UN World Conference on Women in Beijing in 1995, there has been a raft of initiatives, reports and UNSCRs which have attempted to engender peacebuilding. Almost every new initiative or remedy suggested for ensuring attention to gender, however, has generated a new dilemma or challenge for feminists and peace activists, either theoretical or practical, or both. In this chapter I outline the problems of gender-blind peace operations, introducing 1325 as the founding resolution of the WPS architecture at the UN. I also review the initial feminist responses to 1325, which include disappointment and scepticism, which I categorize into concerns over problems of conceptualization, problems of implementation and problems of ambition.[1] Overall, I suggest that peace operations have journeyed from the gender blindness of the twentieth century to a number of gender gaps and gender dilemmas. The remainder of the book takes up these current gaps and dilemmas; this chapter's account of feminist reactions to 1325 in its first decade enables us to understand their origins.

Peace operations pre-2000: the pitfalls of gender blindness

There are several ways in which peace operations pre-1325 failed to advance feminist visions of peace and security. All could be said to stem from a failure of analysis – that is, a failure to understand the gendered nature of war. Peace operations were blind to the way that war *impacts* on men and women differently, the way that it is *experienced* differently by men and women, and, finally, the way that *gender as a relational power dynamic underpins and sustains the war system*. This section briefly elaborates on these three elements of the gendered nature of war, before discussing the interrelated ways in which the failure of the UN and other actors to engage with this reality prevented peace operations from responding effectively to violent conflicts.

Until the passage of 1325 in 2000, gender-disaggregated data on war were almost non-existent, so it is hard to be certain about the extent to which war impacted on men and women differently in terms of suffering death and injury. Nonetheless, feminists have systematically exposed the myth that women were safe on some 'home front' whilst men alone were bravely facing death on the battlefield (Meintjes et al. 2001; Moser and Clark 2001; Turshen and Twagiramariya 2001; Giles and Hyndman 2004; Mazurana et al. 2005). Women have always been at risk in war: as civilians and refugees, perhaps increasingly so in 'new wars', wherein civilians are often directly targeted (Kaldor 2012); and as combatants, a position women have held in almost every war in history (Jones 1997; Kennedy-Pipe 2000; Turshen and Twagiramariya 2001). Recent studies of the available data on gender-disaggregated deaths in war concludes that men are more likely to die during conflict, whereas women die more often of indirect causes after the conflict is over (Plümper et al. 2006; Ormhaug et al. 2009), reinforcing Joshua Goldstein's finding that 'both genders lose in war, although they lose in somewhat different ways' (Goldstein 2001: 402).

Some threats seem to affect women disproportionately, such as conflict-related sexual violence. In Rwanda, between

100,000 and 250,000 women were raped during the three months of genocide in 1994, and UN agencies estimate that more than 60,000 women were raped during the civil war in Sierra Leone (1991–2002), more than 40,000 in Liberia (1989–2003), up to 60,000 in the former Yugoslavia (1992–5) and at least 200,000 in the DRC since 1998 (UN 2014a). Rape can result in unwanted pregnancies, sexually transmitted infections and stigmatization. Meeting the needs of survivors – including medical care, HIV treatment, psychological support, economic assistance and legal redress – is extraordinarily challenging in wartime. Refugees and internally displaced persons (IDPs) are particularly at risk. It is thought that the number of women suffering from some form of sexual violence rose to over 80 per cent in camps for refugees and IDPs resulting from the wars in Sierra Leone and Liberia (Goetz and Anderson 2008: 2). Sexual violence against men and boys is increasingly acknowledged also to have been a feature of many conflicts. In this related form of gender-based violence, predominantly male perpetrators target men and boys of the opposing side as a means of humiliating them through violent subordination and emasculation (Allison 2007; Sivakumaran 2010). Here we see the intersection of race, ethnicity and sexuality with gender, as powerful structures which are drawn upon and reinforced in war.

As well as direct physical violence, 'structural violence', peace scholar Johan Galtung's (1969) term for the denial of basic needs, is an important aspect of war's gendered impacts. Wars cause and exacerbate poverty and inequality through the destruction of livelihoods, infrastructure and communities. Research into the political economy of war zones has identified three overlapping and interrelated economies (Pugh et al. 2004), in which women are rarely the main profit-makers or power-holders (Peterson 2008; Chinkin and Kaldor 2013).[2] Combat economies emerge in war to directly supply and fund fighters and insurgent activities. They are dominated by armed groups and their political supporters and thus predominantly (though not wholly) by men. Soldiers loot, kidnap, smuggle, manipulate aid and expropriate natural resources in order to raise the money to fund their battles. Closely related criminal economies emerge that directly and indirectly supply and fund conflict activities. Here, the agents are primarily motivated by profit-seeking, opportunities which are enhanced in conflict zones as regulatory mechanisms break down, and centralized control is weakened by war, political divisions and/or extensive corruption. The key agents involved are both men and women, but mostly the former. They include petty criminals, conflict entrepreneurs, war profiteers, traffickers, money launderers and those who produce and/or transport trafficked goods. Women are involved, in part, because this economy overlaps with the coping economy as individuals and households pursue illicit activities as an often unavoidable survival strategy. The coping economy encompasses people trying to meet their survival needs in conflict conditions where social stability and traditional livelihoods have been disrupted. It is primarily women who are assigned, and assume, responsibility for sustaining families, households and even neighbourhoods. Moreover, the increase in female-headed households in post-conflict contexts exacerbates the pressures on women to generate coping strategies. Such strategies thus rely increasingly on informal and often illicit activities, including dealing in black market goods; selling organs for transplant; engaging in sex work and debt bondage; and participating in potentially lucrative but high-risk criminal activities (Peterson 2008; also see Justino et al. 2012; Chinkin and Kaldor 2013; Raven-Roberts 2013).

Their participation in these war economies demonstrates that women cannot be thought of only as victims in war; they are actively involved in negotiating survival within and often for their communities. Indeed, women are also often to be found working to facilitate peace and reconciliation at the grassroots (Cockburn 1998; Anderlini 2007; Porter 2007). Women can be victims, perpetrators, survivors and peacebuilders, and these roles are not mutually exclusive (Ní Aoláin et al. 2011: 45). Nonetheless, it is important to note war's devastating impacts on women, particularly women of marginalized races, ethnicities and sexualities, and poor women – in terms of both direct physical violence and indirect structural violence. Indeed, the two are connected with feminist scholars demonstrating how social and economic inequalities increase the likelihood of physical violence, including sexual violence in conflict (True 2012).

This understanding of the links between physical and structural violence links to the second point, which is that war tends to be *experienced* in different ways by women and men. For women, particularly marginalized women, violence may not cease even when there is an end to the fighting between combatants in public spaces. Evidence from post-war situations in every corner of the globe indicates that women face both a continuation of the aggression endured during the war and new forms of violence (Cockburn and Zarkov 2002a; Rehn and Johnson Sirleaf 2002; C. Cohn 2013). Rape continues after war, perpetrated by former combatants and state security forces, who can be both strangers and/or partners (Rehn and Johnson Sirleaf 2002; Pankhurst 2007, 2008). There is also evidence to suggest that domestic violence increases (Sørensen 1998; Meintjes et al. 2001; Rehn and Johnson Sirleaf 2002; Pankhurst 2007). Studies in Cambodia in the mid-1990s indicated that as many as 75 per cent of women were victims of domestic violence, often at the hands of men who had kept the small arms and light weapons they used during the war (Rehn and Johnson Sirleaf 2002: 15). In the coping economy, women are often forced to sell sex for survival (Pankhurst 2007; True 2012). In sum, there is much evidence to suggest that 'while the guns are silent, or the machetes temporarily laid aside, cultural, domestic and structural violence remain' (Vlachová and Biason 2005). Again, the way war is experienced differently for women is not just in terms of direct violence, but also due to the roles women often have as primary carers for the old, the young and the vulnerable. As Christine Chinkin notes, while 'the forms and locations of gendered violence change at the cessation of active conflict, women's relations with war-traumatized children, family members or fighters will placed gendered demands on them' (Chinkin 2003a: 11). For Chinkin, 'post-conflict' is a misnomer: war is rarely over for women in the 'post-conflict' phase.

Feminists have also drawn attention to the role of gender in *driving and sustaining* war. There is a mutually reinforcing relationship between militarism, an ideology which legitimizes violent solutions to conflict and disorder, and patriarchy, an ideology which legitimizes the domination of men over women (Enloe 1993; Cockburn 2007, 2010). Militarism relies on the acceptance of patriarchal notions of masculinity and femininity in order to make militarized responses to conflict appear legitimate, normal or even inevitable. These ideas position men and militaries as endowed with strength, rationality and the ability to use force, and position women and femininities as vulnerable, in need of protection. The gender ideology underpinning war relies on complementary femininities, that is, those that endorse hegemonic masculinity and that assume passivity, vulnerability and irrationality to be an essential part of what it is to be a woman. In this gender order, it appears natural or inevitable that the response to disagreements should be to empower the 'Just Warriors' – the men who protect the weak and vulnerable 'Beautiful Souls' (see Elshtain 1982, 1987) – to exercise authority and use force. As Kimberly Theidon writes: 'Constructing certain forms of masculinity is not incidental to militarism; rather, it is essential to its maintenance. Militarism requires a sustaining gender ideology as much as it needs guns and bullets' (Theidon 2009: 3).

All three of these aspects of conflict zones – the gendered impacts of war, the gendered experiences of war and the gendered drivers of war – were not thought particularly relevant by the UN Security Council before 2000.[3] This blindspot arguably prevented peacekeeping operations from responding effectively to conflicts in many ways. These can be grouped together under three broad headings, although many of the problems are interrelated and overlapping. The first is the way peace operations failed to recognize gender-based violence; the second is the way they failed to recognize and build on women's peacebuilding work; and the third is the way they failed to recognize the nature and extent of the gendered harms of war economies.

Sexual violence in conflict: 'history's greatest silence'

Named by Zainab Bangura, UN Special Representative on Sexual Violence in Conflict, as 'one of history's greatest silences and the least condemned war crime',[4] sexual violence has long devastated the lives and livelihoods of millions of people and threatens collective peace and security. Despite its prevalence and the devastating consequences, outlined above, it tended to be ignored in peace operations before 1325. Over and above the moral and legal grounds for addressing sexual violence, Robert Jenkins and Anne Marie Goetz point to three reasons why failure to address sexual violence undermines peacebuilding. First of all, given that the effectiveness of sexual violence as a tactic of war derives from its ability to destroy the fabric of families and communities, peace operations which do not engage with it cannot support communities in their rebuilding efforts. Secondly, peace operations which fail to establish security so that women, particularly in rural areas, can get to market, or girls get to school, will seriously undermine a post-conflict country's development prospects. Thirdly, the 'delicate process' of instilling a culture of respect for the rule of law is jeopardized when sexual violence in conflict is treated with impunity, resulting in a loss of faith in security services and the government at large. People become less willing to pay taxes and participate in civic life, weakening the prospects for the restoration of effective state authority, let alone accountable governance (R. Jenkins and Goetz 2010: 263–6).

As such, Jenkins and Goetz argue, addressing sexual violence in peace agreements is essential, so that peacekeepers can be trained to detect, prevent and/or respond to it; prosecutors can be instructed to prioritize cases against suspected perpetrators; policy-makers can be charged with designing and administering reparations programmes which tackle sexual violence; and recovery programmes can tend to the specific needs of survivors. Yet parties to conflict rarely raised, let alone prioritized, sexual violence in peace negotiations, and it was rarely mentioned in peace agreements pre-2000 (R. Jenkins and Goetz 2010: 262). In some cases, there was a pervasive sense of denial because both government and rebel fighters had committed sexual violence, creating a strong incentive for all parties to engage in a mutually beneficial conspiracy of silence.[5] Mediators sometimes assumed that sexual violence was a minor issue, and probably an unavoidable, if unfortunate, by-product of war, 'destined to wane when a deal is struck and conflict ends' (R. Jenkins and Goetz 2010: 263).

Indeed, some UN personnel perpetrated sexual violence, abuse or exploitation themselves. Evidence of UN personnel involvement in sexual exploitation exists for almost every UN peace operation of the 1990s (Al-Hussein 2005; Martin 2005; Higate 2007). In their comprehensive survey of the impact of armed conflict on women, Elizabeth Rehn and Ellen Johnson Sirleaf found the association of the arrival of peacekeeping personnel and increased prostitution, sexual exploitation and HIV/AIDS infection to be 'perhaps the most disturbing of everything we saw and learned' (Rehn and Johnson Sirleaf 2002: 61). Rehn and Johnson Sirleaf found evidence of thousands of girls under the age of 16 working as prostitutes, starving families selling their daughters into prostitution, and UN staff – military and civilian – demanding sexual relations with women they employed as domestic workers. They also indicated the devastating consequences of such sexual exploitation: after the operation is over, women who are sex workers or have had relationships with UN personnel are often ostracized by their communities and left to bring up the children of such relationships alone – children who are stigmatized, who are rejected by family and community and who grow up in poverty. Although some internationals established more permanent intimate connections with local women, such relationships could rarely be considered purely voluntary, Rehn and Johnson Sirleaf (2002) argued, as they were often entered into by the women in order to obtain food, housing or jobs.

Women's organizations that tried to tackle the problem of UN personnel using prostitutes repeatedly came up against an attitude that accepted without question a soldier's 'need' for sex (Rees 2002; Higate 2004). For example, Madeleine Rees, head of the Sarajevo office for the UN Office of the High Commissioner for Human Rights (OHCHR) from 1998 to 2006, wrote: 'There is this whole boys-will-be-boys attitude about men visiting brothels. There is a culture inside the UN where you can't criticize it. That goes all the way to the top' (cited in Hipkins 2003). Yusushi Akashi, the United Nations Transitional Authority in Cambodia (UNTAC) head, used the same 'boys-will-be-boys' line to respond to reports of sexual exploitation by the UN there (Martin 2005: 4). Richard Holbrooke, the US Assistant Secretary of State and chief negotiator in the Balkans, reportedly made the comment that 'Human nature is human nature. Where peacekeepers go they attract prostitutes' (cited in Mazurana 2005: 34; also see Mendelson 2005).

The perpetration of sexual violence by military personnel suggested that particular constructions of militarized masculinity needed to be addressed if UN peace operations were to avoid increasing insecurity for women. Indeed, many feminists argued that there was a contradiction inherent in international armed peace operations: the idea that those who are trained in combat and the protection of nation and territory could be used to create peace (Cockburn and Zarkov 2002b; Higate and Henry 2004: 484; Whitworth 2004: 3). Noting that, as a peacekeeper, a soldier is supposed to be altruistic, neutral and capable of conflict resolution in any cultural setting, but that military training and culture are predominantly about learning to be tough, to dehumanize the enemy and to be able to apply overwhelming force, Sandra Whitworth contended that 'the messages that a soldier receives about appropriately masculine soldierly behaviour are fundamentally at odds with what is then expected in a peace operation' (Whitworth 2004: 9). The claim that soldiers are inherently unsuitable for peacekeeping operations was reinforced by research which suggested that they were at best ambivalent about their peacekeeping role (Miller and Moskos 1995; Miller 1997; Segal and Tiggle 1997; Enloe 2000; Razack 2004; Whitworth 2004: 150).

Women as peacemakers: ignoring women's work and neglecting women's potential   The second gender blindspot of pre-1325 peacekeeping operations concerns the potential of women as peacemakers. Despite their informal, community-based contributions to conflict resolution, women were almost never included in formal peace processes (R. Jenkins and Goetz 2010: 262). They were excluded in both deliberate and more subtle, indirect ways. Women suffered from the fact that as they were not the main belligerents or spoilers in peace processes, they were given little attention. In the Arusha peace talks in the late 1990s, for example, Burundian men argued that there was no need for women at the peace table, arguing that, as they could represent women perfectly well themselves, women should go home and bring up their children (Puechguirbal 2005: 5). From the Balkans to Burundi and beyond, there tended to be a focus on ensuring the inclusion of people on the basis of one specific kind of identity – ethno-national – and this worked against the inclusion of women (Byrne and McCulloch 2012: 575). Both local men and international intervening men colluded in this exclusion, viewing women either as irrelevant, or as a group which could be sacrificed in order to stay focused on the important parties (the parties to conflict) or out of 'respect' for local culture, assumed to be inherently patriarchal (Potter 2005; Anderlini 2007; Olonisakin et al. 2011). This 'tyranny of the urgent' move – gender issues can only be discussed after 'more urgent' issues to do with ending the conflict have been settled – is of course familiar to feminists working for change in a variety of contexts where ostensibly progressive groups make unfounded assumptions about women's 'proper roles' or fear gender issues might divide support at a crucial time (Berger 2003).

In peace processes before 1325, there was little interrogation of the masculinities driving war. Instead, male elites arrived to facilitate peace processes between male belligerents – often with their own gender norms and patriarchal behaviours, which, despite cultural differences, bore comparison with the patriarchal views of internal elites – which operated to exclude, silence or nullify women's needs (Ní Aoláin et al. 2011). As a result, not only was an important resource for peace and security overlooked, but women's needs were also often systematically ignored and even deliberately marginalized in post-war peacebuilding efforts (Corrin 2000; Pankhurst 2000; Meintjes et al. 2001; Anderlini 2007; El-Bushra 2007; de Alwis et al. 2013). This exclusion of women from peace processes helps explain why sexual violence was 'history's greatest silence': in peace talks, 'men with guns forgive other men with guns for crimes against women' (Don Steinberg of USAID, cited in R. Jenkins and Goetz 2010: 262). The exclusion of women also led to other important omissions. Examples from Guatemala, Northern Ireland and South Africa indicate that when women are included in peace processes, they bring different sorts of issues to the peace table (Anderlini 2000; Chinkin 2003b; Anderlini and Stanski 2004: 25; Anderlini 2007; de Langis 2011; UN Women 2012b). The key difference can be summed up as an attentiveness to everyday needs, such as food, shelter and livelihoods. This has been suggested to amount to a redefinition or broadening of security to include the provision of material needs as well as freedom from violence (Porter 2007; Ní Aoláin et al. 2011), and will be discussed further in the next chapter.

Failure to realize the gendered impacts of war econo-mies – and policy prescriptions which exacerbate the problems   The third key problem with gender-blind peace operations was that the policies and practices aimed at recon-struction and rebuilding society often ignored women's needs, or pushed women back into traditional subordinate roles (Goldstein 2001; Meintjes et al. 2001; Justino et al. 2012; Jacobson 2013). Gender-blind peace operations rarely recog-nized the gendered nature of the three war economies out-lined above. It is normal in 'post-conflict' to find women heavily represented in the most marginalized sections of society: widows, orphans, rape survivors and disabled people – those with the fewest resources and often the least well trained and educated (Sørensen 1998). 'Transformed house-holds' – households newly headed by a woman, either a widow or caring for a disabled or wounded husband – increase dramatically. The welfare of these households in the post-conflict period is largely determined by the existence of pre-existing gender norms, such as whether women have the rights to own land or property, to travel independently, to speak in public meetings or even simply to appear in mixed settings (Jacobson 2013). Women, especially those who are returning refugees and IDPs, also have particular health needs, partly because of their reproductive roles, partly because may have experienced sexual or other violence and partly because of their roles as prime carers for the young, old and vulnerable. Gender-blind peace operations failed to notice the particular needs of women in the coping economy, and also failed to recognize the particular challenges for many women as the criminal economy in which they may have engaged to survive was challenged by the peace process.

Peacebuilding interventions rarely offered enough support, such as training, education and grants, to support women – with all these particular caring responsibilities and health needs – to achieve sustainable livelihoods. Moreover, they rarely paid attention to the crucial issue of women's rights and access to land, which is a central factor in explaining their relative lack of wealth, security and opportunities. Instead, gender-blind interventions focused on a standard recipe of macroeconomic reforms, including cuts to state services, privatization of state-owned enterprises (SOEs) and the liberalization of trade, a set of policies which actively undermined the potential for women's economic empowerment in post-conflict contexts (as I shall go on to detail in chapter 3). If there were reparations as part of the peace process, they also tended to be gender-blind, exacerbating these economic problems for women.

Disarmament, Demobilization and Reintegration (DDR) programmes are a crucial part of peace operations. As they involve disarming combatants, demobilizing them from their armed groups and reintegrating them into civilian society by supporting them to get jobs and by addressing health needs, they have the potential to demilitarize society and deconstruct militarized masculinities in ways which could be transformative for women and gender equality. Yet pre-1325 peace operations often exacerbated the problems faced by women and girls in situations of conflict through the inappropriate design and implementation of DDR programmes (see, e.g., Douglas et al. 2004; Coulter 2009; MacKenzie 2009, 2012; Mazurana and Cole 2013). Gender-blind peace operations tended to assume that women and girls, if they were thought of at all, were solely victims of war. As a result, female combatants or women who played key support roles did not get the assistance that male combatants received. They often had to fit back into narrowly defined pre-war gender roles, without the support that male combatants received to get longer-term or more rewarding jobs. This also left unresolved any trauma or injury resulting from the conflict. Moreover, opportunities were rarely taken to address masculinities as drivers of conflict. Gender-blind DDR programmes thus often reinforced existing gender inequalities in local communities.

The impacts of the macroeconomic and DDR policies encouraged by the international institutions often coincided with what Donna Pankhurst (2007, 2008) and others have identified as a backlash against women, common in post-conflict contests. Women can be targeted for having gained economic independence from men, for having been employed in male roles, for having adopted urban and educated life-styles in rural societies – leading to calls for them to be forced 'back' into kitchens and fields, even if they were not occupied in such occupations before war. In post-conflict contexts, the state often intervenes in gender politics to the benefit of men – enforcing controls over women's sexuality, failing to ensure women's security and imposing legal restrictions on women's movement, access to housing, jobs, property and land (Rehn and Johnson Sirleaf 2002; Pankhurst 2008). In the Balkans, for example, women's rights to abortion were reduced after the war, compounding the harm of rape (Zarkov 2007). This backlash can be manifested both as spontaneous reactions of individual men or orchestrated by governments– either way, it constitutes forceful, often violent, attempts to define women's roles and rights as secondary to men and to restrict women's behaviour. Gender-blind peace operations did little to anticipate or address this backlash.

By the mid-1990s, peace operations were increasingly sub-jected to these interrelated criticisms from feminist scholars and activists. Feminists were not merely critiquing from the side-lines, however, but were actively campaigning for change in the UN's approach to peace and security. Such advocacy work resulted in a range of measures, including, most signifi-cantly, the adoption of 1325 on Women, Peace and Security on 31 October 2000. The next section turns to 1325 and feminist responses to it, characterizing the transition it brought about in peace operations as being one from gender blindness to gender gaps and gender dilemmas.

UNSCR 1325: a new era of peacebuilding?

UNSCR 1325 calls for international security institutions to address the impact of conflict on women, and to engage women fully in conflict resolution, peacekeeping and peace-building, thus addressing many of the problems discussed in the previous section. Building on the peace activism of women at Beijing in 1995, the largest UN conference ever organized, and the subsequent fears that its energy was failing to have an impact on peace or women's rights on the ground, a group of non-governmental organizations (NGOs) launched an appeal for a Security Council resolution that would formally recognize women's right to participate in peace and security issues and to protection in conflict zones (Anderlini 2000: 6). For many feminists and women's organizations, 1325 represented a 'watershed' – providing a 'critical legal and political framework through which, for the first time in history, women worldwide can claim their space and voice their views on peace and security matters' (Anderlini 2007; also see Cockburn 2007; Reilly 2007; C. Cohn 2008; Tryggestad 2009).

As with all Security Council resolutions, 1325 is binding on all UN member states and other UN entities, creating a range of obligations for national and international actors. It prompted considerable activity in the years following its adoption. The UN Department for Peacekeeping Operations (DPKO) published a Gender Resource Package for Peacekeeping Operations (2004) and a Global Action Plan (2006) which contained concrete policy guidance on gender equality, provided operational support to guide gender mainstreaming and set goals of equal proportions of men and women both at headquarters and in the field. Women's organizations began translating 1325 into various languages, enabling it to be used by women's groups in every continent; states began adopting National Action Plans (NAPs) to facilitate implementation; and many more developments were initiated, as this book goes on to describe. Before doing so, however, I turn to detailing the different ways that feminists have responded to 1325, as it is these concerns that we need to understand in order to assess if more recent additions to the WPS architecture are likely to facilitate sustainable peace and security for all.

It was not long before the high hopes generated by the adoption of 1325 in 2000 had largely been replaced by cynicism amongst feminists, including those instrumental in its genesis (Cockburn 2011). The criticisms of 1325 which emerged over the first decade can be categorized into three broad areas: 'problems of conceptualization' – how gender is articulated in the resolution; 'problems of implementation'– the extent to which the resolution is applied in order to make a difference to women (and sometimes – more specifically – 'gender equality') on the ground; and 'problems of ambition'

– the extent to which the resolution addresses the main barriers to feminist visions of peace.

Problems of conceptualization A major problem with 1325 for many feminists is the way in which, in attempting to highlight the suffering of women during armed conflict and the contributions they often make to peace, it risks essentializing them by positioning them in either of two categories: victim or peacemaker. Many early feminist responses to 1325 argued that the focus on the need to protect women from sexualized violence in the resolution had the unfortunate side-effect of reinforcing the positioning of women as essentially vulnerable and weak (Otto 2009; Puechguirbal 2010a; de Alwis et al. 2013: 177). Although acknowledging the need to address sexual violence, feminists argued that the emphasis in the text on women's need for protection makes women the 'metaphor for vulnerable/victim in war', at the risk of obscuring their agency (Charlesworth 2005: 358). This framing of women does not reflect the complex patterns of gendered agency and harms found in war, which have been outlined above.

Some feminists also responded with concern to the sections of 1325 which stress women's agency – that is, its commitments to support women's participation – arguing that it risked falling into another trap, that of cementing the association between women and peace (Otto 2006; El-Bushra 2007; Charlesworth 2008; C. Cohn 2008; Peterson and Runyan 2010; 243–4; H. Hudson 2012b; de Alwis et al. 2013). This will be discussed further in the next chapter, but, in brief, the claim is that, as with essentializing women as victims, this latter representation of women, as having natural and special abilities for peace, limits our understandings of what women are and do. Feminist scholars argue that women tend to become engaged in peace activities not because of their peaceful natures but as a response to a desperate situation caused by conflict and displacement. The idea that women are somehow predisposed to be peaceful and are naturally gifted as peacebuilders presents a one-dimensional view of their lives. Moreover, basing women's inclusion at the peace table on their supposed natural expertise is for some to include them because of their 'use-value', rather than because it is their right, as equals, to participate in matters of security (C. Cohn et al. 2004; Charlesworth 2008). As Dianne Otto put it: 'If women are admitted [to peace processes] on the understanding that their special contribution arises from their womanly instincts, it follows that their political agency will be limited to what is made possible by that representation and restricted to "feminized" tasks' (Otto 2006: 139), such as caring and compromising. Here Otto is drawing on extensive feminist scholarship which has pointed out that the association of women with peace and moral superiority has 'a long history of keeping women out of power.... Not only are these stereotypes damaging to women, particularly to their credibility as actors in matters of international politics and national security, but they are also damaging to peace' (Tickner 1999: 4; also see Sylvester 1987; Elshtain 1990; Enloe 2002: 23). For not only does the positioning of women as *natural* peacemakers ignore women's agency, their deliberate and risky work to build peace and/or the violence they have perpetrated in wars, feminists argue, it also implies men are naturally or inherently violent. As we saw above, most feminists argue that men are not naturally violent and wars are not the result of naturally violent men. Rather, masculinity and femininity are socially constructed, with masculinity linked in discourse and reinforced through practice and social sanction to the role of the warrior, and it is this gender ideology which has a key role in driving war.

A related and underpinning problem for some feminists is that in 1325 gender is used as a synonym for women, implying that gender is a fixed, objective fact about a person (Vayrynen 2004; Charlesworth 2008; L. J. Shepherd 2008; Willett 2010; H. Hudson 2012b). Thus, for some feminists, through the 'productive discursive power' of its framings, 1325 produces certain types of masculinities and femininities, normalizing binaries and fixed ideas about gender practices (Vayrynen 2010;). This risks undermining the central feminist goal of exposing the social construction and the performative aspects of gender, which not only better capture reality, but open up the possibility of change, of more fluid gender identities and more equal gender relations (Baden and Goetz 1997; Charlesworth 2008). Associating gender exclusively with women allows problems facing women to be understood as the product of particular cultures or a matter of a lack of information, skills or opportunities, rather than the way gender is produced and reproduced through structures of subordination. This dynamic and relational understanding of gender is argued by some feminists to be neglected in 1325, resulting in all the focus being on women, rather than men, masculinities and militarism. Laura J. Shepherd argues that even the stress on *gender equality* is problematic, as it, too, assumes difference, thereby obscuring the discursive mechanisms through which difference is produced (L. J. Shepherd 2008: 131). Particularly problematic for many feminists is the way difference is produced as a binary structure – constructing people into male and female – when reality is more complex. Moreover, the way gender has been conceptualized in 1325 is said to neglect the intersectional analysis so important to feminist theorists, especially from marginalized groups.

Critiques which have focused on the risks of essentialism and binary thinking in 1325 are met with impatience by some feminists, however (see the discussion in C. Cohn et al. 2004). Feminists involved in UN or NGO work to reduce the impact of armed conflict on women and to get more women involved in peace processes have expressed frustration with what seems like abstract theorizing about gender in the face of very real violence and oppression faced by women on the ground in conflict zones, and the obstacles they face not just to get to the peace table but to be heard once there. These feminists tended, in their early reactions to 1325, to focus more on the obstacles to implementation than the problems of conceptualization in the resolution itself.

Problems of implementation   In 2007, Sanam Naraghi Anderlini wryly noted that as a result of 1325, the international community had clearly begun to take notice of women, but that, as the pendulum swung between its extremes, from women as vulnerable victims to women as peacemaking panacea, the rhetoric goes further than any action to support women (Anderlini 2007: 1). She, along with many others (Grady 2010; Jennings 2010; Kanetake 2010; Aroussi 2011), noted that, despite the focus on protection in 1325, sexual abuse was still not adequately addressed in the years following its adoption, especially in refugee camps, and that UN personnel continued to be implicated in the perpetration of sexual exploitation. Many feminists pointed to the problem of political will, arguing that states did not put their money and energy behind the resolution (Whitworth 2004; Puechguirbal 2010b; Willett 2010; Irvine 2013; Olsson and Gizelis 2013). There was no immediate increase in prosecutions, and the establishment of courts did not devote adequate attention to the experience of giving evidence, causing concern to many feminists (Ní Aoláin et al. 2011: 19). The limited nature of gender training for peacekeepers (Peterson and Runyan 2010; Puechguirbal 2010b), one of the measures identified as crucial for tackling sexual violence (Mackay 2005), was another key problem. States were also clearly reluctant to prosecute their own nationals in instances when, as part of a UN operation, they were accused of sexual exploitation (Aoi et al. 2007). Other problems with the protection pillar identified by feminists in the first decade of 1325 included the lack of resources and measures for ratification, compliance and verification; lack of leadership, which meant that no one was accountable in terms of implementation or results; and the lack of resources provided to gender advisers and units who were tasked with protecting civilians from sexual and other violence (Whitworth 2004: 131; Swaine 2009; Puechguirbal 2010b; Willett 2010).

The lack of progress led to subsequent UNSCRs on sexual violence. In 2008, UNSCR 1820 was adopted, which reasserted the need to protect women from sexualized violence in conflict and asserted zero tolerance of sexual exploitation and abuse perpetrated by UN DPKO personnel. A further resolution, 1888 in 2009, created the office of the Special Representative of the Secretary-General on Sexual Violence in Conflict (SRSG-SVC), the creation of UN Action Against Sexual Violence in Conflict[6] and the appointment of Women's Protection Advisers (WPAs) to field missions. These initiatives, and further subsequent resolutions, will be discussed further in the following chapters, but here the point is to note how such developments generated dilemmas for feminists. On the one hand, they increase the likelihood that sexual violence will be documented and prosecuted, and that survivors will have access to services. On the other, some argue that these subsequent resolutions reinforce a UN focus on sexual violence in conflict which is problematic. As well as the risks of reinscribing women as victims and the silencing of male victims discussed above, the focus on the 'extraordinary' violence of conflict risks detracting from 'ordinary' gender-based violence experienced by women and some men. Moreover, it potentially detracts from other insecurities more keenly felt by some, both women and men, in war, such as the loss of a child, separation from children, witnessing harm to children or other loved ones, which 'are felt by many women as harms to the self, more egregious than severe violation of their own bodies' (Ní Aoláin et al. 2011: 47). Although this is a concern which has come to the fore in more recent years, already in the early critiques of 1325 some feminists were drawing attention to the risks of isolating and highlighting sexual violence in conflict as an issue and focusing on the prosecution of perpetrators as the main policy response.

Turning now to consider 1325's second pillar, participation, a key aim was to increase the number of women in all aspects of building peace, including, crucially, as mediators and representatives in the all-important formal peace negotiations. The current situation will be discussed in chapter 4, but, again, initial assessments were not wholly positive. Whilst some pointed to early signs that 1325 was empowering women in areas of conflict throughout the world (see especially C . Cohn 2004), others were more sceptical. Christine Chinkin and Hilary Charlesworth (2006) concluded that the expertise that typically exists in local woman's communities continued to be ignored in peace negotiations, and attributed this to the lack of enforcement mechanisms behind 1325. Noting that when Kofi Annan left office, of his 18 special representatives in conflict areas, none were women, Anderlini argued that despite 1325, when it came to the participation of women in peace processes, the UN continued to suffer from the 'Triple-A' syndrome: apathy, *ad hoc* practices and amnesia (Anderlini 2007: 212). The early evidence seemed to demonstrate that rhetoric about women's contribution to peace was not enough to overcome the obstacles to their participation at the peace table, highlighted above. International negotiators continued to privilege belligerents and ethno-national identities when deciding who needed to be at the peace table. Male participants persisted in resisting the participation of women (H. Hudson 2012b; UN Women 2012b: 1–2). Congolese officials, for example, argued in the run-up to the Sun City peace talks in 2002 that 'war and peace are exclusively the business of men', and that 'women have no right [to participate] as they were not fighters' (Mpoumou 2004: 122).

Some suggest that 1325 may have had the unintended effect of making it harder for women to be included. The fact that the UN was calling for the participation of women enabled local male elites to resist the calls as 'neo-imperial influence', Western elites pushing their ideas about feminism onto the rest of the world. Malathi de Alwis and her co-authors note the irony in the way that women's groups thus suffered because they could be portrayed both as a 'foreign import, a bourgeois elite, unconnected to their country-women' and as being 'no different, so men can easily represent them' (de Alwis et al. 2013). Many feminists argued that UN did not do enough to enable women to get to the peace table, to overcome the practical barriers as well as the prejudice. Women are often busy both surviving and taking care of extended families, making participation in formal peace processes dependent upon support to facilitate their presence (Puechguirbal 2010b: 170). Many also suggest that 1325 failed to pay enough attention to the way women are treated when they are actually around the table, where various norms and strategies are used to marginalize their activities and ideas (Olsson and Gizelis 2013; also see C. Bell 2004; de Alwis et al. 2013: 186).

UNSCR 1325 called for the participation of women in all aspects of peacebuilding, which implies not just formal peace talks but also post-conflict parliaments. Here, feminists note that 1325 seemed to make a difference, helping in the diffusion of an international norm of women's political inclusion, and resulting in an increase in women in parliaments in many post-conflict countries (Hughes and Tripp 2015). Yet they argued that progress was not fast enough (Hughes 2009). Moreover, many were concerned that the formal gain of parliamentary representation does little to enhance women's social and economic standing in society (Ní Aoláin et al. 2011). It seemed that few structural assessments were made as to whether quotas for parliament would actually provide local women with voice, agency and power commensurate with men. Although quotas are important, Fionnuala Ní Aoláin and her co-authors argue that 'attention to women's participation in government must not begin and end with electoral reform. Such a myopic approach fails to see and address the broader site of social, customary and familiar limitations that operate to constrain women's participation in the public sphere' (Ní Aoláin et al. 2011: 236).

Overall, then, many feminists were frustrated with the slow progress in the first decade after 1325. Even for those feminists who were not overly concerned about the risks of essentialism in the conceptualization of gender in the resolution, the lack of resources, political will, accountability and enforcement measures combined to mute the impact of the 'breakthrough' resolution. For another group of feminists, furthermore, 'beneath the failures of these formal mechanisms lie more insidious processes' (Peterson and Runyan 2010: 174). The project of mainstreaming gender into peacebuilding represented by 1325 disregarded 'such sources of structural violence as neo-colonial economic and political relationships and neoliberal economic restructuring that may lie at the heart of the conflict' (Peterson and Runyan 2010: 175; also see Whitworth 2004: 133). As such, the most problematic aspect of 1325 for some feminists could be termed its lack of ambition.

Problems of ambition   Although 1325 is often described as consisting of the '3 Ps', many feminists commenting on the first decade since 1325 argued that the third P had been relatively neglected (Confortini and Basu 2011), and that if serious attention were to be given to the *prevention* of armed conflict, it would become evident that more fundamental issues to do with neoliberal economic structures would need to be addressed by the WPS architecture. As the introduction outlined, peace operations are funded by donors who advocate certain macroeconomic policies for conflict-affected states. Many feminists argue that these neoliberal economic policies make sustainable peace and gender equality impossible, as they exacerbate inequalities (Elson 2002; Benería 2003). Moreover, neoliberalism privileges a certain way of being in the world, *homo economicus*, which ensures that it is predominantly white men who can retain power, wealth and opportunities.

In line with many critical security studies scholars, feminists argue that neoliberal policies are particularly unsuitable for post-conflict contexts, where the imposition of such policies onto weak institutional foundations allows elites to profit through abusing inadequate safeguards and laws and the corrupt appropriation of international aid (Klein 2008; Suhrke 2011). The intervention in Afghanistan, for example, was committed to private sector growth with little attention paid to the way this approach favoured big business, military power-holders and the informal and illicit players of the war economies, and disadvantaged the women producers on the bottom rungs of the social ladder (Kandiyoti 2007b: 192). The power asymmetries in society that are exacerbated by neoliberal reforms, especially if they map onto the warring parties, then make it harder to achieve peace, as women have found in a variety of settings, for example in Palestine (Richter-Devroe 2009; Farr 2011) and Iraq (Gibbings 2011), especially so in contexts where elites benefit from the continuation of conflict and the opportunities it provides for further privatization and appropriation of international aid (Keen 2012). Critical feminist scholars, who aim to demonstrate the way in which weapons manufacturers, construction companies and the armed forces of powerful Western countries – the military-industrial complex – work in alliance to profit from both conflict and post-conflict reconstruction, thus found 1325 to be extremely limited in its ambitions (e.g. Cockburn 2011; Enloe 2007).

Many of the assessments of 1325 at the time of its tenth anniversary highlighted this lack of ambition as the fundamental problem with the resolution and the WPS architecture in general: the provisions of 1325, such as laws to protect women against sexual violence and efforts to include them in peace processes and parliaments, did not help women tackle structural factors such as neoliberalism, which were the underlying cause of their insecurity (Irvine 2013).

In addition, the focus on women's needs, strengths and potential for peace did little to place the reconstruction of masculinities firmly on the agenda as central to peacebuilding; 1325 says little in relation to men and masculinity, their relationship to militarism and war (Cockburn 2007; Charlesworth 2008). Indeed, what many feminists find particularly galling about post-1325 interventions is the way rhetoric about women's rights has been used to justify interventions, thus, they argue, distracting attention from the role of neoliberal macroeconomic policies in fuelling conflict and undermining peacebuilding. Feminists point to the way that women's rights as an issue has often become hyper-politicized, such as debates over the extent to which one should intervene in 'traditional' gender relations, whilst other elements of the peacebuilding package, such as economic liberalization, private sector-led growth and democratic governance, are taken as given (Kandiyoti 2007b: 194). Focusing on how 'others' treat 'their' women not only diverts attention away from sex inequality closer to home, but, crucially, 'exoticizes Third World Women in ways that put the spotlight on cultural restrictions while obscuring other restrictions and obstacles these women face' (Volpp 2001).

Much of the critique of 1325 in its first decade became bound up in critiques of the War on Terror, with many feminists focusing not so much on implementation of 1325 as on the discursive constructions of various gendered identities (barbaric Muslim men, Afghan women as victims, Westerners as civilized humanitarians, etc.) identified in the texts of 1325 and associated resolutions (see, e.g., L. J Shepherd 2008; Pratt 2013). This theorizing raises a dilemma for feminists, as it does not lead to obvious strategies for action – usually a central concern of feminists – in the way a focus on implementation does. Moreover, as many feminist critics of 1325 in its early years were all too aware, to condemn 1325 for its lack of ambition was to criticize one of the few tools on offer for improving the lives of women and girls in areas of conflict. Thus, the move from gender blindness in peace operations represented by the adoption of 1325 has not been a simple tale of linear progress. Rather, as I suggested at the outset of this chapter, with the passing of 1325, the UN moved from gender blindness to a set of implementation gaps, conceptualization challenges and difficult dilemmas. The rest of the book will assess the extent to which the gender gaps and dilemmas discussed in this chapter have been overcome by the development of what is arguably a much stronger WPS architecture, which includes 1325's supporting resolutions, the UN Secretary-General's 'Seven-Point Action Plan' (7-PAP), the UNPBC's commitment to gender, and CEDAW's General Recommendation 30. Of course, it is hard to evaluate success without clarifying what feminists see as the goal of peace-building, so before we turn to the current state of play, it is important first to establish what feminists mean when they talk of peace.

Questions for discussion

1   In what ways and with what consequences were peace-building operations gender-blind before 1325 was adopted in 2000?

2   How did feminists respond to 1325? Which responses do you think are most compelling? Why? What are the implications – theoretical and practical – of the different feminist critiques of 1325?

3   This chapter argues that the WPS agenda generates as many dilemmas as solutions. What are these dilemmas? How could they be resolved?

Suggestions for further reading

Hilary Charlesworth. 2008. 'Are Women Peaceful? Reflections on the Role of Women in Peace-Building'. *Feminist Legal Studies* 16 (3): 347–61.
In this article, Charlesworth critically interrogates the associations between women and peace that she believes are made by the UN WPS agenda, the problem of conceptualization discussed in this chapter. Drawing on empirical evidence from Bougainville, Timor-Leste and the Solomon Islands, she questions whether women are the biggest victims in war, and the source and implications of the claim that they have a special contribution to make to peacebuilding.

Carol Cohn. 2008. 'Mainstreaming Gender in UN Security Policy: A Path to Political Transformation?' In *Global*

Governance: Feminist Perspectives, edited by Shirin Rai and Georgina Waylen. Basingstoke: Palgrave Macmillan.
Informed and insightful account of the successes and limitations of the WPS agenda in the early years. Based on interviews with many of the key women's activists involved in lobbying the UNSC for 1325, Cohn's essay presents a nuanced position recognizing both the promise and the limitations of the WPS architecture.

Carol Cohn, Helen Kinsella and Sheri Gibbings. 2004. 'Women, Peace and Security'. *International Feminist Journal of Politics* 6 (1): 130–40.
This write-up of a conversation between three feminist academics and three feminist activists provides interesting insights into the dilemmas and challenges generated for women's organizations when trying to engage the UN and advocate for a Security Council resolution on Women, Peace and Security.

Sandra Whitworth. 2004. *Men, Militarism and UN Peacekeeping: A Gendered Analysis.* Boulder, CO: Lynne Rienner.
This provocative book on militarized masculinities within UN peacekeeping contains one of the first feminist critiques of 1325, and one that focuses on the problems of implementation and ambition introduced in this chapter. Whitworth argues that with the adoption of 1325, the UN has transformed gender analysis into a series of checklists – number of women peacekeepers, number of mentions of gender in UN missions, and so on – robbing gender analysis of its tranformative potential.

Susan Willett. 2010. 'Introduction: Security Council Resolution 1325: Assessing the Impact on Women, Peace and Security'. *International Peacekeeping* 17 (2): 142–58.
This is an introduction to a special issue of the journal International Peacekeeping *published on the tenth anniversary of 1325, which contains a number of interesting articles worth reading. This introduction typifies the feminist assessment around the 10-year mark: fairly frustrated with the lack of progress on all three of the Ps – protection, participation and prevention.*

Web resources

Conciliation Resources (*http://www.c-r.org/theme-page/gender*)
Conciliation Resources is a peacebuilding organization which works with people in areas of conflict to create opportunities for them to resolve their differences peacefully. The link is to their gender work, which aims to challenge and extend the WPS agenda.

International Alert (*http://www.international-alert.org/blog/new-approach-gender-peacebuilding*)
This blog introduces peacebuilding organization International Alert's important intervention in gender and peacebuilding work: an approach which is more attentive to the intersections of gender, race, class and sexualities than many WPS interventions. It links to a report which focuses on four thematic areas: access to justice, economic recovery, intergenerational conflict and continuums of violence, drawing from field research in Burundi, Colombia, Nepal and Uganda. It aims to demonstrate how the gender, peace and security agenda can practically implement a 'relational' approach to gender.

Saferworld (*http://www.saferworld.org.uk/resources/view-resource/862-masculinities-conflict-and-peacebuilding-perspectives-on-men-through-a-gender-lens*)
Saferworld is a peacebuilding organization which works with local communities and conducts research on peacebuilding issues. The link is to an excellent recent report on masculinities and peacebuilding which demonstrates the importance of the WPS agenda being attentive to masculinities.

Women, Peace and Security Academic Collective (*https://wpsac.wordpress.com/*)
The idea behind this collective of Australian-based academics was to consolidate and extend academic feminist efforts around the UN's WPS agenda for the duration of Australia's term on the UNSC, which was from 2013 to 2014, but the site remains relevant. It contains a rich resource of recent

academic perspectives on the WPS agenda. The collective's mission was not only to advance this agenda but also to extend and challenge it, with the overall objective of using feminist analyses to end violence and militarism at home and abroad.

2
Feminist Visions of Peace

This chapter focuses on how feminists define and envision peace. It is more conceptual than the previous chapter, covering feminist debates about the nature of peace, its relationship to gender equality – in its broadest sense, that is, not just equal treatment of women but the eradication of gendered hierarchies – and how it can be achieved. The chapter thus picks up on Munro's idea that one link between gender and peacebuilding is gender equality as the goal of peacebuilding. Indeed, for many feminists, peace has to *include* gender equality, but cannot stop at that. It has to include a form of gender equality which is beyond liberal feminist ideas of equal treatment, and encompasses the eradication of gendered hierarchies and oppressions. The first part of this chapter considers the debates highlighted in the previous chapter about the risks of essentialism in any attempt to discuss women's role in achieving peace. Feminist women have many insights and an impressive track record in working for peace, but linking pacifism to womanhood is a strategy fraught with risks, potentially preventing both peace and women being taken seriously. This part discusses this dilemma and asks whether feminist visions of peace are always essentialist. The second part fleshes out feminist visions of peace, arguing that feminist peace is inclusive, expansive and transformative. It explores how neoliberal economic policies tend to be antithetical to feminist visions of peace and suggests that although it is not always explicit in feminist theorizing about peace, challenging neoliberalism must be a central part of feminist strategies for peace.

Feminism and pacifism

Feminist women's engagement with pacifism has a long history and includes efforts to prevent the outbreak of the First World War at the Hague Conference in 1915, protesting against nuclear weapons at Greenham Common in the 1980s and opposing the Israeli occupation of Palestine as Women in Black today. This has led to a strong association between feminism and pacifism in many cultures, but the connection raises a number of questions. Are women more peaceful? If so, how? Most feminists think the reasons for women's peace activism lie in the social construction of gender, rather than being rooted in women's biology or any natural predispositions. This has not meant an end to the discussions, however, as feminists have continued to debate whether, how and with what consequences women have come to be associated with peace. This debate is of course part of larger and older feminist conversations about whether, to what extent, how and with what consequences women resemble or differ from men (Confortini 2012: 9).

One common line of argument is that the association of women with peace comes from the evidence that so many women are engaged as peace activists in their own communities (Anderlini 2007; Cockburn 1998, 2007; Porter 2007; de Alwis et al. 2013). Many of these women testify that their motivation is the suffering that they have endured in conflict, or the suffering that they witness through their frequent position as carers for other groups: children, the elderly, people who are sick or disabled. Some feminists have gone further and theorized that this caring role is crucial in explaining not just why women would become peace activists, but also why they might have particular skills and aptitudes for peace work. Sara Ruddick is perhaps the most influential of these theorists. Her *Maternal Thinking: Toward a Politics of Peace* (1989a) argued that the work that women often do in the day-to-day caring for infants was just the sort of work that is necessary in peacebuilding: negotiation, compromise, endurance, patience and fairness. She did not argue that only mothers engaged in such practices, or that mothers found such practices came naturally; she suggested that anyone could and should practise 'maternal thinking' (Ruddick 1983, 1989a, 1989b).

Some female peace activists use a mixture of these arguments to explain why they mobilize as women for peace. From her interviews with more than sixty women's groups for *From Where We Stand: War, Women's Activism and Feminist Analysis* (2007), Cynthia Cockburn identifies three main reasons for their decision to organize as women, and to organize separately from men. Firstly, they wanted to bring greater prominence to the particular suffering of women in war; secondly, reacting to the experience of male-led peace movements, some wanted to develop alternative leadership styles and activist methods; thirdly, they wanted to develop a feminist analysis of war, to build on the insight that the gender ideology that associates masculinity with militarism, in both aggressive and protective guises, and femininity with vulnerability, is a crucial driver of war. With regard to this last reason, Cockburn argues that women peace activists are developing a particular 'standpoint' position on war and conflict. Just as in Marxist thought the working-class standpoint could reveal truths about capitalist society unavailable to the ruling class, so women's lives, different systematically and structurally from those of men, make available a particular vantage point on the 'institutions and ideology that constitute the capitalist form of patriarchy' (Hartsock 1985: 231). For Cockburn (2007, 2010), the feminist standpoint position on war enriches the understanding of peace movements as it reveals the way in which patriarchal gender relations intertwine with capitalism and nationalism in order to drive war. The following description of groups that have developed a feminist standpoint position in order to protest against war draw on her account.

Women in Black (WIB) began in Israel, when peace activists on the left began to think about how to present their opposition to the Israeli occupation of Palestine around the time of the first Intifada in 1987. Taking inspiration from the Argentinian Mothers of the Plaza de Mayo, who silently parade around the Plaza holding photos of their sons who were 'disappeared' during the Dirty War which lasted from 1976 to 1983, and the South African women's Black Sash movement, in which white South African women wore black sashes to visibly declare their opposition to apartheid and their support for black South Africans, they stood in silent protest with signs bearing the words 'End the Occupation'. This practice of women-only silent vigils against war and occupation has since spread all over the world, to at least 300 locations in 30 different countries by 2006 (Cockburn 2007: 52). Many WIB groups have stayed focused on the Israeli occupation, but more recently, many groups have felt driven to mobilize against US/Western war policies. Members attest to the strength they get from knowing they are part of a worldwide women's movement, with a carefully thought-out feminist analysis of the role of patriarchy in sustaining violence and war (Cockburn 2007: 49).

Code Pink is another women's initiative against war, with different tactics but a similar feminist analysis at its core. It was formed in 2002 as a reaction to the impact of the NATO invasion of Afghanistan on civilians, especially women, and the male elites driving both terrorism and the war against it. A small number of American women decided to respond to the simultaneous 'terrorizing' of US civilians through the 'Code Red' clampdowns on civil liberties by launching an alternative 'Code Pink', heading to Washington DC on Vietnam Veteran's Memorial Day in October 2002 to protest the imminent war in Iraq by sporting pink gowns and placards stating 'Support the Vets, Stop the War!' They then embarked on a series of activities which disrupted politics-as-usual in dramatic ways, deploying symbols of femininity such as pink underwear and pink medals in order to draw attention to the gendered ideology behind war, and to advance a particularly feminist message of peace (Cockburn 2007).

Code Pink drew some of its inspiration from the Greenham Common camp in the UK, formed by a group of mostly British women who embarked on a peace march to the Berkshire Royal Air Force base where the UK and US governments had decided to position nuclear weapons and then proceeded to camp there throughout the 1980s. The Greenham Women chained themselves to fences, to which they also attached symbols of femininity and motherhood, such as pictures of their children, teddy bears and baby clothes. They deliberately chose these symbols to legitimize their protest on the basis of their role as mothers to safeguard the planet for their children and future generations, and to declare a specifically feminist analysis of the wrongs of nuclear weapons (Liddington 2005).

Perhaps the best-known explicitly feminist peace movement is one of the oldest, the Women's International League for Peace and Freedom (WILPF) (Cockburn 2007; Confortini 2012). WILPF grew out of a conference instigated by a group of European women as a reaction to the First World War. The Congress of Women was attended by 1,136 delegates from twelve countries: Germany and Austria as well as the allied nations. The congress established an International Women's Committee for Permanent Peace, but its call for a conference of neutral nations to mediate between the belligerent states was ignored. In May 1919, not long after the armistice, women from both the winning and losing side in the war held a second congress to coincide with the meeting of statesmen at Versailles to draft the peace treaty. As the details of the post-war settlement emerged from Versailles, the women's congress issued resolutions strongly criticizing its punitive terms, which they correctly foresaw would lead to poverty and starvation in the defeated countries and give rise to more national hatred and a renewal of war. Again they were ignored, with consequences that are now well known, but they decided to form an organization dedicated to long-term advocacy for peace: WILPF. By the mid-1920s, the organization had 50,000 members in forty countries (Cockburn 2007). More of a formal organization than WIB, Code Pink or the Greenham Common women, it has had consultative status at the UN through the Economic and Social Council since 1948. WILPF was one of the central organizations to advocate for 1325.

Women of all races, cultures and locations have been known to be peace activists. In Somalia, a society said to be made up of five major ethnic clans, women formed a network known as 'The Sixth Clan'. It grew out of a group of women with cross-clan marriages who were ostracized by their own communities and frustrated by their exclusion from peace talks after the devastating impact of war. They explicitly drew on their identity as women in order to mobilize for peace, claiming their clan to be womanhood, the only identity that did not appear to lead to rejection (see Rehn and Johnson Sirleaf 2002: 78; Porter 2007; de Alwis et al. 2013). In 2003, Liberian Women's Mass Action for Peace staged non-violent protests, launched a 'sex-strike' and blockaded the formal peace talks until agreement was reached (Disney 2008). Other examples include the US organization Women Strike for Peace, who pushed their babies in their buggies into city halls and federal buildings to protest nuclear testing in the 1960s; the Committee of Soldiers' Mothers of Russia, or Materinskoe Serdise ('Mother's Heart'), who, angered at the loss of their sons' lives to an unpopular war in Afghanistan, used their maternal authority to question the Soviet state (Enloe 1993: 9–12); and the women in the All-Manipur Social Reform and Development Samaj, who responded to the rape of a young Manipuri girl by soldiers in the Indian Army by adopting a collective position as mothers of the raped girl, and challenging the soldiers to rape them too by taking their clothes off in front of the army headquarters (de Alwis et al. 2013: 175).

Some feminists are wary of claiming that women have any particular knowledge or skills to bring to peacebuilding (see, e.g., Sylvester 1987; Tickner 1992). Amongst these feminists, some see space for 'strategic essentialism' (Spivak 1988) – mobilizing the stereotypes that others have about women's natural skills in order to advance peace. Thus, the political mobilization of motherhood in the examples above may represent an effective tactic rather than an assumption that women are naturally more peaceful. As well as using their role as mothers strategically in order to give their demands and protests moral legitimacy, women's groups may sometimes use the stereotypes about their peaceful nature in order to resolve conflict. The suggestion is that, given that many believe that women have a pacifying presence – around the peace table, as members of security forces or as parliamentarians – this can then become something of a self-fulfilling prophecy. As male participants in a peace process may think of women as non-threatening, more cooperative, more likely to be working towards reconciliation, for example, they react differently to them than they would to other men, also adopting more conciliatory approaches. Perceptions thus become reality. Likewise, as local male populations may perceive women peacekeepers to be less threatening than their male counterparts, they may respond more positively to measures to calm violence (see, e.g., the arguments in Olsson et al. 2004). While there is a lack of abundant evidence to support this, in part this is because of the difficulty of establishing the truth about how perceptions of women have made people act in any conclusive sense. Lack of evidence does not thus totally undermine the claim that some sort of self-fulfilling prophecy can fuel women's effectiveness at peacemaking, leading many to see engaging *as women* an important strategy for peace.

Other feminists, as we saw in the previous chapter, argue that even 'strategic' essentialism is a strategy fraught with risk, as the association between women and peace inevitably leads to the devaluation of both. As Ann Tickner puts it, the 'association of femininity with peace lends support to an idealized masculinity that depends on constructing women as passive victims in need of protection. It also contributes to the claim that women are naïve in matters relating to international politics' (Tickner 1992: 59). Similarly, Judy El-Bushra argues that '[t]he problem is that women's role as mothers provides them with a platform on which to approach and appeal to powerful men, but it simultaneously under-mines their desire to be taken seriously as political players' (El-Bushra 2007, 140; also see Sylvester 1987). This position-ing of women as naïve acts to bar not only women, but also *approaches to conflict which are seen as feminine* – that is, compromise, cooperation and conciliation – from interna-tional relations. Carol Cohn (1987) shows how such prac-tices are coded as feminine and thus rendered inappropriate in the discourse of nuclear strategists, where to express com-passion, empathy or even just awareness of the concrete consequences of nuclear weapons is discrediting and humili-ating. Another pioneer of feminist thinking about war and peace, Jean Bethke Elshtain, agrees that the key problem with the association of women with peace is that it has 'served as the collective projection of a pure and peaceful Other against which a violent male is constructed', the gender ideology described in the preceding chapters. She terms it a 'nasty historic bargain' which allows women to remain removed from the fray while 'boys will be boys'. In other words, any feminist project which presents women as integral to peace 'winds up endorsing – indeed requiring – that which they would oppose' (Elshtain 1982: 342).

It is important to bear in mind these different reasons which lie behind women's association with peace. On one level one could ask 'Who cares? Why does it matter?' and agree to put the reasons behind the link to one side in order to get on with the job in hand: building an inclusive peace. On another level, however, if women's peace activism reinforces ideas of gender difference, that is, that women have particular skills and abilities for peace, it may well undermine long-term aims of a peace which includes gender justice. The following discussion of one particular influential school of thought concerning gender and peace illustrates the problems of assuming and reinforcing gender difference. Suffice it to say here that this is why the issue has remained a dilemma for so long, arguably the central dilemma of feminism: if we mobilize *as women* for change, do we cement the very identity – and the idea of fixed identities – that we have identified as part of the problem? It explains why the conceptualization of women as peacebuilders in 1325 and the other UNSCRs is so troublesome for so many feminists.

An influential argument that has emerged in recent years is that presented by Valerie Hudson and her co-authors (2012) in *Sex and World Peace*. In this work, the authors seek to demonstrate that gender equality is necessary for peace, a formulation which is subtly different from the one argued for in this chapter – that peace has to include the eradication of gendered hierarchies and oppressions. The authors argue that one of the best but overlooked predictors of a state's propensity for war or peace is the level of violence against women within the state. In their analysis, the authors test data on gender equality compiled by the WomenStats Project against indicators of state peacefulness. Gender in this approach is a fixed or at least relatively stable attribute: one is either a woman or a man. Gender becomes largely reducible to sex. Indeed, the terms gender and sex are used interchangeably in the book and differences are identified between fixed categories of men and women, or the 'two halves of humanity' (V. Hudson et al. 2012: 5). Many feminists have taken issue with this understanding of gender. Understanding gender as located firmly within individuals ignores how characteristics *become* feminized and masculinized. Most feminists see gender as produced through practice, through interaction with others as well as in relation to physical embodiment (as we saw in the introduction). Many agree with Cynthia Weber that gender may be 'performed' as difference, but gender cannot be reduced to the dispositions people carry about inside themselves (Weber 1994). Even if not all feminists would go so far as poststructuralist feminists such as Judith Butler (1990, 2004) in understanding gender as infinitely fluid, and instead see an element of fixity due to its relationship to physical embodiment, most agree that gender is best conceived of as a site of social regulation, with power relations deeply implicated in the construction of gender dichotomies. As such, the focus of feminist inquiry must be on how identities are socially produced and reproduced through relations of power and regulation. If we take gender as a 'given', these questions drop out of the picture (Baden and Goetz 1997; Steans 2013). The 'gender as a variable' approach of Hudson et al. has its uses, of course, because it enables us to gain a picture of the material realities of women's lives in broad-brush terms. If we cannot assume men and women to be relatively stable categories, we cannot collect any statistics about their position in society, relative wealth, power and opportunities. However, its use is limited; it gives us only partial purchase on the complexity of gender power relations. It is helpful at 'doing some explaining', but it implies that gender itself does not have to be explained (Steans 2013).

This is important because the assumption of difference underpinning the 'gender as a variable' approach in *Sex and World Peace* has several problematic outcomes (Steans 2013; Holvikivi 2014). At points the authors appear to explain the differences between men and women with reference to socio-biology. For example, they claim that there 'is an evolutionary reason' for the qualities that women across the world are imbued with, such as non-aggression, empathy and lack of competitiveness, and that is that 'women since the dawn of time have had to cope with the predispositions of men' (V. Hudson et al. 2012: 46, 69). Attributing peacefulness and other qualities traditionally associated with women and the feminine to evolution does little to challenge an essentializing view of women (and men). As we have seen, implying that women have a natural predisposition towards peace can undermine their chances of being taken seriously in public life. The authors of *Sex and World Peace* also risk falling into the trap of instrumentalizing women. In their claim that gender inequalities must be taken seriously in order to achieve world peace, women's rights appear to be advocated as a means to an end, whereas most feminists insist that '[a]t the very core of feminism is the conviction that women matter for their own sakes' (Enloe 2013: 15), not because of an impact they have or a role they play. Finally, there are politically problematic neo-colonial overtones to their argument. Hudson et al. construct a narrative whereby enlightened zones of civilization have to introduce the notion of women's rights to barbaric zones of conflict dominated by hot-headed misogynist men. They divide the world into states which are relatively women-friendly and those they describe as 'honor/shame societies' or 'traditional cultures' (V. Hudson et al. 2012: 8, 11, 25). As many of the examples in the book are of faraway men mistreating 'their' women, with a call for the international community to do something about it, the argument contains echoes of Gayatri Chakravorty Spivak's claim that current geopolitics is dominated by a discourse of 'white men needing to save brown women from brown men' (Spivak 1988: 299). Overall, the approach of Hudson et al. arguably diverts us from the ways in which gender-discriminatory norms and practices may be as much a *symptom* as a *cause* of war and violence. As such, we are distracted from the complexity of the causes of both war and hierarchical gender relations, which include the intertwining systems of neoliberal capitalism, patriarchy and a white supremacist nationalism (Pratt and Richter-Devroe 2011: 496). These systems cause war as they are based on violent oppression of others, but they also create gender relations by privileging that which is understood to be masculine over that which is thought to be feminine.

More useful to many feminists working in the area of WPS is an understanding of gender equality and peace as co-constitutive (just as gender hierarchies and war are). Feminists have argued that we need to retain the more complex concept of gender outlined in the introduction, which sees it as being something socially constructed, and emerging out of practice. This, I think, returns us to the thinking of Sara Ruddick and her point that maternal thinking is a practice that anyone, not just biological mothers, can adopt. This focus on practice avoids the slide into essentialism, and an understanding of gender as fixed that can be deployed as a variable to politically troubling effect. Others have noted that maternalism is actually a more malleable, complicated and contingent idea than critics suggest (de Alwis 2012), noting the way it often operates on two levels at once, valorizing the virtues of domesticity, caring and nurturing whilst simultaneously pushing for women to be central to public life, politics, the state, the marketplace and the workplace (Michel and Koven 1993). This active challenge to the boundaries between private and public reveals maternalism to be an active and radical process, not a conservative property of an individual or group. Likewise, in her support for a standpoint feminist position against militarism and war, Cockburn consistently stresses that this position is based not on any supposed nature of women but on practice. For Cockburn, standpoint feminism is an account of the world arising from a group's activities, not their essential nature; it is hard won through struggle (Cockburn 2012: 10). Conceiving of gender as practice, as most feminists do, rather than fixed, enables feminists to negotiate this tricky terrain of campaigning as women, and sometimes as women-only, in order to protest violence and war without cementing the idea of gender dichotomies. It enables an understanding of gender equality and peace as co-constitutive, an important piece of conceptual revisionism which feminists have brought to debates about peace and security. This brings us to the second part of this chapter, which discusses how feminists have conceptualized the idea of peace as inclusive, expansive and in many ways transformative.

Feminist peace: inclusive, expansive and transformative

'Lasting peace'...is an aspirational vision: a society that resolves the conflicts and contradictions within it in a constructive and inclusive fashion and which is thereby rendered relatively immune to mass or systemic violence. In this approach, values such as inclusion or gender equality are an inherent and indissoluble part of lasting peace. Building peace then is a transformative process which comprises, amongst other things, the promotion of women's rights and empowerment. At the same time, the broader processes of peacebuilding can also be used as a means of levering social change. This might include according women a more prominent place in post-conflict reconstruction, as well as the idea of 'reconstructing masculinities' through security sector reform, and promoting a human rights agenda as part of humanitarian interventions and governance reforms.

(El-Bushra 2012: 11)

Judy El-Bushra's description of 'Lasting Peace' drafted for the NGO International Alert captures well several of the elements of feminist visions of peace. It envisions gender equality as an 'inherent and indissoluble' part of lasting peace, rather than a route towards or a consequence of peace. This is important for the reasons outlined above: the risks of essentialism, instrumentalism and inadvertent racism. As opposed to isolating gender equality as a variable, as Hudson et al. do, and testing to see if it leads to peace, conceiving of gender equality as an inherent and indissoluble part of lasting peace enables us to retain the idea that practice of international relations constructs gender relations and hierarchies at the same time that gendered bodies and ideas construct international relations. They are mutually constitutive. States go to war in part because of the valorization of masculine-coded responses to conflicts over resources or identity; war then reinforces the gender ideology which constructs men as protectors, women as vulnerable. Feminists advocate a more positive version of this mutually reinforcing dynamic whereby empathy for others reduces the likelihood of violent responses to perceived threats and also challenges the construction of identity in Self–Other dualistic, oppositional terms. Seeing gender equality as mutually constitutive with peace avoids the instrumentalism involved in Hudson et al.'s argument that gender equality leads to peace, and frames women's empowerment as a goal in itself rather than a route to something else. This framing of gender equality and peace as co-constitutive also moves us beyond the implication in Hudson et al.'s argument that we can rank different countries in relation to gender equality, an approach which is rarely helpful in seeking peace.

El-Bushra's definition for International Alert also envisions peace as inclusive, expansive and transformative, which are three important elements of a feminist peace. It is worth elaborating on each, so that we have a clear understanding of feminist visions of peace in order to assess the extent to which the WPS agenda has been successful at achieving them.

Feminist peace: inclusive   A feminist vision of peace is best conceived of as a process, one which involves people creating their own peace and security. For genuine peace, individuals and communities must be empowered to realize their own security. Moreover, feminists are rarely, if ever, concerned about the liberation of women only. Rather, their emancipatory project tends to involve an understanding of how the international system works to create, support and perpetuate all forms of domination (Confortini 2012: 23). Feminist visions of peace are thus of an inclusive process. Feminists argue that peace cannot involve the demonization or oppression of other groups on grounds of ethnicity, social class, and so on. This has been a particularly explicit focus of feminist theorizing about peace since the 1980s, when black feminists challenged the largely white and middle-class feminist movement for assuming that their concerns were the concerns of women everywhere, and neglecting the particular and cross-cutting oppressions black women faced. In many ways, however, the argument that peace needs to include all races has long been part of feminist theorizing. At the 1919 Women's Congress, mentioned above, Mary Church Terrell declared that white people could 'talk about peace until doomsday, but they could never have it till the dark races were treated fair and square' (cited in Blackwell 2004: 35). Since black feminists introduced the concept of 'intersection-ality' in the 1980s (Crenshaw 1989; also see Hooks 1984, 1989; McCall 2005) to describe the way in which a person's sense of self and ascribed identity are defined by her or his positioning in relation to not one but several dimensions of power – race, class and sexuality as well as gender (Anthias

1998) – the majority of feminists have adopted the approach (see, e.g., Yuval-Davis 2006; Peterson and Runyan 2010; Marchand and Runyan 2011). V. Spike Peterson (2007, 2012) explains that a focus on the multiple axes of oppression facilitates a move away from the traditional dichotomous tendencies of conventional framing and allows identities and subjugations that are inseparable in practice to be considered side-by-side. For an analysis of militarism and war, Cynthia Cockburn (2007, 2010) maintains the concept is indispensable.

This attention to inclusion is why feminists have had such a problem with mainstream definitions of security, as well as with how security policies have been enacted in international relations, and why they have sought to reconceptualize the concept. Mainstream definitions usually see security as a property of a state, achieved through military strength and strong borders. They assume that those beyond the borders are a threat. Feminists have criticized this understanding as being based on dualistic or binary thinking and exclusionary and oppressive practices. Taking US President George W. Bush's response to 9/11 – 'you are either with us or against us' – as a classic example, Elisabeth Porter argues that the traditional security mentality, and the practices, policies and political decisions which follow, are not conducive to peaceful, cooperative relationships because they invite oppositional responses. They assume a ' "self-righteous rightness" about one's own position, and thus miss opportunities for inclusionary politics' (Porter 2007: 48). As such, much feminist work has gone into deconstructing the binaries upon which the discipline of International Relations rests: citizen/foreigner, sameness/difference, free world/axis of evil, Christianity/Islam, friends/enemies and good/evil. Feminists have challenged the role of the key concepts of state and sovereignty in marking insiders and outsiders (Peterson 1992; Tickner 1992; Enloe 1993), and have sought in particular to challenge the rigidity of dichotomies that lead to destructive or 'radical' othering (Hansen 2006), ethnic hatred and exclusion.

Feminists argue that it is not difference *per se* that is problematic. It is the 'way difference is assigned and oppression and exclusion justified' (Robinson 1999: 82). Fiona Robinson and others argue that some form of 'otherness' is necessary to affirm self-identity, to recognize that identity emerges in relation to others who are different from us, but that 'otherness' need not imply inferiority.

> When difference is accepted unproblematically as part of life's rich tapestry, there need be no harm in this 'otherness'. Where difference is seen as inferior, strange, weird or is the justification for violence, the difference of 'othering' is harmful. Harmful 'othering' is based on hierarchically valued dichotomies which are not simply opposites 'but rather mask the power of one side of the binary to control the other'. (Porter 2007: 48, citing D. Bell 2002: 433)

Likewise, for many feminists along with critical peace and security scholars (e.g. Curle 1971; Lederach 1998), what is problematic is not conflict – as a culture without conflict would never change or progress – it is the use of violence and oppression to resolve it.

Feminist approaches to peace involve challenging dualisms and dichotomies through practising humility, openness, dialogue, reconciliation and care (Porter 2007: 63–6). They interrogate the privileging of masculinized definitions of security problems and solutions, and propose alternatives which draw on personal experience and relationships, on concrete contexts and inclusive solutions. They stress that 'emotions of care and sympathy lie at the heart of the ethical life' (Nussbaum 1999: 14). Empathy enables respectful negotiations with contentious others because we can recognize involuntary similarities across difference as well as differences that mark independent identity (Sylvester 2002: 119–20). 'Empathy is the willingness to enter into the feeling or spirit of something and appreciate it fully – to hear other's stories and be transformed by our appreciation of their experiences' (Sylvester 1994: 96). L. H. M. Ling describes this transformative process as the creation of hybrid subjectivities, which compel the recognition that the 'Other exists in part *within* the ... Self' and that the Self needs to 'concede that its own survival and subjectivity depend on learning from the Other' (Ling 2002: 286). In a similar vein, Robinson argues that we need to focus on caring about others in ways that make us rethink 'our own attitudes about difference and exclusion by locating that difference within relationships, thus dispelling the claim that any one person or groups of persons is naturally and objectively different' (Robinson 1999: 164–5).

Feminist peace: expansive   Feminist concepts of peace start from the evidence gathered from conflict zones which suggests that war is experienced by women differently from men in many respects. It does not affect all women the same way, of course, but, as a result of the challenges associated with their role as the prime carers in most societies and their particular vulnerability to sexual and gender-based violence, war is often experienced as a continuum by many women. That is, there is no obvious point at which violence starts and ends, and there is no clear distinction between violence per- petrated by an armed combatant, a civilian stranger or an intimate partner. Rather, violence impacts upon women in both private and public spheres, both before and after the formal declaration of war and the signing of any peace agree- ment. This is also true for many men, of course, especially those in marginalized racial groups and sexualities, or in lower socio-economic classes. It is important to remember that although it offers opportunities for some, war is experi- enced for the most part as horrific by the majority, whatever their gender. For all marginalized groups, the implication is clear: peace needs to go beyond the notion of formal peace agreements. NGOs working with women on the ground in conflict-affected areas report that the broad range of ingredi- ents women identify as necessary for addressing social differ- ences and building sustainable peace form an 'intricate tapestry' including but not confined to social justice, women's rights, co-existence, tolerance, participatory democracy, transparency and non-violent dialogue (Porter 2007: 36). Researchers also stress that a crucial component of women's definition of peace is the emphasis on meeting the material needs that further a sense of security (De La Rey and McKay 2006; Pankhurst 2007; Porter 2007; Ní Aoláin et al. 2011).

Many also highlight the centrality of sustainable develop- ment to feminist visions of peace (Harcourt 1994; Detraz 2014). Noting that resource scarcity and degradation are often the starting point of resource-related conflicts – with at least 18 such conflicts identified by the UN Environment Programme since 1990 (UN 2013) – and the way that both environmental change and conflict have gender-differentiated causes and consequences, many feminists increasingly acknowledge the importance of environmental protection and sustainable development as part of any peace which involves challenging gendered hierarchies. Primarily because women are the majority of the world's poor, they are more dependent for their livelihood on natural resources (UN 1997; True 2012). In times of increasing scarcity and degradation of land and water, exacerbated in recent decades by climate change, those who lack income and power – many of them women – often lose their rights to use those existential resources. Those tasked with the responsibility to secure water, food and fuel face the greatest challenges. Recognizing that inequalities and violence are exacerbated by resource scarcity and degradation, many feminists have identified sustainable and inclusive development as an essential component of peace (WILPF 2014).

Peace is not thus just the absence of war. For feminists, it includes the economic and social empowerment of women and other marginalized groups: freedom from want as well as freedom from fear.[1] In this respect, feminist peace shares much with the concept of Human Security, which also focuses on the long-term continuous threats to security, often highlighting the structural bases of problems, and the need for people to be active in the process of achieving their own security.[2] Feminists stress the gendered power relations underpinning insecurities which Human Security scholars often neglect; they also complicate the notion of 'people-centredness' at heart of the Human Security concept, arguing that there is a need to clarify what is meant by 'people', especially when there are multiple and competing interests of different people (Tripp et al. 2013: 27–33). However, the two approaches share many of the same understandings and prescriptions: they are agency-oriented, people-centred and bottom-up perspectives with a commitment to tackling the root causes of insecurity (Tripp et al. 2013: 27). Similarly, although adding the crucial insights about the need to tackle the gender ideology sustaining war, feminist peace also shares features with the 'positive peace' (Galtung 1996), 'just peace' (Lederach 1999) and 'emancipatory peace' (Richmond 2006) advocated by many critical peace and security scholars, which also emphasize local ownership, a bottom-up approach and a stronger concern for social welfare and justice (also see Pugh et al. 2008; Cooper et al. 2011).[3]

There is no doubting that feminist definitions of peace are broad and complex, creating challenges for policy-makers. As one NGO puts it:

> [P]eacebuilding is a process made up of inter-locking, interdependent elements, including looking after the security of ordinary people, ensuring stable and proficient governance, giving people access to justice in an increasingly fair society, healing the wounds of war and making it possible for people to enjoy an adequate and stable standard of living. Each of these elements is equally important – there is no single, magic key. (Banfield 2008: 5)

Feminist peace involves women and other marginalized groups enjoying their full human rights, economic and social as well as civil and political (Tickner 1992: 129). Women and other marginalized groups have to be able not only to meet their everyday needs, but also to have enough to make life worth living – sustainable livelihoods, leisure time and security for their dependants. Most feminists agree that this requires a state which can facilitate employment opportunities and which can provide healthcare, education, justice and a safety net for those who cannot work. As such, for many feminists, peace by definition then needs to tackle neoliberalism. This links us to the third key element of a feminist peace, that it is transformative.

Feminist peace: transformative   This delineation of feminist visions of peace makes clear that peace involves nothing less than transforming the structures of neoliberalism. As such, feminists note the irony in the association between peace and passivity, as if peace were the easy option (Tickner 1995). We considered the feminist critique of neoliberalism briefly in the previous chapter, as failure to tackle it has been the major 'problem of ambition' feminists have articulated in relation to 1325. This section expands on these concerns, detailing the ways in which neoliberal economic prescriptions are inimical to feminist visions of peace. In neoliberal economic frameworks, which have dominated the global economy since the late 1970s, the underlying assumption is that reducing state intervention in the market and increasing global competition results in a more efficient allocation of resources and higher rates of growth. Inflation control through a combination of tight monetary and fiscal policies tends to be the overriding objective of macroeconomic policy. Structural policies focus on the reduction of the role of the state, the promotion of private enterprise, the deregulation of labour markets and the removal of capital controls. Neoliberal policies have had a profound global impact since their adoption in the late 1970s. One generally accepted result is that they have exacerbated inequalities in most countries of the world (Chossudovsky 1997; Cramer 2006; Duffield 2007).[4] Neoliberalism, for many feminists, constitutes a form of structural violence, with a particularly profound impact on women and other marginalized groups (Marchand and Runyan 2011; WILPF 2014).

This is firstly because neoliberal policies entail cuts in public expenditure, such as cuts to healthcare, education, childcare, parental leave, food subsidies and prenatal nutrition, which means cuts to the services women in particular rely upon (Elson 1991; Sparr 1994; Benería 2003; Young et al. 2011). As women are often the ones to stay home to care for the sick, children and the elderly, even if they do not have any health issues themselves, they suffer disproportionately from any reduction in public spending. If they have to give up work in order to care for others because the state no longer will, they lose their income. Secondly, women in employment are often concentrated in the public sector, so are more likely to lose their jobs, and, moreover, the social and welfare benefits linked to jobs, as neoliberal reforms include scaling back jobs in the public sector in particular (Waylen 2007: 181; Young et al. 2011). Women's cooking, cleaning and caring roles in the household also mean they are particularly badly affected when public goods and services such as water and power are privatized as part of neoliberal reforms. Government cuts can also force women into the paid labour force to be able to afford healthcare or education for their children, compensating for state cuts, and thus they make them tolerate precarious or hazardous conditions they would not otherwise accept (Benería and Feldman 1992).

The liberalization of trade required by neoliberalism tends to result in low wages in the export sector, particularly women's wages in labour-intensive industries such as the garment trade or electronics manufacturing, in order to keep exports competitive (Standing 1989; Çagatay et al. 1995). The resultant poverty can lead women to be trafficked or to engage in unsafe work in order to survive (True 2012). Market-oriented neoliberal policies also tend to be detrimental to women in that they shift resources into male-dominated corporations, markets and institutions (Connell and Pearse 2015: 139). The use of public money – aid or revenue generated through tax – to provide support for the private sector tends not to benefit women to the same extent as men because of the obstacles women face in accessing resources and markets (Elson 1991; Sparr 1994; Haddad et al. 1995). If peace and security involve freedom from want as well as freedom from fear, then it is not hard to see why many feminists find neoliberal economic policies hostile to peace.

Undoubtedly it is in women's interest to have markets regulated by law, that monopolistic patterns are undone and that corruption in the economic sphere is fully addressed. Feminists do not tend to assert that all forms of capitalism are problematic and would concede that some interventions in post-conflict economies might be important for sustainable development of the economy (Benería 2003). They object, however, to the framing of corruption, monopolistic practices and inefficiencies as inherent problems of the global South, problems which can be cured by the intervention of the more rational, efficient, advanced and moral global North. Monopolies and corruption in post-conflict contexts are as much the product of the legacies of colonialism, war economies and donor practices of bribing as they are of any local customs (Hawley et al. 2000).

When the IFIs first introduced neoliberal policies to the global South through Structural Adjustment Programmes (SAPs) in the 1980s, they initially ignored the gender implications. This changed over the years, but the tendency became to try to add social policies on, without addressing the way in which the macroeconomic policies at the heart of the agenda are gendered (Elson and Çagatay 2000). Thus, just as SAPs were replaced in the 1990s by Poverty Reduction

Strategy Papers (PRSPs), which claimed to be a more pro-poor approach to development whilst remaining neoliberal in their overall prescriptions, policy documents which began to mention gender in the 2000s did not attempt to challenge neoliberalism. When gender is considered in World Bank and International Monetary Fund (IMF) documents, the governments of developing countries and so-called 'traditional arrangements' tend to be blamed for any disadvantage to women, rather than global capitalist structures and processes (Bergeron 2003: 409). For example, women's triple roles (as income earners, carers and community managers) have been acknowledged by the World Bank since at least 2000, but there is little acknowledgement of the role of neoliberalism in causing or exacerbating women's triple burden (World Bank 2012). Instead, social structures in developing countries, or outdated gender roles of breadwinner and homemaker, are held responsible for the unequal socioeconomic relations between men and women (see, e.g., Narayan and Shah 2000; Kabeer 2009; Roberts and Soederberg 2012). In reality, however, it has been the unequal power relations between poor countries and the World Bank which have played a defining role – it is hard to adopt women-friendly policies whilst cutting the state. The work feminists have carried out in order to catalogue the damage these policies do in post-conflict countries in particular will be detailed in the following chapter. Here, it is sufficient to note that, although it is not always explicit in feminist scholarship on peace and security, feminist visions of peace would seem to require a paradigm transformation from the current neoliberal economic model of development which prioritizes profit over people and exacerbates inequalities, while supporting militaries and patriarchy, and furthering war and conflict, environmental degradation and climate change (WILPF 2014).

Conclusion

Peace is generally conceived of by feminists as inclusive, expansive and transformative – not just the absence of war but the ability to live a fulfilling life. It involves replacing hierarchical dualistic ways of thinking with inclusivity and empathy. It is best conceived of as a process rather than an objective state of being, and, moreover, a process that subjects must participate in themselves – peace cannot be achieved by external actors alone. Most importantly, perhaps, it means freedom from want as well as fear, an end to poverty and injustice as well as physical violence (Pettman 1996; Tickner 2001). Almost by definition, then, it means challenging the current neoliberal global economic policy framework. In that sense, feminist peace is revolutionary; critical in Robert Cox's sense of the word, where theorizing is concerned to stand apart from the prevailing order, interrogate its origins and find ways of transforming it, rather than ensuring a more efficient or effective version of existing power relations (Cox 1981). Feminist peace activism aims to understand 'both how social change happens in the context of defining structures and how such change can be emancipatory – that is, how it is effectively transformative of unjust structures' (Confortini 2012: 21).

The next chapter considers the neoliberal underpinnings of the international community's efforts to build peace since the end of the Cold War. It builds on the depiction of neoliberalism set out in this chapter as antithetical to feminist peace, by considering concrete examples of 'liberal peacebuilding' projects in detail, and how their neoliberal assumptions and prescriptions have impacted upon women and other marginalized groups. This paves the way for chapters 4 and 5, which consider current peacebuilding activities in order to assess whether it is possible for the WPS agenda, with its considerable reinforcements since 1325, to challenge neoliberalism and thus bring about the feminist visions of peace outlined in this chapter.

Questions for discussion

1 What is the connection between feminism and peace? Is it a necessary connection? Are there risks in making such a connection?

2   What are the differences between seeing gender equality as a route to peace or a goal of peace, in theory and in practice?

3   How do feminists envision peace? How does this differ from non-feminist versions of peace? Do you think feminist visions of peace are too broad to be conceptually coherent and/or translated into practical policies? Or do you agree that peace must be more than the absence of war? What is your preferred conceptualization of peace?

Suggestions for further reading

Lourdes Benería. 2003. *Gender, Development, and Globalization: Economics as If All People Mattered*. New York: Routledge.
This is a great introduction to feminist economics from one of the pioneers of the field. It provides an excellent overview of the gendered paradoxes and harms generated by neoliberal development and globalization.

Cynthia Cockburn. 2007. *From Where We Stand: War, Women's Activism and Feminist Analysis*. London: Zed Books.
Readable and rich, this account of women's peace activism explores the connection between women and peace and contains detailed accounts of various influential peace movements, including WILPF and its advocacy for 1325 at the UN. Unlike the many scholars who are wary of the risks of associating women and peace, Cockburn is a staunch defender of women's particular contribution to make to peacebuilding but builds this case on their 'standpoint' as women, rather than any 'natural' qualities or dispositions.

Catia Cecilia Confortini. 2012. *Intelligent Compassion: Feminist Critical Methodology in the Women's International League for Peace and Freedom*. New York: Oxford University Press.

Confortini also focuses on WILPF, but provides a longer historical perspective than Cockburn, tracing WILPF's development through the last six decades. Intelligent Compassion *goes beyond a historical account to offer important theorizing on the possibility of emancipatory agency in women's peace activism, so is useful for thinking through how feminist visions of peace might be achieved.*

Elisabeth Porter. 2007. *Peacebuilding: Women in International Perspective.* Abingdon: Routledge.
Porter draws upon positive examples of women's peacebuilding around the world to demonstrate the importance of recognition, inclusion and tolerance. She thus provides a good example of a feminist advocating the inclusive, expansive and transformatory version of peace that I have argued is characteristic of feminist visions. She critically interrogates the entrenched dualisms, or the 'othering', of contemporary global politics in a richly theoretical text which argues for a broader understanding of peace than that found in the UN WPS architecture.

Web resources

Powerful Synergies (*http://www.undp.org/content/undp/en/home/librarypage/womens-empowerment/powerful-synergies.html*)
This webpage links to an important 2013 publication from the UNDP, Powerful Synergies: Gender Equality, Economic Development and Environmental Sustainability, *a collection of papers by scholars and practitioners that explore the interconnections between gender equality and sustainable development across a range of sectors and global development issues such as energy, health, education, food security, climate change, human rights, consumption and production patterns, and urbanization. It is a useful source for thinking through the connections between peacebuilding, environmental security and gender. The publication provides evidence from various sectors and regions on how women's equal access and control over resources not only improves the lives of*

individuals, families and nations, but also helps ensure the sustainability of the environment.

WomanStats Project (*http://www.womanstats.org/*)
Though problematized by many feminist scholars for its use of gender as a static variable, as this chapter discussed, the data here remain a useful source of information on the status of women in the world. The project aims to provide comprehensive statistics on a range of measures of women's lives, and to facilitate understanding of the linkage between the situation of women and the security of nation-states.

Women's International League for Peace and Freedom (*http://www.wilpfinternational.org/*)
One of the most influential and long-standing women's peace organizations, WILPF promotes political, economic and social justice for all. It has been a key advocate for the inclusive, expansive and transformatory peace described in this chapter.

3
Feminist Critiques of Neoliberal Peacebuilding

This chapter focuses on the neoliberal prescriptions for post-conflict reconstruction which accompany most peacebuilding operations. Feminists share with other critical security scholars concerns about the in-built assumptions of donors about the necessity of neoliberal economic reforms as part of the peacebuilding package. Feminist scholars shed light in particular on the gendered nature of these assumptions and their gendered consequences. They do so by using gender as an analytical tool, the second connection between gender and peacebuilding, in Jean Munro's framework (see introduction). At one level, using gender as an analytical tool means asking how conflict or peacebuilding operations impact differently on men and women. At another, gender analysis can be used as a tool to see how the world operates according to logics and structures which are both gendered and gendering. This chapter is attentive to both these ways that feminists have used gender as an analytical tool to explore peacebuilding. It engages in more detail with the feminist critique of peacebuilding outlined in previous chapters, namely that even with – or, for some, particularly as a result of – the adoption of 1325 and all the many other initiatives to mainstream a gender analysis, peacebuilding constitutes a form of neo-imperialism.

The chapter first focuses on the requirements made of post-conflict states in terms of economic and governance restructuring and details the problems associated with these neoliberal economic prescriptions in post-conflict settings from a feminist perspective. It then turns to three mini-case studies of peacebuilding interventions – Mozambique, Bosnia-Herzegovina and Afghanistan – to illuminate the gendered harms caused by the imposition of neoliberal policies. The final section outlines the arguments of the many feminists who have focused on the narratives used to justify peacebuilding interventions in order to demonstrate the role gender plays in elite legitimations of 'the liberal peace'.

Neoliberal policies in post-conflict contexts

What have feminists had to say about the neoliberal agenda underpinning peacebuilding in conflict-affected countries? Many feminists argue that neoliberal policies are advocated by donors for post-conflict contexts despite not being designed for them and in the face of all the evidence that even in non-conflict-affected areas they have failed to promote inclusive and sustainable growth. Feminists also share with critical security and international political economy (IPE) scholars (Pugh et al. 2004; Cramer 2009) the concern that neoliberal policies do not fully grasp the particular features of war economies, something which is essential for (re)constructing war-torn countries.[1] Instead, the donors have encouraged liberalization policies in a way that implies a 'blank slate' on which to design a new economy, as if the three intertwining war economies – combat, criminal and coping – did not already exist. Since these economies are profoundly gendered, as we have seen, this insistence on ill-suited economic policies has particularly detrimental impacts on women (together with other marginalized groups) in post-conflict contexts. Most of the feminist scholarship focuses on women in the coping economy (Meintjes et al. 2001; Pankhurst 2008; Jacobson 2013), but for a fuller analysis of the gendered impact of neoliberal policies, it is worth paying attention to all three war economies.

The many interests that some agents have in perpetuating war economies make transforming them very difficult. Those who have benefited from looting and black market activities that the chaos of war facilitates are inevitably hostile to peace. The challenge, Christopher Cramer argues, is to develop policies and institutions that contribute to long-term structural change and fair and sustainable economic development. Policies need to consolidate those dimensions of the war economies that have the potential to contribute to this goal, of which there are few, and to tackle the dimensions which benefit belligerents, criminals and elites, of which there are many (Cramer 2009: 129–30). The World Bank's 'Breaking the Conflict Trap' (2003a) assumes neoliberal economic policies will meet the challenge. The evidence suggests, however, that such policies aggravate the gendered inequalities and devastation caused by the combat and criminal economies, and intensify the desperation of the women who dominate in the coping economy.

Neoliberal policies offer incentives to the mostly male agents in the combat economy to keep fighting because they rarely offer the alternative livelihoods necessary to persuade them otherwise. Furthermore, when IFIs insist on privatization, those in key positions in the war economy who have been able to accumulate wealth are best placed to be able to benefit. In neoliberal economic theory, privatization liberates enterprise from the shackles of bureaucracy often found in SOEs, releasing the entrepreneurial spirit and enabling greater efficiency, generating new investment, expanding output and bringing about rising productivity and employment. In many post-conflict states, however, in patterns which are both profoundly unjust and risk a return to war, the resources which are allocated through liberalization (privatization of SOEs, incentives to encourage foreign direct investment [FDI]) are more often than not captured by belligerent or criminal groups, those who were the main beneficiaries of the war economy. These are rarely women. Research indicates that privatization has produced more corruption, not less, in Angola (Le Billon 2001; Cramer 2002), Afghanistan (Goodhand 2004), Bosnia (Pugh 2005; and see below) and beyond. Neoliberal policies shrink the state, and in the absence of strong central authority and reliable law enforcement, 'there are few incentives for entrepreneurs to make the shift toward longer-term productive activities' (Goodhand 2004: 65). In post-conflict countries, neoliberal policies often mean that a very small group of domestic actors benefits – elite men with international contacts (Greenberg and Zuckerman 2009: 5) – in the combat and criminal economies.

Meanwhile, the strategies used to survive in the coping economy, dominated by women, tend to be undermined by neoliberal policies. Such policies, as discussed in the previous chapter, reduce the ability of families and households to meet their essential needs – emotional and material. Many studies have shown that narrowing the role of public provision shifts the costs and the workload of social reproduction from the paid to the unpaid economy, with negative consequences for women's health and well-being, and for girls' opportunities to develop their capabilities by having access to education (Elson and Çagatay 2000). In other words, cuts in social spending in post-conflict settings hit women and girls disproportionately, for a number of interrelated reasons: firstly, because of women's role in society as carers for the widowed, orphaned, disabled, injured and vulnerable, of whom there are many in the aftermath of war; secondly, because they are often made homeless by war, so have to carry out that caring role as refugees or IDPs; thirdly, because they are likely to have complex health needs, especially if they have suffered from sexual violence, so suffer disproportionately if health services are cut; fourthly, because girls are likely to be first to be pulled from school if subsidies for education are cut; and, fifthly, because women's employment opportunities are more likely to be curtailed as it is the public sector, a relatively high employer of women, in which the most swingeing cuts are implemented (Waylen 2007; Greenberg and Zuckerman 2009; Jacobson 2013). The privatization of public services and utilities also curtails the entitlements of women in post-conflict contexts, as it tends to disrupt fair and affordable access to power and water. Whilst it is important to acknowledge that the state delivery of water and power pre-war in many states in the global South rarely benefited women, privatization arguably increases further the considerable burden of time and work on women in obtaining water and fuel, commonly designated their duty in rural areas (Jacobson 2013).

The post-conflict reconstruction projects advocated as part of peacebuilding tend to be macro in scale, such as major infrastructure, mining or drilling projects, or micro, the provision of microfinance schemes or small-scale income generation projects. The former provide employment opportunities primarily to men; the latter often specifically target women. The success of such 'microfinance' schemes for women is debated,[2] but there is some consensus that a key problem is that its micro-level means that it is rarely a route out of the coping economy for women (Kabeer 2009: 83–4; Karim 2011; Roodman 2012; Hickel 2015). In post-war contexts, problems such as the low purchasing power of the populace, uncompetitive local markets owing to unregulated imports and limited tourism scupper many microfinance initiatives (Pupavac 2005: 401). When the credit on offer is on a larger scale, women are often overlooked, in part because they are burdened enough in the coping economy, and in part because of donor ignorance about their skills and desires (Greenberg and Zuckerman 2009: 14). Women are thus pushed into the coping or survival economy, with a lower likelihood of escaping poverty.

A further example of the way in which neoliberal policies exacerbate gender inequality and women's hardship in the aftermath of war is in land reform. Lack of access to land has long been recognized as a key factor in explaining the relative poverty and lack of opportunities for women and other marginalized groups, particularly indigenous people. Land reform could be a policy which works to provide these groups with economic security and increased equality with elite men. In post-conflict states, however, the World Bank tends to promote 'market-friendly' land reform: that is, individual private ownership of land. Whilst the World Bank is ostensibly aiming at tackling undemocratic and unequal access to land with this policy, it can worsen the situation for marginalized groups in post-conflict contexts. It drastically reduces or removes completely the multiple and collective forms of land use on which women and other marginalized groups have relied in places such as Mozambique (Jacobson 2013: 234).

Through the positioning of particular people into particular positions in the global economy, neoliberal policies reproduce gender roles. That is, neoliberalism does not just have gendered impacts, but is productive of gender itself. This is important to note because, whilst most of the advice given to post-conflict countries assumes the sort of fiscal policy which might be appropriate for a typical service-delivery state, post-conflict states have to go beyond service delivery and be transformatory. They need to challenge those roles. They need not only to deliver services, but also to build institutions, invest in people, regulate the combat and criminal economies which have grown up during the war and transform the laws, policies, and cultures which discriminate against women and other marginalized groups. This requires revenue beyond that which would be required in a non-conflict-affected state. Donor countries and agencies insist that a flourishing private sector will generate sufficient revenue through tax. In practice, in post-conflict contexts, this rarely happens, for several reasons. Firstly, trade policy is liberalized in order to encourage inward investment and growth of exports by simplifying and reducing the taxes on both, thus reducing the revenue going to the state. This undermines prospects for improving governance, state capacity and service delivery, let alone any more ambitious goals of structural change (Cramer 2009). Secondly, there is the corruption mentioned above, whereby armed groups and criminals avoid paying tax on the profits made by their acquisition of resources made available through the sale of national resources or SOEs. Not only do elites not pay their share of tax, they often sell off resources at vastly undervalued prices for bribes, robbing the state of the revenue sorely needed by the majority population (Watkins 2013). Thirdly, the development policies insisted upon by IFIs often reinforce dependence on a narrow range of primary commodities, where there is minimal profit to be made (Cramer 2009).

Cuts in public expenditure mean cuts to and controls on the services upon which women and other marginalized groups particularly depend post-conflict, such as justice and health. Reducing public spending also means cuts to the precise areas which could be transformatory for women and girls affected by conflict: education, childcare and the creation of decent livelihoods (Jacobson 2013). IFIs and other donors are thus accused by some of 'organized hypocrisy' by advocating a purist version of the neoliberal model designed to 'lower both trade barriers and financing for welfare programmes in ways that would not be accepted in Western capitals' (Cooper et al. 2011: 2005).

We move now to consider some cases of post-conflict states to illustrate the gendered consequences of neoliberal peacebuilding in more detail. The aim is to demonstrate the links between macroeconomic policies insisted upon by donors and gender inequalities and insecurities felt at all levels of society. This analysis suggests that the feminist critics of 'the liberal peace' are right to point to its neoliberal underpinnings as undermining prospects for peace. This then sets the scene for following chapters, which focus on whether the strengthened WPS agenda is managing to significantly improve the security of women, girls and other marginalized groups in this neoliberal context.

Case studies of the liberal peace

Mozambique   Mozambique suffered three decades of almost continuous war from the early 1960s to 1992, first liberating itself from its Portugese colonial master and then enduring a 'Cold War proxy war of destabilization' (Hanlon 2010: 79) from 1981 to 1992 as the United States and South Africa supported a guerrilla force, Renamo, to contain the leftist Frelimo liberation movement. As Frelimo, in the late 1970s, owed some of its popularity to bringing independence, free movement and an expansion of health and education, Renamo targeted schools, health posts, the economic infrastructure and transport as part of a strategy to undermine the government. Passengers were burned alive in buses to make people afraid to travel; schools were attacked, and teachers and pupils kidnapped and killed to make people afraid to use the Frelimo education system (Hanlon 2010). The decade-long war was a heavy assault on Mozambique's social and economic infrastructure. From a mid-1980s population of 13–15 million, 1 million people died (7 per cent of the population) and 5 million (one-third of the population) were displaced or made refugees in neighbouring countries; damage was estimated at US$20 billion; and Mozambique's gross domestic product (GDP) was estimated to be only half of what it would have been without the war (UNICEF 1989; Hanlon 1996). The number of basic health posts had increased from 326 at independence to 1,195 in 1985, but 500 of these were closed or destroyed by Renamo, as were 60 per cent of all primary schools and more than 3,000 rural shops, most never reopening (Hanlon 1996).

A peace accord between Renamo and the government was signed in Rome on 4 October 1992. Mozambique, with its economy devastated by war and debt, had already been a recipient of aid and IMF and World Bank SAPs since 1984, but as part of the peacebuilding project, these intensified. In order to rebuild and reconstruct society, Mozambique needed funds, but nearly all donors made aid conditional on the recipient having programmes with the IMF and World Bank, which gave those agencies the power to dictate the policies. In many of the ways outlined above, these policies privileged small groups of elite men and disadvantaged women and other marginalized groups.

Although there were not extensive combat and criminal economies as both sides were war-weary after so many years of fighting (Hanlon 2010), the neoliberal policies imposed on Mozambique turned a country where corruption was relatively rare into one where, by the early 1990s, it was endemic. Joseph Hanlon argues that the World Bank and other donors were so committed to turning the Frelimo government towards free-market capitalism that they pushed loans onto private businessmen they knew would not repay them (Hanlon 2010: 87). The policy adopted by Mozambique from the early 1990s was to encourage FDI, in line with donor requirements. Most investment was in large projects in the mineral-energy sector – a US$1.5 billion aluminium smelter, a gas pipeline for export to South Africa and titanium and coal mines. The evidence suggests that these mega-projects have created few jobs and, because of tax exemptions, contribute little to public revenue (Virtanen and Ehrenpreis 2007). Moreover, the jobs created in these projects have mostly been in the traditionally male occupations of construction and transport (Castel-Branco 2008), so have offered little in the way of employment for women (Hanlon and Smart 2008). This problem was compounded by liberalization of Mozambique's cashew nut production, which forced factories largely employing women to close (Hanlon 2000; Cramer 2009), and the way that urban women in Mozambique were the first to be laid off when the public sector was trimmed and when 'unprofitable' industries were wound up (Espling 1999; Sheldon 2002). The IFIs imposed cuts in government spending, including sharp cuts in wages – nurses and teachers, professions dominated by women, fell below the poverty line in 1992, below the abject poverty line (then US$50 per month) in 1993 and below US$40 per month in 1996 (Hanlon 2010: 86).

The closure of state farms, cooperatives and agricultural marketing boards forced women back to subsistence production (Hanlon 1996; Hanlon and Smart 2008), a time-consuming and demanding existence which constituted life for 95.3 per cent of working women in Mozambique in 2008 (Fox et al. 2008). The closure of the grain marketing board, ending storage facilities and guaranteed prices, shifted all of the risk onto farmers still recovering from war, making commercial farming less viable (Hanlon 2010: 88).

The resultant poverty hampers women's ability to challenge social relations, which perhaps explains the persistence of gender-based violence for women in Mozambique. Data show that 54 per cent of all women in Mozambique have been abused (UNICEF 2011: xxiv). Mozambique has one of the highest rates of child marriage in the world: 18 per cent of Mozambican girls aged 20 to 24 are married before the age of 15 and 51 per cent before the age of 18 (UNICEF 2011: 148). There is alleged to be widespread sexual abuse in Mozambique, particularly in schools. According to the Ministry of Education, 80 per cent of girls report that sexual abuse occurs in schools and communities, 70 per cent report that teachers use sexual intercourse as a condition for promotion between grades, and 50 per cent state that not only teachers abuse them but also boys in their peer group (UNICEF 2011: 115). The case of peacebuilding in Mozambique provides good evidence, then, that the aid used to finance post-conflict reconstruction is dependent on a set of neoliberal economic prescriptions which have acted to undermine the country's development and exacerbate insecurities and inequalities in society, particularly those that are gendered.

Bosnia-Herzegovina The 1992–5 conflict in Bosnia-Herzegovina, as the Federal Republic of Yugoslavia (FRY) imploded, touched virtually every sector of the country, devastating the economy and the social fabric of society. Of a pre-war population of 4.4 million, a million people sought refuge abroad, while another million were displaced internally (Dahlman and Ó Tuathail 2005). Ten years after the war ended, 20 per cent of the population lived below the poverty line, nearly 30 per cent lived in houses without adequate property rights, about 25 per cent had only basic education, 20 per cent were underemployed or unemployed and more than 15 per cent were in poor health. Poverty was felt most acutely in rural communities, especially by women. Farmers lost 50 to 60 per cent of their assets and 90 per cent of their livestock. Buildings were ruined and water and electrical power facilities destroyed. The nation's GDP fell to half its pre-war level (IFAD 2010).

The negotiation of a peace agreement in 1995 took place five thousand miles away from Bosnia at an airbase in Dayton, Ohio. The negotiators, as usual, were the male war leaders – the beneficiaries of the combat and criminal economies, whose main interest was to retain the power, territory and wealth they had gained during the war. The Dayton Peace Accord set up a complex political system, dividing the territory along ethnic lines. Funding for reconstruction was dependent on the typical package of neoliberal reforms. The male leaders of each faction were thus in pole position to benefit, and, as soon as privatization of SOEs and public utilities began, they started to use their ill-gotten gains to buy up shares at discounted prices. Monopolies, corruption and capital flight ensued, and those who had been the drivers of the war got exceedingly rich while women and other marginalized groups were forced into the coping economy (Orford 1997; Cockburn and Zarkov 2002b; Cockburn 2014).

We can see how the neoliberal reforms demanded of Bosnia after Dayton exacerbated gendered insecurities and inequalities in two overlapping policy areas: microfinance and employment. Before the war, many women, at least in urban areas in Bosnia, were highly skilled and qualified. If they were not already working in the public sector in, for instance, service provision, public administration or public companies, or setting up their own business, they tended to have such aspirations. The microfinance initiatives which have dominated the post-war economic development strategy recommended by donors, however, forced many to set their sights lower, on more small-scale endeavours, often involving return to the land. Microfinance was heavily promoted, especially to women (Walsh 1997; Pupavac 2005: 397–8), while other alternative financial systems (e.g. Small to Medium Enterprise Development Banks, which might have capitalized on Bosnia's strong industrial enterprise sector and technological and institutional infrastructure) were either disallowed or undermined (Pupavac 2005; Bateman 2010). Microfinance is not the sole cause of increased poverty for women, of course. The widespread poverty in Bosnia-Herzegovina is largely an outcome of the war, which caused extensive damage and led to high unemployment. However, microfinance – as discussed in the previous chapter – rarely offers a sustainable development strategy, especially for women, and can be seen to have made things worse for many women in agriculture in Bosnia.

For example, many women were encouraged to buy a cow to provide milk, in a project which is characteristic of the flaws of microfinance. While this was largely celebrated by the international community, seen as a means by which individuals could support themselves, it led to an over-supply of milk, which subsequently led to a decline in prices (Bateman and Chang 2009: 8). Moreover, the initiative was not good for the sector as a whole. Larger, more sustainable dairy farms testified to lower levels of profitability because of the over-supply, and could not invest in new stock and equipment (Bateman and Chang 2009: 9). The focus on microenterprise during the post-war period led to the 'deindustrialization and primitivization of the average local economy', which 'effectively set back the region's development chances by decades' (Bateman 2010: 102). As the majority of the recipients of microfinance loans were women, they suffered disproportionately. This approach can be contrasted with the socially transforming impact of the massive expansion of public sector employment in the FRY after the Second World War, which offered many opportunities for women to build sustainable careers (Pupavac 2005: 402).

Another policy advocated in post-war Bosnia and Herzegovina was the 'Jobs and Justice' initiative, introduced by the High Representative Paddy Ashdown in 2002 with the intention of creating 60,000 jobs. It was based, however, on the neoliberal assumption that the free market will create the jobs as long as it is 'liberated' to do so, through the privatization of industries and the attraction of foreign investment. As a result, the actual policies were aimed at the fiscal architecture of the state; there were no policies aimed directly at job creation (Pugh 2006: 282–3). Many Bosnian women thus lost their jobs as a result of the policy, as they were employed in higher numbers in the public sector, which faced cuts as part of the liberalization approach. Moreover, women left widowed by the war (women-headed households rose to 25 per cent) found it harder to seek employment because of cuts to state-funded childcare. By 2007, only 35 per cent of women in Bosnia-Herzegovina were employed, among the lowest levels in the region, and women earned 20 to 50 per cent less than men (IFAD 2010). The inability to earn a living along with the decrease in social spending caused by neoliberal austerity measures has had a knock-on effect on women's social standing in society. Women who once held prestigious positions in public life are now relegated to their homes, engaged in domestic duties (IFAD 2010). Furthermore in another common feature of coping economies, many women have been forced or deceived into prostitution since the wars broke out in 1991 (Cockburn and Zarkov 2002b; Jennings and Nikolić-Ristanović 2009).

Just as in Mozambique, it is clear that the neoliberal reforms insisted upon by donors for Bosnia and Herzegovina benefited the male elites in the combat and criminal economies, whilst pushing women and other marginalized groups into the coping economy. Almost a quarter of a century later and the situation has little improved, leading to a wave of protests across the country in 2014 and a demand for the redistribution of wealth (Arsenijevic 2014).

Afghanistan   Afghanistan has been the site of superpower intervention throughout its history, as is well documented (Rashid 2002, 2009; Barfield 2010). The most recent phase began immediately after the 9/11 terrorist attacks on the

United States, when NATO announced it would launch air strikes if the Taliban government ruling Afghanistan from Kabul did not give up the terrorist leader responsible for the attacks, Osama bin Laden. The intervention in Afghanistan thus did not start out as a peacebuilding operation, but the NATO states increasingly stressed peacebuilding elements in order to justify the intervention as it proceeded, claiming that it was about stabilizing Afghanistan in order to facilitate security for its citizens, including particularly for women.

The funding for the stabilization and state-building mission was dependent upon the usual mixture of neoliberal reforms. Afghanistan's economy was already very weak, but the reforms have consolidated its almost total dependency on aid or foreign investment (Kühn 2008; Suhrke 2011). The United States and the World Bank insisted upon the liberalization of the economy of Afghanistan almost immediately after the post 9/11 invasion in October 2001 (World Bank 2003b, 2005; Kandiyoti 2007b). Under Presidential Decree No. 103 (2005), the Afghan Ministry of Finance began assessing the economic viability of various SOEs, recommending that only eight of 64 enterprises should remain state-owned while the other 56 should be divested – through privatization, liquidation, corporatization or other mechanisms. The World Bank also helped Afghanistan produce a new Minerals Law in 2005 which provides the framework for private development of the previously state-owned mines (World Bank 2004). Afghanistan is resource rich in iron, copper, cobalt and gold – worth billions of dollars (Risen 2010) – but the neoliberal framework for the development of the extractive industry, alongside corruption, has limited the revenue available for public spending. As with Mozambique and Bosnia-Herzegovina, it is those who had already secured power and resources through the combat and criminal economies in Afghanistan, the male leaders of the warring groups, who have been able to benefit from this massive privatization project, primarily through corruption (Giustozzi 2007). Since the West intervened in 2001, it has, according to evidence given to the British House of Commons Foreign Affairs Committee, channelled millions of dollars to Afghan power-holders it deems politically expedient, regardless of their records. Many Afghan elites, including those suspected of corruption, continued to receive large sums of money from various international actors. Afghanistan is the world's greatest recipient of aid, US$20 billion in the past decade, but relatively little reaches those in the coping economy. Ten years after the intervention began, US$3 million a day was said to leave Kabul airport corruptly to be used to buy property in Dubai (S. Jenkins 2011; Gall 2012).

The interrelated factors of corruption, ongoing insecurity and neoliberal reforms mean that Afghanistan raises inadequate sums in revenue (World Bank 2014). This weak tax base undermines efforts to transition from a war to a peace economy, as there has been little fiscal foundation upon which the state can support services or engage effectively in governance more generally. The liberalization process, which has benefited elites, exacerbated corruption and been harmful for the majority of Afghan citizens, has been particularly damaging for women and other marginalized groups in the coping economy, who are hardest hit by the public sector cuts encouraged by the donor community (Kandiyoti 2007a, 2007b). Deniz Kandiyoti concludes that state building in Afghanistan is premised on the principle 'that institutions must be put in place to ensure "good governance" in a manner that delivers just enough "state" to allow basic security for the functioning of markets and private-sector-led growth' (Kandiyoti 2007a: 505). A more transformative state is not considered an option. As in the cases of Mozambique and Bosnia, the neoliberal reforms demanded by donors are not the only cause of women's poverty and inequality. Fundamentalist Islam and the legacies of Cold War interventions have also combined to make Afghanistan 'the worst place in the world to be a woman' (Bowcott 2011). Yet neoliberal policies make it harder for women and other marginalized groups to challenge gender inequality. With educational and economic opportunities for women thwarted, and the power of male elites, often former warlords, consolidated, Afghan women are doubly penalized by the neoliberal policies of peacebuilding. In sum, the intervention in Afghanistan provides further evidence that many peacebuilding projects are undermined by donor insistence on neoliberal economic reforms.

Feminist scholars have been prominent in criticizing the neoliberal underpinnings of the peacebuilding endeavour. A particular preoccupation in feminist International Relations scholarship is the way that peacebuilding is described and justified in the discourse of the UN and other multilateral organizations by means of a gendered and racialized 'victim–rescuer' model. The next section turns to detail the arguments of feminists that have focused on this discourse and the harms it does. It aims both to highlight the significant contribution of this scholarship and to argue that there is a need for feminist analyses of peacebuilding to go beyond identifying the discourse and concluding that neoliberalism is the problem, and to focus more on solutions, by way of bringing material realities and institutional practices back into our sights.

The seductive narratives of peacebuilding

Feminist scholarship has drawn attention to the way in which, in dominant media and policy narratives about peacebuilding, analysis of the causes of conflict is confined to the global South, and these 'failed states' are found to be in need of rescue by the bearers of civilization, the more advanced states of the global economy. Inspired by post-colonial scholarship, many feminists argue that these narratives draw on colonial imaginings of a white male hero who is associated with attributes including freedom, authority, civilization, power, democracy and wealth, an identification strengthened by its opposition to a second essential character in the narrative, the object of the imperial gaze: the black, native or colonized subject (Orford 1999: 684–8). At the height of the British Empire, promotions of tourism, such as the World's Fairs of the 1890s, 'preached that white men's manliness fuelled the civilizing imperial mission and in turn, that pursuing the imperial mission revitalized the nation's masculinity' (Enloe 1989: 27). As such, colonial projects have always depended on this racialized, imperial masculinity (Nagel 1998). For many feminists, peacebuilding narratives are the continuation of this same narrative.

Criticism of peacebuilding interventions as neo-colonial rose to a crescendo in the wake of the invasion of Afghanistan in 2001. Countless feminists found the US and UK government assertions that the intervention was motivated in part by the need to protect Afghan women's human rights as a particularly galling case of powerful Western elites attempting to justify and legitimize, through a claim to superior moral and civilizational values, an operation which was actually aimed at reinforcing Western hegemony (Abu-Lughod 2002; Tickner 2002; Cloud 2004; Jabbra 2006; Nayak 2006; Youngs 2006; Eisenstein 2007; Thobani 2007; Bhattacharyya 2008; Khalili 2011).[3] The narrative of 'saving brown women' (Spivak 1988; see previous chapter) was particularly prominent in the United States, with President George W. Bush stating that 'the central goal of the terrorists is the brutal repression of women – and not only the women of Afghanistan...that is the reason this great nation, with our friends and allies, will not rest until we bring them all to justice' (G. W. Bush 2001). Laura Bush declared that 'the fight against terrorism is also a fight for the rights and dignity of women' and '[c]ivilized people throughout the world are speaking out in horror...because our hearts break for the women and children in Afghanistan' (L. Bush 2001). At around the same time, a video previously ignored by CNN of a woman being beheaded by the Taliban at Kabul stadium was suddenly picked up by the network and repeatedly broadcast, along with other horror stories of how Afghan women were treated. Some women's organizations in the United States added their voices to the chorus, seeking the opportunity to capitalize on the apparent new-found concern for Afghan women after many years of their advocacy on the issue being ignored (Ferguson 2005; Russo 2006).

The effect of this, many feminists argued, was to cast Afghanistan as inherently backward, misogynist and uncivilized, and its women in need of rescuing by NATO. As Jasmin Zine puts it, '[T]he archetypal image of the deprived and debased Muslim woman was resurrected to perform her duty as a signifier of the abject difference of Muslims; the barbarity and anti-modernism of Islam and its essential repression of women; and most importantly as camouflage for US interventions' (Zine 2006: 34). Many feminists argue that the focus of these narratives ends up being not about women at all; it becomes about white men and Muslim men and how they treat 'their' women (Hunt 2002; Bhattacharyya 2008; Al-Ali and Pratt 2009). Muslim men are portrayed as 'dangerous foreigners, terrorists, and threats to public safety' and, with the obsessing over cultural and religious treatment of women, Muslim women are rendered 'victims of their anachronistic faith, lacking agency and voice' (Zine 2006: 30). Crucially, this 'consistent resort to the cultural' distracts from the role of geopolitics and the global economy in causing the insecurities, inequalities and hardships of life in Afghanistan (Russo 2006: 560). Poverty and violence in Afghanistan have clear roots in the legacy of colonialism and Cold War-era interventions, which exacerbated poverty, funded Islamist groups and flooded the country with weaponry (Hirschkind and Mahmood 2002; Kandiyoti 2007b). Yet in the dominant policy and media narratives these factors are neglected and the poverty and violence in Afghanistan are attributed to 'Afghan culture'.

This critique did not emerge only in the wake of the 2001 intervention in Afghanistan, however. Feminists have been prominent amongst critical scholars who have argued that all interventions which claim to be peacebuilding or humanitarian are problematic in this way. For example, feminists focusing on the UN peacekeeping operation in Somalia in 1993 focused on the way in which the Canadian peacekeepers saw themselves as civilized, advanced and heroic, and Somalia as backward, inherently violent and beyond saving (Razack 2004; Whitworth 2004). This sense of righteousness made it seem reasonable for these soldiers, as representatives of 'civilized nations', to intervene to build peace as if they had nothing to do with the cause of the conflict in the first place, which is hard to argue in the case of the Horn of Africa. The famine and conflict in Somalia can be linked to the devastation caused by the SAP introduced into Somalia in the 1980s, which contributed to a crisis in Somali agriculture and extreme austerity measures imposed on social spending (Chossudovsky 1997). Yet in dominant narratives of peacebuilding the causes of the violence were portrayed as the ancient hatreds of primitive warring tribes. As Sherene Razack describes the narrative: 'Warlords and ethnic nationalism, indisputable scourges of our age, are often pictured as though they have risen up from the landscape itself and not out of histories in which the West has featured as a colonizing power.... [H]istory is evacuated and the simplest of story lines remains: the more civilized states have to keep less civilized states in line' (Razack 2004: 16, 48). As Razack and Sandra Whitworth detail, the Canadian peacekeepers were angered and frustrated when not all Somalis were grateful for their intervention, and, for two soldiers at least, this anger led to the torture and murder of a 16-year-old Somali boy. In the tribunal which followed, and the considerable national soul-searching in Canada, the narrative that 'saving Somalia' was an impossible task, one incredibly hard on 'our soldiers' given the violence and backwardness of that country, proved resilient. Crucially, this discourse not only distracts from the role of Western powers in causing the violence, but it perpetuates the idea that Western models of economic reform are the solution. For Whitworth, inherent in the peacebuilding narrative is the idea that 'the well-ordered rational, liberal, free market North brings peace in a variety of ways, not least by delivering through peacekeeping the very principles of rationality, liberalism, and free market economics so clearly absent in the anarchic global South' (Whitworth 2004: 25).

Likewise, Anne Orford identifies in the discourse of media, legal and policy texts on the interventions in the Balkans the same gendered narrative which ignores almost completely the historical context of rapid and massive global economic change which contributed to the violent disintegration of the former Yugoslavia. Balkan national leaders, including the Serb nationalist Slobodan Milošević, came to power as the IMF's neoliberal stabilization programme radically altered the nature of Yugoslav constitutional and political arrangements, causing significant and unstable new alliances in the region (Orford 1997; also see Cockburn 1998). Orford argues that the constant linking of violence to local passions and chaotic nationalism in the way that the disintegration of Yugoslavia was described in Western narratives masked the 'more far-reaching forms of violence that are now conducted through massive restructuring and social upheaval in the name of free trade or economic liberalism' (Orford 1999: 710).

For many feminists, the text and framing of 1325 and other elements of the WPS architecture continue this narrative (Whitworth 2004; Barnes 2006; Pratt 2013). For these feminists, 1325 is too silent on structural violence caused by the global economy. Sheri Gibbings (2011) tells a story about

Iraqi women who were welcome at UN to discuss their activism for peace, but who caused offence when they began to talk about neo-imperialism, capitalism and war. Nicola Pratt (2013) argues that in the very language of 1325, gender may be taken seriously, but because it is achieved by reinforcing ideas of zones of peace and progressive values and zones of violence and misogyny, this gain is achieved at the cost of a 'reinscription of racial sexual boundaries, evocative of the political economy of imperialism' (Pratt 2013; also see Barnes 2006; Whitworth 2004; L. J. Shepherd 2008; H. Hudson 2012b; Nesiah 2013; Pratt and Richter-Devroe 2011).

This critique has been important in drawing our attention to the big picture – the gendered harms of the neoliberal underpinnings of peacebuilding – and demonstrating the way that Security Council resolutions do not just require policies and actions but also construct narratives and identities. However, it also contains some limitations.

As I argued in the introduction, much of the feminist scholarship on WPS follows the structure of acknowledging that 1325 has achieved some things, but ultimately cannot achieve feminist visions of security because of the dominance of neoliberalism in the current world order.[4] There is a risk of determinism in such a position, and some of the scholarship tends towards a totalizing account of peacebuilding wherein interventions are always, inevitably going to make thing worse for women and other marginalized groups because they are always, inevitably going to be neoliberal and re-inscribe gendered and racialized hierarchies (see, e.g., Razack 2004; Pratt 2013; Welland 2015). This is perhaps due to an over-reliance on analysing texts and discourses for evidence of gendered logics in feminist International Relations scholarship, where many, despite a theoretical commitment to discourse analytical tools which assume that discourses are never fixed and that there is always then the possibility of change, often in practice reach the conclusion that every policy, initiative and action in the WPS agenda is the continuation of imperial relations. The dominance of narrative approaches may be due to the unconvincing but incensing 'saving brown women' narrative used by the Bush administration as the justification for invading Afghanistan. In any case, it is important at this juncture in the WPS agenda for feminists to rediscover their focus on the practices, initiatives and institutions on the ground, and their material effects, as well as the gendered logics in discourse.[5]

Conclusion

That neoliberal policies rest upon gendered assumptions, reinforce gendered hierarchies and rely upon gendered discourses for their legitimation has been well established, as this chapter demonstrates. If peacebuilding is to benefit gender equality, bringing about the peace described in the previous chapter, it must attend to these realities. This chapter has argued that although feminists have been at the forefront of developing sophisticated critiques of peacebuilding, claiming that the WPS agenda stands little chance of success because of the ways it reinforces the civilizational discourse of white men saving brown women from brown men, these critiques risk becoming too totalizing in their conclusions. It was suggested that this might be in some ways due to a tendency to focus on the narratives and discourses that construct global politics, which, whilst important, do not capture the full picture – both of the gendered harms of neoliberalism, which were detailed at the start of the chapter, and of the potential of the WPS architecture, which we turn to consider in the next. Given that the WPS architecture has been considerably strengthened in recent years, has there been any corresponding progress in any post-conflict settings? Has it begun to overcome the problems of conceptualization, implementation and – most crucially – ambition outlined in the first chapter? In what ways precisely is the WPS agenda hindered by or surmounting the neoliberal contexts within which it operates?

Questions for discussion

1 What is meant by war economies, and how are they gendered?

2   How do neoliberal reforms imposed on post-conflict countries as part of peacebuilding impact upon gendered war economies?

3   What do feminists mean by saying peacebuilding is characterized by Spivak's phrase 'white men saving brown women from brown men'? Do you find this argument compelling? If so, does it apply equally in all examples of peacebuilding?

Suggestions for further reading

Christine Chinkin and Mary Kaldor. 2013. 'Gender and New Wars'. *Journal of International Affairs* 67 (1): 167–87.
This article analyses the gendered experience of 'new wars' and presents an interesting argument that the construction of masculinity in new wars, in contrast to the heroic warrior of 'old wars', is much more contradictory and insecure.

Christopher Cramer. 2009. 'Trajectories of Accumulation through War and Peace'. In *The Dilemmas of Statebuilding: Confronting the Contradictions of Postwar Peace Operations.* Abingdon: Routledge.
Cramer provides a good overview of the way neoliberal reforms tend to benefit those in the combat and criminal economies at the expense of those in the coping economy. He does not focus on gender specifically, but the chapter is a good introduction to how neoliberal economic policies play out in post-conflict contexts, drawing on examples from Mozambique and Afghanistan in particular.

V. Spike Peterson. 2008. ' "New Wars" and Gendered Economies'. *Feminist Review* 88 (1): 7–20.
In this article, Peterson introduces a feminist perspective to the literature on war economies, providing a compelling case for their gendered nature. This article should have provided a framework for policy-makers, but, to my knowledge, it has not been taken up by any peacebuilding institution in order to inform post-conflict reconstruction policies.

Vanessa Pupavac. 2005. 'Empowering women? An Assessment of International Gender Policies in Bosnia'. *International Peacekeeping* 12.3: 391-405.
This article considers international policies intended to further the economic empowerment of women and demonstrates how they are undermined by broader neoliberal prescriptions for the post-war state.

Sherene Razack. 2004. *Dark Threats and White Knights: The Somalia Affair, Peacekeeping and the New Imperialism.* Toronto: University of Toronto Press.
A fascinating account of the Canadian peacekeepers in Somalia, which is persuasive in its account of the neo-imperial underpinnings of the endeavour, but which also risks a totalizing and overly pessimistic analysis of peacebuilding.

Web resources

DAWN: Development Alternatives with Women for a New Era (*http://www.dawnnet.org/feminist-resources/analyses/peg*)
DAWN is a network of feminist scholars, researchers and activists from the economic South working for economic and gender justice and sustainable and democratic development. On the page linked to here, DAWN monitors and analyses the systematic processes of economic globalization and trade liberalization and their impacts on poor women of the South. It works closely with other global development networks for greater accountability and radical restructuring of institutions like the World Bank, the IMF, the UN system and (from 1999) the World Trade Organization.

Oxfam (*http://politicsofpoverty.oxfamamerica.org/2015/02/uneven-benefits-unequal-burden-women-and-extractive-industries/*)
Oxfam has recently focused on the gendered impact of the extraction of minerals, oil and gas that is often recommended as a central economic development strategy for post-conflict countries. This blog post summarizes Oxfam's concerns, and links to a variety of other reports and analyses on the

links between extractive industries and threats to women's security.

UN Women Watch Feature on Gender Equality and Trade Policy (*http://www.un.org/womenwatch/feature/trade/index. html*)
An overview of the gendered dimensions of trade policy, which, although not focused on post-conflict contexts, covers relevant debates. Presents a fairly optimistic view of the potential of modifying the current economic system in order to enhance gender equality, but contains a good overview of the issues.

World Bank's 'Breaking the Conflict Trap' (*http://elibrary. worldbank.org/doi/abs/10.1596/978-0-8213-5481-0*)
A research report on the links between poverty and conflict which is claimed by some to demonstrate a shift in World Bank thinking towards a more pro-poor approach, but which is still felt by many critical security and feminist scholars to be very much within the neoliberal framework.

4
Protection, Participation and Prevention in Practice

This chapter considers the extent to which current peace-building efforts have overcome the problems, dilemmas and obstacles outlined in previous chapters. More specifically, it asks if current efforts to engender peacebuilding with the WPS agenda are taking us towards the feminist vision of peace outlined in chapter 2, and, crucially, if they are addressing in any significant way the neoliberal underpinnings of mainstream peacebuilding outlined in chapter 3. Most feminists have long argued that the project of gendering something – or 'gender as an approach', in Munro's typology – is about more than *adding women* to previously male-dominated institutions. It is about recognizing gendered inequalities and the gender ideology that underpins a phenomenon, in our case, war, and trying to challenge them. It involves reconstructing masculinities and femininities and transforming the unequal relations between men and women. More than that, recognition of the importance of intersectionality means that any effective project has to involve transforming unequal relations between different races, classes and sexualities too. This chapter considers how the extant WPS architecture – bearing in mind the measures taken to strengthen it post-2008 – is achieving this more thoroughgoing and transformative understanding of engendering peacebuilding as a feminist project. Taking protection, participation and prevention in turn, and also considering the gendering of security sector reform (SSR) as a strand of the WPS agenda which has recently gained in importance, the chapter assesses the extent to which current peacebuilding efforts have overcome the gaps and dilemmas outlined in previous chapters. It focuses in particular on specific aspects of peacebuilding in the DRC, Syria, Burundi and Liberia to explore the current status of the WPS agenda, whilst recognizing that this approach leaves out some other equally important aspects and areas.[1] The web resources listed at the end of the chapter point to the routes by which readers can explore further, make comparisons and draw their own conclusions.

Protection of women and girls from violence

In chapter 1, we saw how a major concern of feminists with the protection pillar of 1325 was the lack of accountability and monitoring measures, the limited funding for training soldiers about the protection of civilians against, *inter alia*, sexual violence, the limited funding for justice systems so that perpetrators could be prosecuted, and the lack of willingness of states contributing troops to UN peace operations to prosecute their own nationals in cases where they were accused of perpetrating sexual violence. In sum, there were concerns about lack of resources and political will. Some feminists also had concerns about the focus on protecting women – that it essentialized them as victims – and about focusing on tackling impunity of perpetrators – because it privileged a legal response when women affected by conflict might have different priorities. The level of activity at the UN Security Council over the last 15 years indicates that some of these concerns, those related to political will, have at least been heard. In order to strengthen the UN response to protection of women and girls, against sexual violence in particular, several further resolutions have been adopted.

Although 1325 had already identified sexual violence as a tactic of war that required a security and political response, four subsequent resolutions adopted between 2008 and 2013 strengthened the UN's response considerably. UNSCR 1820, adopted in 2008, required the Secretary-General and his envoys to raise the issue of sexual violence when seeking to resolve conflicts, thus compelling the UN's peacekeeping bureaucracy to make ending conflict-related sexual violence central to their work (Goetz 2014). Within the UN this took institutional form in the creation of the cross-UN collaboration UN Action Against Sexual Violence in Conflict, which was intended to make sexual violence no longer just a 'women's issue' or a matter for humanitarian agencies but a key priority for peace and security work across the organization. Comprising 13 UN entities, it has linked UN force commanders with women peace activists and victims of sexual violence, inventoried best practices by peacekeepers in detecting and preventing sexual violence, developed and disseminated innovative scenario-based training for military peacekeepers, convened peacemakers and mediators to discuss the neglect of sexual violence in peace negotiations and to produce guidance to address it, and developed early-warning indicators specific to conflict-related sexual violence.

UNSCR 1820 was followed one year later with UNSCR 1888, which called for a Special Representative of the Secretary-General on Sexual Violence in Conflict (SRSG-SVC), a team of rule-of-law experts on the issue and the deployment of women protection advisers in peacekeeping missions. Further strengthening of the UN's response was provided by UNSCR 1960 in 2010, which called for field-based monitoring, analysis and reporting arrangements to provide the Security Council with up-to-date information on trends and perpetrators; and UNSCR 2106, adopted in 2013, which reiterates that all actors, including not only the Security Council and parties to armed conflict, but all member states and UN entities, must do more to implement previous mandates and combat impunity for these crimes. In addition to these resolutions, Foreign Ministers of the G8 launched a Declaration on Sexual Violence in April 2013 at their meeting in London. Together with SRSG-SVC Zainab Bangura, the G8 committed to the development of a Comprehensive International Protocol on the Investigation and Documentation of rape and sexual violence in conflict. Ministers also promised to review national doctrine and training provided to police and military personnel to better equip them in dealing with sexual violence within conflict zones to which they are deployed. This was followed in June 2014 with a UK government-hosted Global Summit to Tackle Sexual Violence in Conflict. With the celebrity endorsement of actress and UN Goodwill Ambassador Angelina Jolie, it brought immense media attention to the issue and a considerable turnout – 1,700 delegates and 123 country delegations including 79 ministers – in its efforts to continue the momentum of action to tackle sexual violence in conflict.[2]

This summit capped off five years of what could be said to be unprecedented activity, but to what effect? A pertinent case to examine in order to answer that question is the DRC, as war's impact on women there has been particularly brutal (Peterman et al. 2011; Trenholm et al. 2011). For decades the DRC has been caught up in a spiral of armed conflict. The legacies of colonialism and Cold War interference include severe poverty, insecurity and an almost total lack of functioning state infrastructure, despite the DRC being one of the world's most resource-rich countries (Stearns 2011). Invasions sparking consecutive conflicts in 1996–7 and 1998–2003, fuelled by foreign interests over Congolese resources, have played a significant role in destabilizing the economy and governing institutions. The DRC's human development index remains the next-to-lowest on earth (186th of 187 countries surveyed in 2013). IMF and World Bank policies have in many ways exacerbated poverty, insecurity and inequality, as they have encouraged economic reforms which further undermine state infrastructure and facilitate corruption (Martin-Prével 2014a). Despite numerous peace accords and the presence of the world's largest UN peacekeeping mission, the United Nations Organization Stabilization Mission in the DRC (MONUSCO), fighting continues in the east between various armed factions (Deleu 2015). Sexual violence has been a dominant feature of the conflict (Meger 2010; Leatherman 2011), leading Margot Wallström, then UN SRSG-SVC, to call the DRC 'the rape capital of the world' (BBC 2010).[3]

The WPS architecture and global attention on sexual violence in conflict helped put pressure on MONUSCO and the government of Joseph Kabila in the DRC to do more to tackle these crimes. In 2006, the government passed a relatively far-reaching law broadening the definition of sexual violence and promoting stronger penalties for perpetrators. In 2009, the country developed a National Strategy on Gender-Based Violence, and in March 2013 the government and the UN signed a Joint Communiqué outlining concrete actions the government would take to eradicate these offences. In October 2014, Kabila appointed a Special Representative on Sexual Violence and Child Recruitment. Despite these initiatives, however, the prevalence of sexual violence remains shocking. A peace deal in February 2013 prompted hopes for some calm, but 2014 saw a revival of violence, with the UN Population Fund (UNFPA) recording 11,769 cases of sexual and gender-based violence between January and September in the provinces of North Kivu, South Kivu, Orientale, Katanga and Maniema. Of these cases, 39 per cent were considered to be directly related to the dynamics of conflict, and were perpetrated by armed individuals (UNSC 2015). Whilst these figures could be due to an increase in reporting, it is clear that sexual violence continues to be a major cause of insecurity for civilians, boys and men as well as women and girls, in the DRC.

There have been efforts to ensure access to justice for some of these victims. A number of UN agencies and NGOs have instigated programmes focused on providing better access to justice, training police to investigate crimes of sexual violence and to pay special attention to the safety and security of victims, and ensuring that victims of sexual violence receive reparations for the harm they have suffered. A UNDP project in the Kivu Provinces and Ituri District, for example, has established clinics to provide legal and medical assistance to victims, including legal aid. It has trained the judiciary, too, in how to prosecute those responsible. It has also trained and supplied mobile courts so that trials can be held as close to the crime scene and complainant's home as possible. Through this work, in 2010 and 2011, the UNDP claimed to have monitored over 6,500 sexual violence crimes, seen 650 of these cases go to court by the end of 2011 (with dozens more in 2012), resulting in a conviction rate of almost 60 per cent (UNDP 2014a). This can be contrasted with the OHCHR's claim that of the 14,200 rapes reported in South Kivu alone during 2005–7 (before the newer resolutions), only 2 per cent of the perpetrators were ever pursued (UN Women 2012c: 11). In 2014, military tribunals convicted 135 individuals – including 76 members of the armed forces, 41 members of the national police and 18 members of armed groups – of sexual violence crimes (UNSC 2015).This work to bring perpetrators to justice indicates some advancement on the WPS protection agenda, but, with rape continuing at a reported rate of 40 women and girls every day in the DRC (Nallu 2015), not at an adequate pace. Moreover, in isolated areas, where the justice system is weak or absent, civilians may resort to informal practices between the families of the perpetrator and the victim to 'close' the case, including marriage (UNSC 2015).

Furthermore, the follow-on resolutions reinforce an understanding of sexual violence as a weapon of war which is best tackled through the prosecution and conviction of perpetrators, a framing which is of concern to some feminists (Ní Aoláin et al. 2011; Eriksson Baaz and Stern 2013), as we saw in chapter 1. In the Congolese case, feminists have pointed to three problems with this approach. Firstly, it does not provide what victims of sexual violence often prioritize as their needs. When local women are asked what it would take for them to feel secure, the answers are often not the donors' priorities – tackling the impunity of perpetrators by strengthening the justice system – but being able to secure work, support their families and send their children to school without discrimination (Ní Aoláin et al. 2011: 61; Autesserre 2012: 216; Eriksson Baaz and Stern 2013). Other populations who have suffered but not from sexual violence often find it hard to secure services at all (Autesserre 2012: 17). Secondly, this approach has meant that in order to access services, Congolese women have had to identify themselves as victims of sexual violence, which has led to them being ostracized from their family and/or community (Ní Aoláin et al. 2011). Thirdly, the 'sexual violence as a weapon of war' approach arguably fails to capture the links between ordinary violence and conflict violence that are crucially important in addressing sexual violence (Ní Aoláin et al. 2011; Autesserre 2012: 217). There is some evidence that *civilian* rapes in Eastern Congo increased by 17 per cent whilst rapes committed by soldiers *decreased* between 2004 and 2008 (Bartels et al. 2010), yet there is still a strong presumption that 'sexual violence in war is a thing apart, an experience capable of being parsed out from the "regular and normal" violence that accompany women's lives in many societies' (Ní Aoláin et al. 2011: 46). The problem is, as we saw in chapter 1, that gender-based violence does not end with the ceasefire. The construction of violent and misogynist cultures and gender roles in peacetime and the justice system more broadly need to be tackled in order to tackle sexual violence. The approach that has been privileged by the UN's WPS agenda arguably does not do enough in this regard.

Thus it is clear that even as more effort is put into tackling sexual violence in war, the dilemmas outlined in chapter 1 have not disappeared and have perhaps intensified. On the one hand, framing sexual violence as a weapon of war has been useful both for grabbing the attention of the world's policy-makers and for improving protection on the ground (Goetz 2014). Not least because some victims of sexual violence live in remote areas which can only be reached by armed patrols, some feminists maintain that militaries have an important role to play in advancing the WPS protection agenda, and that the 'weapon of war' framing has been useful for engaging militaries in this work (see UN Women 2012c). Others remain concerned that this framing reinforces the myths that sexual violence only happens in war, that it is about militarized masculinities in wartime rather than gender relations more broadly, and that it is a harm which can be tackled with international humanitarian law alone. As Anne Marie Goetz (2014) puts it:

> Sexual violence in war is now out of the ghetto. But the security and law enforcement focus may have encouraged the notion that sexual violence in conflict can be addressed without intensifying the political project of ending gender inequality that produces sexual violence even in peacetime. Advocacy language suggesting 'it's not about sex/women/ gender, it's about war' may have helped to convince the Security Council that this was a subject requiring their attention, but may also have unwittingly downplayed the importance of the feminist emancipatory projects of empowering survivors, and ensuring that protection and recovery efforts contribute to transformation in gender relations.

Even those feminists who are sceptical of the 'weapon of war' framing concede that a commitment to tackling impunity is crucial (Ní Aoláin et al. 2011; Autesserre 2012). At the same time, they urge more attention to important contextual issues, such as the practicalities of women's lives in DRC:

> Victims, who may be raising children that resulted from their rapes, or who may be unable to have more children because of the violence, may, for example, continue to live in the same communities as the perpetrators, who have returned from war to their families. As we craft remedies, we must account for these differing, potentially conflicting, realities which themselves may reflect divergent constituencies: a need for punishment, a need for rehabilitation for both victims and perpetrators, and a need for national reconciliation. (Ní Aoláin et al. 2011: 20)

Fionnuala Ní Aoláin and her co-authors argue that as well as constantly reasserting the centrality of law in confronting such violations, and continually improving the process and creating laws which respond to what women perceive as broadly harmful to them, it is important to think about other mechanisms which can work in synergy with the law to build a gender-sensitive peace.

An example of work which meets these broader needs of survivors of sexual violence in conflict is gender-sensitive reparations. Rather than just provide legal justice, they provide resources to women, and sometimes to the community as a whole, in order that women are economically empowered to rebuild their lives. The Congolese government's 2009 National Strategy to combat Gender-Based Violence includes a commitment to provide reparations, but reports in 2013 indicated that it had yet to pay out any of the money awarded by the courts to survivors (Parmar and Mushiata 2012). The UN Joint Human Rights Office, however, has since stepped up its efforts to encourage the government to meet its obligations under international law to provide reparations, has provided grants to NGOs to support survivors (OHCHR 2013), and in June 2014 produced with UN Women a Guidance Note on Reparations for Conflict-Related Sexual Violence (UN 2014b).

Reparations are no panacea (Rubio-Marín 2006, 2012). Chief amongst the stumbling blocks is resourcing them, as the DRC example illustrates well, but innovative solutions have been proposed. Truth Commissions in South Africa, Sierra Leone, Timor-Leste and Liberia have, for example, recommended legislation that would tax businesses that profited from repression or the protection of armed groups during a conflict, and in the Philippines, legislation has been drafted so that part of the funds recovered from the assets amassed through corruption by Ferdinand Marcos during his dictatorship can be used to finance reparations (UN Women 2012a). What is promising about reparations for many feminists is that they have the potential to bring about structural reforms (Ní Aoláin et al. 2011; True 2014). They can be linked to legal reform, for example, such that women can be awarded rights to hold property. They can be paid to the whole community, rather than only to individuals. This is important not just to avoid divisions within the community, but because reparations can be used in this way to fund education, healthcare and livelihood support (Ní Aoláin et al. 2011: 191). A benefit of gender-sensitive reparations of a slightly different nature is that they can be used to foster women's social capital and knowledge of their rights through a process of asking women themselves what form of reparation best meets their needs, thus including them, empowering them and challenging the idea of women as eternal victims in ways which could have long-lasting effects on their place in society (Ní Aoláin et al. 2011: 264).

It is also fair to say that there has been more focus in recent years in work on sexual violence in conflict on challenging masculinities to complement the work on promoting access to justice for women. The UNDP has trained over 2,200 soldiers in the DRC on the laws regarding sexual violence and the criminal responsibility of commanding officers (UNDP 2014b). UNICEF runs discussion groups for adolescents in the DRC to talk about sexual violence, one aim of which is the deconstructing of masculinities (UN Secretary-General 2014). NGOs, too, increasingly focus on the need to deconstruct and reconstruct masculinities and incorporate this more sophisticated approach into their protection projects (see, e.g., El-Bushra 2012). This is happening on a small scale, but represents progress nonetheless.

This progress has to be seen in its wider context, of course, and here it is important to note the framework of a neoliberal macroeconomic development strategy in the DRC. This framework, which encourages FDI as a route to economic growth, has undermined the tax revenue the DRC requires to provide the access to justice, health and education so desperately needed. The neoliberal model has also undermined the building of a responsive and legitimate state infrastructure more generally through the facilitation of corruption. The DRC is rich in key resources such as cobalt, copper, diamonds, tantalum, tin and petroleum. FDI in the DRC rose from US$72 million in 2000 to US$3.3 billion in 2012, but the tax incentives offered, combined with corruption amongst DRC elites, have undercut the tax revenue which the mining of these resources could generate (Martin-Prével 2014a). Five hundred companies operate in the DRC to exploit these resources, but revenues from oil and mining added up to just 5 per cent of the country's GDP in 2012 (EITI 2013). Undervaluation of assets when selling mineral licences to foreign investors is a central part of the problem. This practice cost the DRC more than US$1.3 billion in revenues between 2010 and 2012 (Watkins 2013). Likewise, the vast majority of logging revenues in the DRC were lost to tax avoidance and other illegal financial arrangements, with the Treasury receiving only 10 per cent of its dues under Congolese law in 2012, depriving it of more than US$11 million (Global Witness 2013a). As argued in the previous chapter, post-conflict countries need to be able to raise enough revenue to transform society, including in terms of securing justice for victims of sexual violence, and the combination of neoliberal reforms and corruption make this impossible. Aid, too, is undermined by the current economic system: Africa is said to lose twice as much in illicit financial outflows as it receives in international aid (Watkins 2013).

This story of gains, limitations and remaining obstacles to achieving protection of women, girls and other marginalized groups in the DRC is one which shares features with many other conflict-affected areas where sexual violence has been rife, from Afghanistan to Colombia to the Philippines. Sexual violence differs in its nature and prevalence in different contexts, but the DRC illustrates well the challenges in addressing it. A significant amount of energy has been expended on tackling sexual violence in armed conflict, but the evidence from a variety of conflict zones demonstrates there is a long way to go (Buss et al. 2014). Some feminists argue that the initiatives around prosecution of perpetrators, training of peacekeepers and access to justice and reparations for victims are starting to achieve results. Others suggest that the UN's efforts still often miss the two vital aspects which feminist scholarship has highlighted as crucial: an emphasis on reconstructing masculinities and a focus on the economic security of women to resist and recover from sexual violence. It is thinking about these challenges, and the sort of macroeconomic development approach which would enable them to be met, that arguably represent crucial areas of future work for feminists focused on the WPS protection agenda.

Participation in peace processes

In terms of the participation of women in peace processes, we see a similar picture of considerable UN activity to strengthen the WPS architecture, and a complex scenario of small wins and remaining obstacles and barriers. Participation in formal 'Track 1' peace processes is crucial for women as this is where agreements are forged which will shape the future of a country and have long-term effects on its population. Although Track 1 negotiations are not the only important element of building peace, without access to this formal process, the considerable work that women often do building peace in more informal ways at the community level is undermined. As chapter 1 outlined, UNSCR 2122 (2013), along with the Secretary-General's 7-PAP (2010), was adopted in part as a response to feminist concerns that the participation of women was being neglected in comparison to their protection. Both place emphasis on the importance of including women and gender analyses in order to reach a sustainable and inclusive peace.

As we saw in chapter 1, the adoption of 1325 did not seem to make much impact on the number of women who were included in peace negotiations in the years following. UN Women's survey of 31 major peace processes between 1992 and 2010 found that, of the 17 cases for which such information was available, women only accounted for 9 per cent of the negotiating parties and 4 per cent of the signatories. Has the strengthening of the participation elements of the WPS architecture since 2010 made any difference? Syrian women would be unlikely to answer in the affirmative. As one of the world's most recent and most devastating conflicts, Syria offers us a good case to test the effectiveness of the extant WPS participation agenda. The evidence is not heartening. Although there have been peace talks, Syrian women have been largely excluded from Track 1 negotiations in Geneva, both the first peace conference in June 2012 (Geneva I) and the second in January 2014 (Geneva II). This is despite the many ways in which they have demonstrated their particular role in building peace, their experience at negotiating local ceasefires, at getting humanitarian aid through to those who need it, and their commitment to negotiating a sustainable, inclusive peace settlement as the basis for a new constitution (Williams 2014). The frustration of WILPF's Secretary-General Madeleine Rees is palpable. 'It's as if', she noted, 'the Security Council Resolutions which reflected the need to bring the voices of others into the discourse were passed in a vacuum, that our minds could not actually catch up with what they purported to bring about' (Rees 2014). UN Women gathered 47 Syrian women to meet Lakdhar Brahimi, the UN's Special Envoy to Syria, in advance of Geneva II. Women's organizations WILPF, Code Pink and Madre also organized a roundtable for these women to share strategies for effective advocacy for peace with Nobel Peace Prize-winning women from Northern Ireland and Iran (Enloe 2014). These efforts resulted in both the government and opposition being encouraged to include women in their negotiating teams at the last minute. The women selected, however, were not those with the relevant experience on the ground and were unknown to peace activists (Enloe 2014).

As we saw in chapter 1, feminists stress the importance of ensuring representation for women's organizations, who, as part of civil society, are an important constituency to have at the table. Their long-standing exclusion makes it difficult to demonstrate the difference their inclusion makes, but there are suggested correlations between the organized participation of women's groups and greater attentiveness to gender in the resulting text of the agreement (UN Women 2012b). Brahimi said he supported the inclusion of women, but did little to facilitate it in Geneva, seemingly unable to move beyond the accepted wisdom that you must focus on getting representatives of the most violent and intransigent groups around the table so as to cultivate potential spoilers. Of course, peace agreements do require elite bargains between key belligerent groups, but genuine peace also requires an inclusive and open peace process if it is to result in peace and security for all groups in society and avoid reinforcing the very dynamic which is in need of resolution, the idea that there are two implacably opposing sides. Syrian women have resisted this binary narrative, recognizing that it does not represent the Syria they know (Cockburn 2014; Enloe 2014; Rees 2014; Williams 2014). Feminists point out that focusing only on the two sides in Syria has meant cultivating the groups who have been responsible for human rights violations on a massive scale: the regime has violated international humanitarian law, ignored the International Criminal Court and used chemical weapons against its own citizens; and the opposition includes criminals and jihadists funded by Gulf States (Rees 2014). It has meant excluding those who have suffered most and who have demonstrated commitment to peace – women's groups and other civil society organizations (Williams 2014).

Owing in part to the WPS agenda, the barriers to women's inclusion have shifted. Where once the inclusion was a matter of gender blindness – the UN did not think of including women – there is now, thanks to feminist persistence, little chance of ignoring women. Similarly, where once they used explicit arguments that women were not qualified as they were not fighters, now men, of the international community at least, have to pay lip-service to the importance of the inclusion of women. Nonetheless, in the Syrian case, it appears we have not moved much beyond lip-service. Both parties have included a small number of women, but as Cynthia Enloe (2014) asks:

> [S]hould feminists be pleased or not that at the last minute the men leading each of the warring sides added a few women

to their official rosters? To answer this salient question, one has to be able to tell what is mere 'window dressing'. Then there's a follow-up question to answer: Can even a token be turned into something substantive?

Recent research on the specific question of translating presence into results during peace negotiations beyond Syria finds that the dangers of co-option are real, but that women's participation can make a difference (McLeod et al. 2014; Waylen 2014). As has been found to be the case in women's representation in parliaments (Lovenduski and Norris 2003; Paxton and Hughes 2007), substantive change often requires an ongoing commitment from feminist activists on the outside both to support women's representatives and to call them to account. It requires that women be present at all levels and at all stages of the peace process; if they are not involved at the earliest stages, they will not be able to shape the agenda and purpose of the negotiations (C. Bell 2004).

As well as the *barriers put in the way* of women, there are also *obstacles preventing* Syrian women's participation in peace negotiations.[4] In Syria, as in all societies, women have traditionally shouldered the bulk of caring responsibilities, which explains their relative absence from positions of power and authority in public life today. This has limited their opportunity to be in positions where they could influence the peace process. More directly, Syrian women have been targeted by the warring parties, and in areas where extremist Islamic groups have taken control, they are in danger if they leave the house without a male guardian (Benjamin 2014; Cockburn 2014). Women inside Syria thus face considerable obstacles when it comes to making their needs and priorities clear to the international actors responsible for peace talks. The devastation caused to infrastructure means that it is harder to communicate across divides and with the outside world (Barsa and Williams 2014). That the UN needs to do more to facilitate women's participation in peacebuilding by tackling these structural impediments to women's participation has been stressed by feminists throughout the progression of the WPS agenda. The scale of the challenge is huge. By July 2015, the conflict in Syria had driven at least 7.6 million people from their homes – almost half the population were either refugees or internally displaced (UNHCR 2015).

The Syrian case thus illuminates the way in which work on the economic and social rights of women, enabling them to overcome the obstacles to their participation, is as crucial as a focus on pushing for their civil and political right to participate in peace talks. Again, it is important to be mindful of the economic context, the root causes of the poverty and inequalities in Syria. One of the triggers for the protests against the ruling regime in November 2011 was the inequalities caused by Assad's adoption of neoliberal policies, which cut public sector employment and social spending and enabled those close to power to amass huge personal fortunes through the privatization of SOEs. In 2010, whilst the average citizen in Syria made about US$2,600 a year, Assad amassed a personal fortune of between US$550 million and US$1.5 billion (Inman 2012; S. Cohn 2013). The Syrian peace talks have focused on the religious divide between the two main groups and have neglected the underlying inequalities and poverty that risk undermining any peace agreement. By contrast, Syrian women have stressed the need for the economic empowerment of women and other marginalized groups as a crucial part of their blueprints for peace (Williams 2014), highlighting the importance of their voice at the table.

The Syrian example resembles other recent cases (e.g. Sudan and South Sudan) where women are largely excluded from formal Track 1 negotiations, despite the strengthening of the participation elements of the WPS architecture. It remains the case that some of the most prominent examples of the inclusion of women in different aspects of the peacebuilding process, such as El Salvador, Guatemala, Northern Ireland and South Africa, precede the passage of 1325 (Domingo et al. 2014: 12). Yet there are signs of progress. By 2012, of the nine processes of active negotiation under UN auspices, six negotiating teams had at least one woman delegate, up from 2011, where only four women participated in the 11 negotiating teams. An example would be Colombia, where in November 2013, President Santos announced the appointment of two women, María Paulina Riveros and Nigeria Rentería, to sit at the peace table in Havana, where the Government of Colombia and the Revolutionary Armed

Forces of Colombia were meeting to put an end to 50 years of conflict. Were these women merely tokens? Not necessarily. Both were lawyers with track records in women's equality and human rights issues, and Nigeria Rentería was specifically charged with bringing the views of women's organizations to the table. Perhaps more important than their appointments, however, were complementary initiatives taken in the Colombian peace talks in 2014, such as the inclusion of delegations of survivors of the armed conflict, and representatives of women's organizations and the lesbian, gay, bisexual, transgender and queer (LGBTQ) community, who were able to present their proposals for possible post-conflict scenarios (UN Women 2015). A sub-commission on gender was subsequently established in September 2014 in order to integrate the voices of women and gender perspectives in all of the accords reached at the table, and to develop proposals for 50–50 representation of men and women in the political party lists of candidates for public office (UN Women 2015).

In terms of UN appointments to mediate negotiation, again, the picture is of gains and remaining challenges. There was a noted increase in women experts on the UN mediation support teams over 2011 and 2012 (they were included in all 12 processes tracked in 2012). Of 11 active negotiation processes co-led by the UN in 2013, eight at had least one senior woman negotiating delegate. Gender experts were deployed to 88 per cent of UN co-led conflict resolution processes in 2013. Also, the UN has appointed the first two women to senior mediator and envoy positions in ongoing peace processes and agreements. Nigerian politician Aïchatou Mindaoudou Souleymane became the first woman UN chief mediator when she was appointed as Acting Joint African Union–United Nations Special Representative for Darfur in 2012 and former Irish President Mary Robinson was appointed as Special Envoy to the Great Lakes in 2013. The African Union has also appointed women to powerful mediating positions: in January 2014, Bineta Diop, Founder and President of NGO Femmes Africa Solidarité, was appointed Special Envoy for Women, Peace and Security of the Chairperson of the African Union Commission.

As we saw in chapter 1, one of the reasons it matters so much that women are participants in the peace process is because of evidence that it increases the prospects of their participation in politics in the post-conflict period, the subject of the next section. Indeed, peace treaties often end up becoming the base from which future constitutions are drafted. This is an area of contention for feminists. Some argue that it is vital that the two processes are separated, so that constitution building can take place in a careful, democratic and inclusive process on home soil, unlike peace talks, which are often held in 'neutral' distant territory (Cockburn 2014). Others accept the two will be linked, and see the opportunities this provides – if, and only if, the peace talks can be made to be more inclusive. Bosnian women, still suffering from the consequences of their exclusion from the Dayton Peace Agreement in 1995, have urged Syrian women to ensure that the two are kept separate (Cockburn 2014), but in Guatemala, women were frustrated that many of their demands which were included in the 1996 peace accords (UN Women 2012b: 8) have still not been implemented, in part because the peace accords were *not* used as the basis of the new constitutions (Domingo et al. 2014: 16; Castillejo 2011). Christine Bell and Catherine O'Rourke (2010) note that even where strong gender provisions are included in the text of peace agreements, 'the relationship between peace agreement text, implementation of its provisions, and durable peace, remains largely unknown and contested'. In terms of the specific link between participation in peace processes and participation in parliaments, however, the evidence suggests that the former has been an important factor in bringing about the latter, with women in Burundi, Nepal and Timor-Leste all using peace talks in order to argue for quotas for women in post-conflict legislatures.

Participation in parliaments and governance

Here we turn to the case of Burundi, which illustrates well both the importance of including more women in formal politics and the limitations of this as a strategy for building peace. Women had to work hard to be included in the peace talks for Burundi, which ran from 1998 to 2000, having been initially excluded for many of the same reasons described in the Syrian case above. As a result of their perseverance, the efforts of Nelson Mandela as negotiator and the UN, however, women were eventually included and 60 per cent of their demands were included in the final peace agreement, the Arusha accords. One of the things they called for (along with the classification of rape as a crime against humanity; the recognition of the specific vulnerability of women and children when defining repatriation policies for refugees; and the guarantee of women's rights to property, land ownership and inheritance) was the adoption of a 30 per cent female representation for parliament and governing bodies (Castillejo 2011: 4). The quotas led to an increase in women's representation from 20 per cent during the transition period to 31.35 per cent in 2005, and then 32.1 per cent in 2010. Women's representation within the government also grew, reaching 42 per cent in 2010 (Sow 2012).

Has women's representation made a difference to the process of building an inclusive peace in Burundi? The picture is, once more, one of gains and opportunities along with continuing challenges and disappointments. In terms of gains, women in the Burundian parliament were able to pass several important provisions favouring gender equality. For example, the 2009 reformed penal code now gives a clearer and more precise definition of rape and gender-based violence, providing a statutory basis for heavier sentences against such crimes. Women also obtained an amendment to the Penal Code, making domestic violence punishable by law. Moreover, there is evidence that Burundian women feel more confident, and that gender dynamics within the household have to a certain extent shifted away from rigid and hierarchical relations. Among respondents to an International Alert study, 82 per cent believed that the increased representation of women had introduced positive changes in terms of gender relations and the social status of women (Falch 2010: 30; Sow 2012). The perception is that the right to make their voices heard in the political sphere has contributed to giving more freedom of speech to women in general, in the household and at community level (Sow 2012: 25). This perhaps helps explain how women at the local community or *colline* level are making a difference to peacebuilding, mediating in disputes and reducing domestic violence (UN Women 2011: 77). With support from UN Women, women in Burundi have also managed to join the *Bashingantahe*, a circle of elders who play a central role in conflict resolution at community level and now total 40 per cent of such committees. As well as increasing awareness of sexual and gender-based violence and women's rights, this has led to a shift in attitudes towards inheritance, with male leaders on record advocating for equal inheritance laws (UN Women 2011: 77).

Women in the Burundian parliament have not, however, been able to achieve the changes that would help transform their lives, around issues of land and property rights in particular. Life is still tough for the majority in Burundi, which remains one of the poorest countries in the world, ranked 180th out of 187 countries worldwide in the 2014 UNDP Human Development Index. Burundi has nickel reserves, tea and coffee plantations, and possible opportunities in tourism, but the majority of Burundians live in acute poverty, with very high levels of unemployment and malnutrition on the increase. Around 90 per cent of its people are subsistence farmers, and around half of the national budget is financed by donors (World Bank 2015). With 67 per cent of the population under the poverty line, the country is still repaying US$3.36 million annually in debt servicing to donors.

What are some of the factors explaining the difficulty in translating women's presence in the parliament into a meaningful difference in women's lives on the ground? The first is that women in Burundi are rarely united in their motivations. The women who worked together to lobby the peace talks for the quota are divided on many issues, so once the immediate goal of quotas was achieved, it was hard to remain in solidarity, to privilege their common interests as women over their divergent interests which result from an ethnic, class or political perspective. Some of the particular structures of democracy in Burundi make it harder for women to privilege that common interest. There are ethnic quotas for parliamentary seats as well as gender quotas, and the experience has been that when they clash, it is the ethnic loyalties which are viewed as more important. In 2007, the President of the National Assembly and the Vice-President of the Senate, both women, were removed from office and replaced by men (Sow

2012). Furthermore, as politicians usually have to have party support in order to be effective, women parliamentarians in Burundi are usually loyal to party lines (Castillejo 2011). This has at times undermined their ability to advocate for women-friendly legal change on such issues as polygamy and land reform (Domingo 2012). Many male MPs in Burundi fear that reforming land ownership and inheritance laws will put too much pressure on the land, and mean an end to the practice of using land as part of a patronage system which male elites use to retain power and privilege, and thus they vehemently resist change. Even with the quotas, women MPs are still in a minority, which makes challenging these majority male views difficult. The quota system does not apply to senior roles in political parties, so it is hard for women in Burundi to get into positions of power in parliament and government.

Women MPs have mostly been assigned departments such as communication and sociocultural affairs, which do not hold the purse-strings (Nanourou and Wilson 2014: 9). The ministry in charge of gender issues in Burundi has been chronically underfunded, receiving less than 1 per cent of the national budget in 2012 (Sow 2012).[5] Some argue that women are deliberately given the least powerful departments because they are there to appease foreign investors and are not respected by their peers in the parliament (Nanourou and Wilson 2014: 10; Falch 2010: 30–1). Women parliamentarians need structures in place to enable them to overcome the same obstacles detailed above when discussing women's participation in peace talks: poverty, an unfair share of caring responsibilities, insecurity, illiteracy and lack of confidence and experience owing to their long-term exclusion from formal politics. Finally, there is only so much an MP can do – macroeconomic policies are largely determined by external funders. As a result, Burundi remains one of the poorest countries in the world, with both physical and structural violence combining to make life hard for ordinary Burundian women. Peace is very precarious indeed, with the 2015 elections precipitating renewed violence (Howden 2014; Tertsakian 2014)

The case of Burundi illustrates well the *importance and the limitations* of quotas for women in parliaments as part of peacebuilding. There is evidence of similar gains in terms of legislation around gender-based violence and the beginnings of a shift in how women are viewed in other post-conflict countries where quotas are in place, such as Afghanistan, Timor-Leste, Guatemala, Nepal, Rwanda and Uganda. There is evidence too, however, in each of these places, of the barriers to turning the presence of women into substantive gains for women and a gender-sensitive peace (Tripp et al. 2009; Castillejo 2011; Byrne and McCulloch 2012; Domingo et al. 2014). In Afghanistan, for example, female MPs have struggled to be effective in the absence of the networks and influence of their male peers (Kandiyoti 2007b). This has led to difficult dilemmas for some, who report the need to develop alliances with key power-holders, who can include warlords. They have also faced many of the other constraints faced by Burundian women – finding it challenging to build solidarity when coming from very different ethnic, religious and socio-economic backgrounds, needing to toe the party line, being assigned to marginal departments and needing to overcome perceptions about a women's proper role in society. In Afghanistan, the latter is particularly acute, with female MPs facing violence and intimidation as a result of their prominence in the public sphere.

Crucially, it has proved difficult in almost every post-conflict context for women to translate their presence in parliaments into a focus on women's *economic* empowerment sufficient to challenge the imposition of neoliberal policies by the donor community. As we saw in previous chapters, informed by the case of Afghanistan, many feminists are sceptical that quotas can make a difference in post-conflict contexts. Malathi de Alwis and her co-authors conclude that 'it remains moot whether such drastic, external interventions regarding women's rights [quotas] can be sustained without adequate, organic support from among those in power or from within a devastated society, most of whose intellectuals and liberal leaders have long fled that country' (de Alwis et al. 2013: 185). Indeed, pressure from the international community can also have the effect of entrenching polarized positions between traditional power-holders and women's rights advocates (Kandiyoti 2007a, 2007b). For some feminists, this backlash makes quotas a flawed policy (Al-Ali and

Pratt 2009). Others draw optimism from the limited gains that women's representation in parliament has achieved in post-conflict contexts such as Burundi, Rwanda and Uganda, and consider quotas a necessary, if insufficient, step to building an inclusive, gender-sensitive, sustainable peace. All possibly agree that more attention needs to be paid to the *substance* of women's inclusion and incorporation – the difference women representatives can make – as the mere presence of women in different aspects of peacebuilding is not enough to ensure feminist visions of peace.

Engendering SSR and DDR

The Geneva Centre for the Democratic Control of Armed Forces (DCAF), an international foundation mandated to enhance security sector governance through security sector reform, offers the following definition of SSR: 'the political and technical process of improving state and human security by making security providers more effective and more accountable, within a framework of democratic civilian control, rule of law, and respect for human rights'.[6] The importance of SSR has increasingly been emphasized in international engagement with post-conflict countries. In February 2007 the UNSC stressed that 'reforming the security sector in post-conflict environments is critical to the consolidation of peace and stability, promoting poverty reduction, rule of law and good governance, extending legitimate state authority, and preventing countries from relapsing into conflict' (UNSC 2007). It can thus be seen as an activity which encompasses all '3 Ps' of the WPS agenda. The importance of including a gender perspective has been increasingly recognized. The UN SSR concept emphasized gender as one of its guiding principles, and whilst 1325 did not directly address such reform, 1820 directly makes the link between justice, SSR and gender in processes supported by the UN.[7] The Organization for Economic Cooperation and Development – Development Assistance Committee (OECD–DAC) handbook on SSR of 2007 added a new chapter in 2009 to set out the significance of gender equality to this area of work, particularly in post-conflict settings, and the challenges and entry points for gender issues. Feminists within DCAF have been at the forefront of pushing for the engendering of SSR, claiming that 'SSR is a process of transformation: sometimes rapid, sometimes gradual and incremental. It brings opportunities – and responsibilities – to create more inclusive and less discriminatory security sector institutions. SSR strategies that promote the recruitment of women in security services, and ensure that women participate equally in security decision making, contribute to creating an efficient and legitimate security sector (Bastick 2008; see also Mobekk 2010). Engendering SSR matters because the sector has a key role in defining the distribution of power and resources in society (Domingo et al. 2014). Multiple policy platforms and toolkits now exist to enshrine the centrality of gender awareness in DDR and SSR (see, e.g., Bastick and Valasek 2008).

Efforts to engender SSR in Liberia provide a good case for us to evaluate the extent to which this work is crucial to contributing to feminist visions of peace, as it is often cited as a success story. Two civil wars, from 1989 to 1996 and from 1999 to 2003, destroyed much of Liberia's economy, especially the infrastructure in and around Monrovia (Dennis 2005). Between 1987 and 1995, Liberia's GDP dropped 90 per cent, one of the world's worst economic collapses, and by 2005, Liberians' average income was a quarter of income levels in 1985 and one-sixth of average income in 1979 (IMF 2008). Between 1989 and 2003, the war displaced nearly 1 million Liberians and killed approximately 250,000, out of a population of about 3 million. Militias conscripted an estimated 15,000 children (Tate 2004) and 22,500 women (Harsch 2005). Of the 4,501 Liberians surveyed in 2011, 77 per cent had been displaced during the war, 35 per cent had been attacked with a weapon and 20 per cent had been abducted. More than half of Liberian women were sexually or physically assaulted during the war (Bacon 2012).

Women were central to ending the war, forming the Women in Peacebuilding Network (WIPNET) in 2002 and beginning a Mass Action for Peace campaign which drew in women from all sectors of society, including social worker Leymah Gbowee, who was to go on to become joint winner of the Nobel Peace Prize in 2011. These women were not included in the peace talks in Ghana in 2003, but took their Mass Action to Accra and made their demands known, even resorting to bodily blocking the delegates in the hall and obstructing the entrance when rebel leaders threatened to walk out (DCAF et al. 2011: 22). Their actions resulted not only in an agreement, but in one which included language on the protection and promotion of women's human rights (Tripp et al. 2009: 204–5).

One important strand of WIPNET's work since has been to insist that gender be taken seriously in the processes of SSR and, relatedly, Disarmament, Demobilization and Reintegration (DDR). In December 2006, WIPNET and others called on their government and the international community to increase the role of women in SSR by engaging women-led civil society organizations in transforming public perception of the military and police, strengthening disarmament and recruiting women for the armed forces and police (Bastick 2008: 158). The following year, they made concrete recommendations as to how the SSR process could be more effective and responsive to gender issues, including that: penal reform address the needs of male, female and youth prisoners; training for the security forces include trauma counselling; and anti-corruption measures combat requests for sex as well as for money. They also underlined that women should be recognized and more extensively involved in 'managing security risks', given their skills, for example, in advancing local reconciliation, connecting local communities with national government and reaching out to youth (Bastick 2008: 158).

This pressure resulted in several initiatives regarding the Army and the Liberian National Police (LNP), both important organizations for reform owing to their perpetration of serious human rights violations throughout both civil wars. Firstly, a 20 per cent quota for women's inclusion in the police and armed forces was established; secondly, a Women and Children Protection Unit (WACPU) was established in the LNP, with officers specially trained in the handling and management of cases of sexual and other forms of gender-based violence; and, thirdly, a recruitment programme for the LNP was established, with literacy programmes for women included so that the pool of female recruits could be expanded without lowering essential qualifications (N. F. Hudson 2009: 109; DCAF et al. 2011).

The women also called for a more gender-sensitive DDR process. The UN's initial plans for demobilizing combatants resulted in chaos when 12,000 fighters presented themselves with their weapons at a cantonment site in Monrovia which could only accommodate 1,000 (DCAF et al. 2011: 22). WIPNET worked with the UN Mission in Liberia to design a more localized and responsive DDR process, one which would seek to make things safer and more effective for the many female former combatants, given that women and girls were thought to have comprised up to 38 per cent of the 38,000–53,000 combatants eligible for DDR in 2004 (Douglas et al. 2004). Measures included separate transport, separate registration lines and separate medical examination, dining, sleeping and recreation areas for male and female ex-combatants. In addition, reproductive health and gender-based violence screening and services were identified as priority activities. Finally, access to DDR was not based on the holding of weapons, but all women 'associated with fighting forces' were eligible for enrolment. By February 2005, 2,370 women and 2,440 girls (24 per cent of all participants in the DDR programme) had been disarmed and demobilized. By the end of 2006, 13,223 of the women had been 'reintegrated', mainly into agriculture, formal education and vocational training (DCAF et al. 2011: 23–4).

Many feminists thus cite Liberia as an example where engendering SSR and DDR is an important step towards sustainable and inclusive peace. They point to a number of important gains. Firstly, some identify an increased reporting of gender-based violence because women who were targeted in the civil war, or suffered abuse in fighting forces, became more comfortable reporting these crimes to women security personnel (Cordell 2010: 35). Secondly, observers have noted that girls have been inspired by the female faces they see in the police and security sector and see greater future employment opportunities available to them (True 2014). In the month following the UN's deployment of its first all-female peacekeeping contingent, made up of 103 Indian policewomen, in January 2007, the LNP received three times the usual number of female applicants (Bastick 2008: 159;

Cordell 2010: 43; Ford and Morris 2010). Thirdly, some suggest that participation in the security sector has imbued some Liberian women with public trust and legitimacy (Salahub 2011). Even while the outcomes are acknowledged to be gradual, some feminists argue that engendering SSR in Liberia is beginning to alter the local political economy by redressing the socioeconomic power imbalance between women and men (True 2014).

Other feminists are more sceptical. Some look at the Liberian experience and note that including women did not mean that society and security forces questioned or modified traditional roles (Jacob 2008: 65–6). Nor, they claim, did it lead to a rethink in the understanding of security, along the lines suggested in chapter 2: the Comprehensive Peace Agreement agreed at Accra fixed the mission of the new army in state-centric traditional security terms, and as a result, some feminists argue, by privileging representation over empowerment, SSR only includes more women within a fundamentally masculinist institution (H. Hudson 2012a: 97–8). WACPU is argued by some to be based on the essentialist logic that women are better able to deal with violence against women owing to innate caring qualities (H. Hudson 2012a; Mobekk 2010), undermining policewomen by discounting the training, skill and perseverance required to do the job well. The claim that responding to sexual violence is a discredited, feminized aspect of SSR is disputed, however, with evidence that this element of police work is valued: WACPU is said to have acquired something of the prestige of an elite task force, in part because donor support has ensured that it is better equipped than some of its counterparts (UN Women 2012d: 5).

SSR is broad-ranging in its scope and ambition, as the above definitions make clear, and is not just about enhancing the capacity of security providers to respond to gender-based violence; it is a crucial but extremely challenging aspect of peacebuilding. Even regarding that more specific aim, the evidence suggests that there is a significant way to go before SSR will achieve security for women and girls. Sexual and domestic violence still affects hundreds of thousands of Liberian women and girls, and, to a significantly lesser extent, men and boys, and WACPU cannot reach them all, particularly those in rural areas (Schia and de Carvalho 2009: 8). Although there has been an increase in reports to the police, and over half sexual and domestic violence cases reported to the police result in arrests, few are tried in court and convictions are rare because the justice system is severely under-resourced. The special court created to prioritize cases of gender-based violence has only one judge, severely limiting the cases upon which it can adjudicate; as a result, prisons are almost entirely full of inmates awaiting trials and the majority of victims are prevented from attaining justice (Dziewanski 2012). This suggests that engendering SSR in Liberia has struggled to overcome the obstacles caused by poverty, insecurity and damage to infrastructure exacerbated by the civil wars. This assessment is reinforced by Helen Basini's (2013) finding that the attempt to engender the DDR process was much stronger in the area of Disarmament and Demobilization than in the more developmentally focused Rehabilitation and Reintegration areas, which required a significant shift of resources and power to women in order for them to rebuild their lives. The Liberian case thus provides further illustration for a key feminist concern: the level of attention given to gender and women in SSR and DDR policy documents is not matched by human and financial resources allocated to ensuring effective engendering of SSR and DDR in the field (Mobekk 2010). As this summary of the Liberian case indicates, effective engendering of SSR and DDR involves the provision of significantly more resources to increase the capacity of the justice system, for education and health services, and to provide women, girls and other marginalized groups with the power and resources they need in order to live secure lives.

Whilst work on the economic empowerment of Liberian women exists (UN Women 2014), it tends to be in the form of small-scale income-generating projects, rather than the structural changes required to ensure the state has sufficient revenues to invest in justice, education, health and job-creation schemes. Meanwhile, two factors combine to exacerbate poverty and inequalities. The current macroeconomic policies are not working. Liberia derives 76.9 per cent of its GDP from the agricultural sector, and its industry is largely dependent on production of natural resources, such as rubber, palm oil, timber and diamond mining. Over a period of three years, between 2008 and 2011, it implemented a series of 39 reforms to improve the 'ease of doing business in the country', leading to its classification among the top 10 global reformers of the World Bank's 2010 Doing Business ranking. This resulted in considerable FDI, but the reforms implemented, along with corruption and smuggling, have undermined the potential tax revenue. Investors have simultaneously undermined local communities' potential to sustain their livelihoods through the acquisition of large swathes of land for palm oil and rubber production (Friends of the Earth International 2013; Martin-Prével 2014b: 8). Across all sectors, there is evidence that laws have been broken in virtually every natural resource deal since 2009, enabling government ministers to benefit from the sale of natural resources and undermining Liberia's revenue base (Global Witness 2013b). More than 40 per cent of the country's land has been granted to foreign concessions – including logging, palm oil, rubber and mining companies since 2006 (Global Witness 2013b) in what has been termed 'the new colonialism' of the land-grab across Africa (Ford 2012).

Meanwhile, the Ebola virus hit Liberia particularly badly in 2013–14 (O'Carroll 2014). As the crisis emerged, Liberia had only one doctor for every 100,000 patients in a population of 4.4 million. Infected people were driven to health centres with no spare beds, only to be turned away, return home and create 'flare-ups' of deadly fever in their villages (Agence France-Presse 2014). As with any health emergency, the Ebola crisis hit women particularly hard because of their role as carers for the sick and vulnerable. The macroeconomic policies imposed on Liberia and the Ebola emergency are intimately related. Despite Liberia having one of the world's highest ratios of FDI to GDP in the world, and a growth rate of over 10 per cent for years, the state has little revenue to invest in healthcare, and, left to the private sector, the healthcare system is said to be 'in a desperate state' (Dearden 2014). A system whereby investment is enticed through tax breaks which undercut revenue appears both counterproductive and unjust. Together with corruption, it has left Liberia and other post-conflict West African states ill equipped to cope with the health crisis of Ebola. The reason that Ebola became an epidemic, health campaigners thus suggest, 'lies not in the pathology of the disease but in the pathology of our society and the global political and economic architecture' (People's Health Movement 2014). The Liberian Finance Minister reported in October 2014: 'The government has already lost revenue equivalent to 25% of our annual receipts. While images of hospitals and dying patients saturate the international media, it is the hidden story of closed schools, unpaid teachers, underfunded security forces and absent local services that could threaten the very fabric of Liberian life' (cited in Konneh 2014). It is this context that feminist scholars and activists have to keep in their sights, whilst also being attentive to the importance of significance of small steps, when evaluating the effectiveness of recent efforts to reform the security sector.

Prevention: the neglected pillar

We saw in chapter 1 that a part of the feminist critique of 1325, its lack of 'ambition', was connected to the neglect of what many feminists see as the most important of the '3 Ps', prevention (Confortini and Basu 2011). UNSCR 1325 affirms 'the important role of women in the prevention and resolution of conflicts', but the prevention pillar has often been narrowly interpreted in practice to mean preventing sexual violence against women or, at best, integrating gender perspectives into early warning systems, community-level mediation and disarmament initiatives. There has been very little attention given to activities which might constitute prevention of armed conflict in a more fundamental sense: addressing the underlying drivers of conflict such as the inequalities and injustices rooted in economic and political structures. Some feminists have argued that the UN's WPS agenda needs to pay more attention to these inequalities and injustices and the ways in which they are gendered (C. Cohn 2008; Confortini and Basu 2011; Saferworld 2015).

A 2010 UNDP report (Budlender 2010) analyses the funding of peacebuilding projects, and is revealing about the priorities of both donors and recipient governments. Analysis of the allocation of donor state funding for peace operations shows a disproportionate focus on political security and humanitarian assistance and a relative neglect of economic security and development. The assumption has been that later assistance will focus on these latter areas. Significant resources have been allocated to SSR, DDR and the law and justice sector more generally, as well as some immediate humanitarian needs. Strikingly, at least 60 per cent of peacebuilding budgetary allocations have gone towards the salaries of military contractors serving as UN peacekeepers. Significantly less is allocated towards reconstruction aid, and when it is, the UNDP found in the four post-conflict countries analysed (Timor-Leste, Sierra Leone, Kosovo and South Sudan) that there had been only very limited resources allocated to promote gender equality or women's specific needs. Despite the existence of considerable gendered inequalities in all four countries, such as in access to education and health, to water and to economic opportunities, less than 5 per cent of activities and only 3 per cent of budget lines mentioned either gender equality or women's needs. Women were also excluded from the planning of economic reconstruction and not one of the countries had an economic policy adviser with gender budget analysis training and skills. This crucial report illustrates clearly the way in which tackling the structures at the root of conflicts is neglected by the UN system, despite the WPS agenda.

Conclusion

Consideration of these aspects of peacebuilding reveals considerable activity to enhance the protection of women and girls in armed conflict and the participation of women in peacebuilding. It exposes a mixed picture of small wins and opportunities with many remaining challenges. Underpinning many of the challenges is the lack of resources which are required to make many of the initiatives more effective. This lack of resources, I have suggested, is connected to the macroeconomic development strategies insisted upon by the donor community funding peacebuilding. These economic policies, combined with the corruption they encourage, undermine the revenue base of states – revenue which is required in order to fund the services identified as so crucial to achieving security for women and other marginalized groups: justice, education and health. More energy is being directed at addressing physical violence than structural violence, but for women and other marginalized groups in conflict-affected areas, these two forms of violence cannot be separated so easily.

Many feminists reviewing progress of the WPS agenda to date conclude that a key problem is lack of resources (Budlender 2010; O'Gorman 2014). Yet this concern is often expressed as a call for more funds to be devoted to women's specific needs and gender equality projects when arguably there is a need for a more fundamental challenge to the economics of peacebuilding. There needs to be more explicit attention to the way that neoliberal macroeconomic policies have direct impact on budgets and public finance, to the detriment of women's rights and security. The next chapter turns to ways of addressing this omission. It considers the necessity of a challenge to the neoliberal model of post-conflict reconstruction in order to achieve the economic empowerment of women and other marginalized groups in post-conflict contexts.

Questions for discussion

1   What initiatives have been implemented since 2000 to improve the protection of women and girls in armed conflict? To what extent have they succeeded? What dilemmas have been generated?

2   What are the various obstacles and barriers preventing women influencing and participating meaningfully in peace processes? To what extent has the WPS agenda enabled women to overcome these barriers?

3   What is the potential for gender-sensitive SSR and DDR to contribute to feminist visions of peace?

Suggestions for further reading

Doris Buss, Joanne Lebert, Blair Rutherford, Donna Sharkey and Obijiofor Aginam, eds. 2014. *Sexual Violence in Conflict and Post-Conflict Societies: International Agendas and African Contexts.* London: Routledge.
A useful overview of sexual violence, by researchers, civil society and community activists working on Africa. It covers policy responses as well as causes and contexts of sexual violence. An excellent mix of empirical evidence and conceptual debates.

Pilar Domingo, Rebecca Holmes, Alina Rocha Menocal and Nicola Jones. 2014. 'Assessment of the Evidence of Links between Gender Equality, Peacebuilding and Statebuilding: Literature Review'. Overseas Development Institute.
A contemporary overview of the literature on gender and peacebuilding, usefully organized into challenges, barriers and opportunities of a number of different aspects of peacebuilding.

Maria Eriksson Baaz and Maria Stern. 2013. *Sexual Violence as a Weapon of War? Perceptions, Prescriptions, Problems in the Congo and Beyond.* London: Zed Books.
This is a provocative book by two feminist scholars who have considerable experience of researching sexual violence in the DRC and who are two of the very few to have interviewed perpetrators. In this work they take issue with the framing of sexual violence as a 'weapon of war', arguing that it serves to disguise the prevalence of sexual violence in 'peacetime' and distracts us from other forms of violence in war.

Jana Krause and Cynthia Enloe. 2015. 'A Wealth of Expertise and Lived Experience: Conversations Between International Women Peace Activists at the "Women Lead To Peace Summit" Preceding The Geneva II Peace Talks on Syria, January 2014'. *International Feminist Journal of Politics* 17 (2): 328–38.
This article contains a fuller account of the experience of Syrian women who have been excluded from the Geneva-

based peace process despite their conflict-resolution and humanitarian work on the ground.

Web resources

Conciliation Resources, Women Building Peace (*http://www. c-r.org/accord-project/women-and-peacebuilding-insight*) Accord Insight *is a publication from peacebuilding organization Conciliation Resources, and this edition presents nine articles that examine the roles women have played in addressing violence and building peace. The publication documents women's first-hand peacebuilding practice: the challenges they faced, the opportunities they created and the lessons they have drawn from their experiences.*

DCAF's Gender and Security Programme (*http://www.dcaf. ch/Programmes/Gender-and-Security*) *DCAF works with security institutions to help them create structures, policies and procedures to better integrate gender, and with civil society organizations and legislatures to improve their ability to be effective advocates and overseers of security institutions. This webpage contains links to their publications on gender and SSR, dating back to 2005.*

OECD–DAC Handbook on Security Sector Reform (*http:// www.oecd-ilibrary.org/development/the-oecd-dac-handbook -on-security-system-reform_9789264027862-en*) *The* OECD-DAC Handbook on Security System Reform: Supporting Security and Justice *provides guidance to operationalize the 2005* DAC Guidelines, Security System Reform and Governance. *It contains a chapter on gender, which was added in 2008. It aims to provide the tools to encourage a dialogue on security and justice issues and to support a SSR process through the assessment, design and implementation phases.*

Office of Special Representative of the Secretary-General – Sexual Violence in Conflict (*http://www.un.org/sexual violenceinconflict/*)

Crucial website for up-to-date statistics and information about responses to sexual violence. The case of DRC outlined in this chapter can be usefully compared and contrasted with other cases by using this website.

Peace Agreements Database (*http://www.peaceagreements. ulster.ac.uk/*)
The Peace Agreement Database provides details of over 640 peace agreements signed since 1990, addressing conflicts that affect over 85 jurisdictions. The database can be searched to find which peace agreements mention gender and women.

UNDP Report on the Price of Peace (*http://gender-financing. unwomen.org/en/resources/p/r/i/price-of-peace-financing-for-gender-equality-in-post-conflict-reconstruction*)
This report interrogates the extent to which post-conflict reconstruction initiatives allocate resources to promote gender equality, to address women's needs and to involve women in decision-making around strategies and related resource allocations. It finds that less than 5 per cent of activities and only 3 per cent of budget lines mentioned women's needs, reinforcing the argument that the WPS agenda is undermined by lack of funding and the neoliberal model of development.

United Nations Disarmament, Demobilization and Reintegration Resource Centre (*http://www.unddr.org/key-topics/ gender/introduction_5.aspx*)
This website presents the UN's work on integrating gender into DDR, including training resources.

5
Gendering Alternatives to Neoliberal Peacebuilding

The previous chapter painted a complex picture of gains and challenges when we consider current efforts to implement the WPS agenda. There has been progress, but many of the issues feminists highlighted about the limitations of 1325 continue to cause concern. The scale of the challenge is clear in each of the contexts we have considered. A key factor in explaining the poverty and inequalities which remain in all post-conflict settings is the continued insistence of donors on an orthodox neoliberal macroeconomic framework (chapters 3 and 4) as essential to peacebuilding. This approach has exacerbated poverty and inequalities, hampering women's attempts to make a difference and the realization of feminist visions of peace (chapter 2). Of the many obstacles to engendering peacebuilding, neoliberal policies stand out as central to the slow pace of progress.

The UN has increasingly recognized the importance of women's economic rights over the course of the 15 years since 1325, in part because of sustained feminist pressure. As chapter 2 demonstrated, many feminists have long high-lighted the detrimental effect of structural violence and its impacts on gender equality and peace. Increasingly, many feminists are making this a more specific call, translated into specific demands of the WPS architecture. Indeed, some of the most exciting feminist work in the field of gender and peacebuilding focuses on this dimension, on addressing the economic empowerment of women as part of peacebuilding. This work will be the subject of this chapter. It focuses on what is required in order to capitalize on the gains and overcome the obstacles discussed in the previous two chapters in order to realize the peace discussed in chapter 2.

The first section details the way in which the most recent developments in the UN WPS agenda pay more attention to the importance of the economic and social rights of women in peacebuilding. The second details the work of scholars such as Jacqui True (2013, 2014) and Fionnuala Ní Aoláin, Dina Francesca Haynes and Naomi Cahn (2011), who advocate a new approach to peacebuilding which places women's economic empowerment at its centre. The third section considers Uganda as a case of a post-conflict country which demonstrates both the potential of and the missed opportunities in its attempts to include women's empowerment in building peace. The fourth section suggests avenues for future feminist research and advocacy which could be productive in challenging neoliberalism.

New UN developments

As we saw in chapter 2, feminist visions of peace demand an attention to the economic dimension. Peace means having economic security and opportunities, not just the absence of war. Indeed, 'peacebuilding is a process made up of interlocking, interdependent elements, including looking after the security of ordinary people, ensuring stable and proficient governance, giving people access to justice in an increasingly fair society, healing the wounds of war and making it possible for people to enjoy an adequate and stable standard of living' (Banfield 2008: 5).

The UN can be seen to have increasingly recognized the need to focus more on the economic empowerment of women as part of peacebuilding over the course of the 15 years since 1325. Although 1325 does not explicitly mention economic rights or empowerment for women, and attention has been most focused on the '3 Ps' of protection, participation and prevention,[1] UNSCR 1889, adopted in 2009, breaks new ground in making explicit mention of the need to support women's socioeconomic rights in post-conflict settings. In addition, since 2010 the Secretary-General has reported on a fourth pillar, relief and recovery, which allows for more attention to be paid to social and economic issues. Although not representing a commitment to the economic empowerment of women in itself, it has the potential to encourage more focus on social and economic empowerment of women and other marginalized groups. Also in 2010, the Secretary-General introduced the 7-PAP, which has as its seventh point the commitment to including women in economic recovery. It pledges to ensure 'women's equal involvement as participants and beneficiaries in local-development, employment-creation, frontline service-delivery and DDR programmes in post-conflict situations'. The 7-PAP also committed the UN to allocating 15 per cent of any UN-managed funds in support of peacebuilding to be dedicated to projects whose principal objective is to address women's specific needs, advance gender equality or empower women (UN Secretary-General 2010).

UNSCR 2122, adopted in September 2013, picks up on this theme, and, along with increasing measures on protection and participation, considers gender equality and women's empowerment to be central to international peace and security, underlining that the economic empowerment of women greatly contributes to the stabilization of societies emerging from armed conflict (UNSC 2013). It explicitly recognizes the interconnectedness between development issues such as economic empowerment and security from physical violence. It notes that 'sustainable peace requires an integrated approach based on coherence between political, security, development, human rights, including gender equality, and rule of law and justice activities', as well as 'the need to address the gaps and strengthen links between the UN peace and security in the field, human rights and development work as a means to address root causes of armed conflict and threats to the security of women and girls'.

On the same day that 2122 was passed, the Committee on the Elimination of Discrimination Against Women adopted its general recommendation on women in conflict prevention, conflict and post-conflict situations, General Recommendation 30. This adoption represents an important step forward as it makes a strong statement about the importance of the economic participation of women. It promotes an integrated approach to women's rights encompassing both their civil and political rights and their economic and social rights. By placing the implementation of the Security Council WPS agenda within the broader framework of the implementation of the Convention and its Optional Protocol, this move should provide a stronger framework to ensure and promote women's social and economic rights in conflict prevention, conflict and post-conflict situations. The general recommendation provides authoritative guidance to states, and to some extent non-state actors, on how to implement obligations under the Convention. Not only does CEDAW General Recommendation 30 strengthen 1325, but through 1325, CEDAW becomes relevant to non-signatories such as the United States and Sudan, non-state territories which cannot sign, such as Palestine, and non-state armed groups (CEDAW 2013).

As the entity devoted to development, the UNDP has unsurprisingly consistently paid more attention to the need for women's economic empowerment, and has recently devoted attention to linking this work up to the UNSC WPS agenda. Central to its 2008 Eight-Point Agenda for Women's Empowerment and Gender Equality in Crisis Prevention and Recovery is the idea that war sometimes provides opportunities for women and gender equality if societies can 'build back better' (UNDP 2008). It argues that women must be given equal opportunities to livelihoods, including access to land and credit; that rebuilding in key sectors such as transportation, shelter and healthcare must specifically benefit women; and that women must be engaged in decision-making on government budgets and resource mobilization. In addition, the UNDP has acknowledged that 'business as usual and traditional types of livelihoods enhancement do not necessarily lead to women's economic empowerment' (UNDP/BCPR 2011: 11), and has called for a minimum of 30 per cent of temporary employment posts created in early post-conflict settings to be reserved for women. More recently, the UNPBC held a high-level meeting in New York in 2013 dedicated to the theme of Women's Economic Empowerment for Peacebuilding. A Declaration resulted from the meeting which stressed the importance of 'assisting post-conflict countries in creating favourable conditions that can generate decent jobs for women, nurture their business skills, encourage them to join the workforce, and deliver the financial services that these women need, both in the formal and informal sectors' and 'enhancing their engagement in political and economic decision-making at early stages of recovery processes' (UNGA and UNSC 2013).

New feminist approaches

Feminist scholars, too, are increasingly focusing on the need for the WPS architecture to pay more attention to the economic empowerment of women. Jacqui True has argued that efforts to enhance the protection and participation elements of the WPS agenda will flounder without equal, if not more, effort to work on women's economic empowerment: 'Putting SCR 1325 into practice by promoting women's participation in peace processes', she writes, 'depends on efforts to change the gendered social and economic inequalities that currently constrain their participation and underlie their vulnerability in conflict and post-conflict settings' (True 2014: 247). The examples in the previous chapter clearly demonstrated this to be the case.

As True points out, if key economic and social rights such as those to land and housing, to transact in one's own legal name, to equality in marriage, to employment opportunities and equal pay and to freedom of mobility are not secured early enough after conflict, then many women who are already poor and marginalized will be denied opportunities for both economic and political participation in peace and reconstruction (True 2014: 248–9). This is because women's capacity to access economic resources after conflict affects their access to justice and physical security. She argues that '[t]he challenge for the UN is to bridge the gap between the interdependent political and economic security pillars of peacekeeping in order to achieve the protection, participation and prevention goals of the SCRs on women, peace and security and create gender-equal and lasting peace' (True

2014: 248). The gender bias and discrimination in post-conflict societies explored throughout this book show how the failure to address social and economic rights has particularly detrimental impacts on women's security. True argues for a feminist political economy perspective that takes into account the 'material as well as the cultural and normative basis of gender inequalities and of insecurity, including all forms of gender-based violence' (True 2014: 244). She insists that, contra the arguments of the feminists discussed in chapter 3 that peacebuilding is an inherently neoliberal endeavour which is only legitimized by gender mainstreaming, there is a way to improve peacebuilding's economic impacts on women and other marginalized groups. The route to avoid is one of grafting gender mainstreaming onto interventions that maximize the role of the market and minimize the role of the state in economic recovery. Rather: 'Reconceptualizing peace operations through a feminist political economy framework means transforming the underlying structures of socio-economic inequality that affect women's and men's differential insecurity and vulnerability to violence and poverty after conflict' (True 2014: 244).

True is not alone in arguing that it is time for a new approach. Fionnuala Ní Aoláin and her co-authors (2011) call for what they call Social Services Justice (SSJ). Recognizing the key point, discussed in chapter 2, that women often conceptualize security in terms of meeting everyday needs, they argue that social services should become a critical aspect of any peacebuilding endeavour. They suggest that the concept of social services can serve as a bridge between the recognition of the immediate needs of the population and long-term development. When post-conflict programmes are grounded in the recognition of and response to the daily realities of life in a post-conflict country, where abstract notions of legal accountability and impunity can be a distant dream, then they will be truly attentive to gender. Acknowledging that, for women, the transformation from 'conflict' to 'peace' is generally partial and exclusionary, they argue that when women are in control of their finances, their needs are better met, as are their family's. The three broad goals of SSJ are thus to respond to daily needs of the population, ranging from livelihoods to health to education; to expand the focus of justice and accountability mechanisms to account for daily needs of victims of conflict *and* their visions of justice; and to dismantle conflict-perpetuated hypermasculinities and open space for women and men to thrive in the post-conflict environment. The importance of all three goals is backed up by the evidence surveyed in this book. Ní Aoiláin et al. make the point that SSJ is no easy solution; the list of women's needs and fears in post-conflict contexts is a long one and the challenges are immense, but this change in approach is necessary and can help meet those challenges.

Although there are differences in terminology and emphasis, it seems to me that these authors are advocating the same thing. Indeed, this call for the UNSC WPS architecture to focus more on the economic pillar of peacebuilding builds on the long history of feminist scholarship which has called for more attention to be paid to the economic empowerment of women and other marginalized groups as a crucial part of what it means for them to be secure. Such scholarship is new perhaps in its specific attention to the UN peacebuilding architecture and the need for the WPS agenda to focus on women's and other marginalized groups' economic rights, but it is not new in its underpinning insights. Indeed, the call to reconceptualize the notion of security to encompass economic and social rights could be said to be the origination of feminist International Relations. Thus it has long been acknowledged that 'women are disproportionally victims of structural violence and that it is gender inequalities that are often responsible for women's particular vulnerability' (Tickner 1995: 51). The work of Sheila Meintjes and her co-authors (2001) in conflict contexts in the 1990s/early 2000s led them to argue for a need to move beyond a perceived dichotomy between a 'rights'- and a 'needs'-based approach to post-conflict reconstruction for women. The needs-based approach, they argued, was often too focused on physical and immediate needs, and missed the importance of justice for women; the rights-based approach, on the other hand, was often too narrowly focused on tackling the impunity of perpetrators and did not address what women need for survival and security. They concluded that '[n]either framework recognises the real need women feel for social transformation rather than reconstruction of the past' (Meintjes et al. 2001: 4). More recently, Nadje Al-Ali and Nicola Pratt have urged for a redefinition of security 'away from the deployment of militaries and security services and towards the fair distribution of resources to enable people's access to livelihoods and to ensure political and social justice, regardless of nationality, gender, class, ethnicity/race and religion' (Al-Ali and Pratt 2009: 20). All these scholars, using slightly different terminology, have argued for the necessity of keeping both the political and economic pillars of security in mind.

V. Spike Peterson and Anne Sisson Runyan convey something similar in their claim, drawing on Nancy Fraser (1995), that security for women and other marginalized groups requires a 'politics of recognition' *and* a 'politics of redistribution' to minimize both inequalities and grievances (Peterson and Runyan 2010: 234). The former, a focus on respecting identities often through the reward of political and civil rights, is no use, and can even be damaging, without the latter, which focuses on ensuring economic and social rights through the redistribution of wealth.

What has been relatively neglected is a focus on exactly how this is to be achieved in peacebuilding contexts. There has arguably not been sufficient feminist theorizing about how small steps to empower women and other marginalized groups economically through the WPS agenda would not just be ameliorative (in the face of an immovable neoliberal structure) but could also be scaled up to transform the global economic system. Likewise, although in mainstream peacebuilding literature (Lederach 1998; Gizelis and Kosek 2005; Francis 2010; Richmond 2010; Ramsbotham et al. 2011) there has long been an extensive focus on the importance of working with and empowering local people, particularly in terms of economic and social rights, there is not always an explicit focus on how these activities can be developed into a challenge to neoliberalism.

It is not that feminists lobbying the UN on the WPS agenda have neglected to push for women's economic empowerment. It is not that they have forgotten the insights of feminist scholarship, particularly from those working in development and IPE. The fact that the WPS architecture has focused on protection and participation – and sometimes in practice quite limited understandings of the two – is largely due to the difficulties inherent in trying to negotiate feminist change inside large bureaucracies (C. Cohn et al. 2004; Cockburn 2007; C. Cohn 2008). Moreover, there has perhaps been another obstacle – more theoretical – for some feminists in advocating for the economic empowerment of women as part of the WPS agenda. Feminists and other critical security scholars have been sceptical of the way that donor governments have linked insecurity and poverty together, into what they term the security–development nexus (Duffield 2010; MacKenzie 2012). They argue that Western governments construct a particular relationship between security and development whereby poverty and underdevelopment in the global South is positioned as a security threat to the North. This, they claim, distracts attention from the role of Western nations, discussed in previous chapters, in the causation of poverty, inequalities and insecurity (historically through colonialism and today through neoliberalism) and suggests that the solution is to spread 'the liberal peace'. One could say that whilst post-conflict contexts were once seen as not yet ready for development and in need of security measures *before* any attention could be paid to economic empowerment, increasingly donor governments and the UN acknowledge the links and seek to address both *at the same time*.[2] This was the approach of 'Breaking the Conflict Trap' (World Bank 2003a), discussed in chapter 3. Thus, marginalized groups become instrumentalized – have their poverty and insecurity addressed in order to make citizens in the global North feel safer, and because it supports the global neoliberal system that we all depend on, rather than out of respect for human rights (Duffield 2010: 1). The way to deal with poverty, according to donors and IFIs, is to integrate marginalized groups, including women, into neoliberal economies so as to enhance growth. There is no acknowledgement here of the role of neoliberal growth in causing poverty, inequalities and conflict in the first place. As many feminists and critical security scholars argue that this 'solution' will enhance the power and wealth of elites disproportionately in comparison to the poor and marginalized, they are wary of the linkages made between poverty and insecurity (Stern and Öjendal 2010; MacKenzie 2012).

A similar tension exists in the way that the World Bank and IFIs have positioned the economic empowerment of women as 'smart economics'. The World Bank has increasingly turned its attention to the economic empowerment of women, but has based its position on arguments that investing in girls and women promotes a society's economic growth. Many feminists have been concerned because of the way that this instrumentalizes women – sees their economic empowerment as a route to an end, rather than being an end in itself (see, e.g., Roberts and Soederberg 2012). Equally problematic is the end to which they are put. In the World Bank's vision, women's economic empowerment becomes about making the system more efficient – a system which is at the root of women's poverty and exclusion in the first place. In other words: 'Women are enlisted as footsoldiers to serve in battles whose aims are not related directly to their interests' (Chant and Sweetman 2012: 524). Meanwhile, the World Bank can claim any improvement in 'growth' as success.

It is hard to say whether fears of contributing to this instrumentalization of women's economic rights and to a problematic policy agenda have directly influenced the feminist organizations lobbying the UN on the WPS agenda. Feminist scholars such as True and Ní Aoláin et al. do not address the security–development nexus or these critiques of it. Their position appears to be that the fact that *donors* might conflate security and development in problematic ways in order to legitimize a neoliberal agenda should not entail that feminists neglect the links between development and security, particularly for women and gendered inequalities. They are fairly consistent in linking development and security, arguing that any analysis of women's lives on the ground demands that peacebuilding starts paying more attention to women's economic rights. The conceptualization of development that Ní Aoláin et al. adopt indicates a certain care to avoid the approach of 'empowering women as smart economics' as they focus on the 'right to development' as laid out in the UN Charter, the Universal Declaration of Human Rights, the Convention on Political and Civil Rights and the Convention on Economic and Social Rights, not on development's contribution to growth (Ní Aoláin et al. 2011). True explicitly insists upon the importance of linking both security and development, arguing: 'Conceiving of political stability and socio-economic development as separate may advance the security and rights of some groups, but it cannot advance women's security and rights, given the disproportionate poverty and discrimination they experience, especially in post-conflict settings' (True 2014: 253).

It is increasingly recognized that tackling war economies, including the illicit trade that sustains combat and serves personal enrichment during war, is essential if the violence is to be tackled. Economic recovery is crucial in improving a conflict-affected country's chance for peace. This recovery, however, must be sustainable, just and gender-sensitive. As has been detailed throughout this book, neoliberal models of economic development deepen inequalities, with particularly detrimental impacts on women and other marginalized groups. Moreover, the misuse of public resources, elite control of economic opportunities and unequal access to employment opportunities associated with neoliberalism all fuel grievances and even cause violent conflict to break out (Nafziger and Auvinen 2002). Foreign companies investing in conflict-affected regions can further exacerbate tensions or create fresh ones. Building a peace economy, where all groups, including women and other marginalized groups, have access to 'decent work'[3] opportunities is an essential ingredient for consolidating and sustaining peace in the long term. While there is emerging awareness that a country's economy is often closely entwined with its conflicts, and that conflict-affected and fragile countries cannot simply be subjected to 'economic development as usual', it is less clear what alternative approaches are required and how these could enhance chances for lasting peace rather than focusing purely on economic growth as the end goal (for an overview of the challenges and dilemmas, see Pugh et al. 2004; Ballentine and Nitzschke 2005; Fischer and Schmelzle 2005; Turner and Pugh 2006). The majority of interventions, as we saw in chapter 3, continue to follow orthodox aid, trade and investment paradigms. Donors might fund gender-sensitive peacebuilding projects, inspired by 1325, but the same donor's geo-political interests often lead it to support military expansionism and/ or neoliberal policies that are at odds with overall peace and security in the very same country. The UN, donor countries, and international NGOs need to grapple with neoliberalism head-on if they are to achieve feminist visions of peace. Yet, as International Alert notes, 'The tendency for development assistance to pride itself on technocratic content, whilst remaining silent on geo-political dynamics, is a major problem in international relations today, and highlights the need for agencies genuinely committed to peace and conflict-sensitivity to take a much more strategic overview of their own work, even if this means grappling with difficult political issues' (Banfield 2008: 11).

Case Study: Uganda

This section takes Uganda as an example of a post-conflict state in which to examine the challenge of achieving women's economic empowerment. It discusses the importance and potential of focusing on economic empowerment, along with the missed opportunities in the Ugandan case. Northern Uganda went through a bloody conflict that lasted for over 20 years as armed groups such as the Lord's Resistance Army (LRA) resisted the government in the south. The conflict escalated in 2002–3 in response to a Ugandan military offensive and millions were displaced. This conflict had devastating economic consequences in the region, caused the destruction of economic infrastructure and resulted in high casualties. Since the 2006 Juba Peace Talks, there has been relative calm and the chance for the Ugandan government, supported by international donors and institutions, to begin the process of building peace.[4] Various programmes for the region's reconstruction and development were set up at the end of the war by the government, international development agencies, the private sector and international NGOs. The usual emphasis given in government policy to the centrality of the private sector as an agent for growth and development in the country is apparent in the Peace, Recovery and Development Plan (PRDP), Ugandan government's flagship programme for the rehabilitation of Northern Uganda (as of 2014 absorbed into the National Development Plan, which outlines a 30-year strategy for the socioeconomic transformation of Uganda).[5] The Ugandan government has launched initiatives to try to promote and facilitate investment in the region by Ugandan and foreign enterprises, hosting conferences and trade fairs, and setting up industrial parks. As previous chapters have highlighted, however, private sector investment is not always good for development, peace or women and other marginalized groups.

As was the case in Mozambique, discussed in chapter 3, the long-term development initiatives encouraged by the PRDP are likely to generate employment for men more than women, and to have other gendered consequences. Considerable investment is being provided to Uganda in order to develop the recently discovered oil, for example, but the jobs which such oil exploration and drilling generate tend to be only available to men. Meanwhile, women will suffer equally or disproportionately from the risks that the discovery of oil tends to generate in developing countries. Early evidence suggests significant violations of Ugandan people's rights, through the pollution of land and the appropriate of land without due compensation (Pinnington 2014). Moreover, the sexual exploitation of young girls has been documented as a result of the influx of oil workers with economic power (Pinnington 2014). The potential benefit from the discovery of oil is said by many to be huge, but this is entirely dependent on democratic control over the distribution of the profits (Diamond and Mosbacher 2013; B. Shepherd 2013; Pinnington 2014) and Uganda's government has a poor track record in managing public funds (Diamond and Mosbacher 2013). Also, despite the UN's International Panel on Climate Change warning about the need to stop burning fossil fuels in order to prevent climate change, there are few voices in Uganda talking about the need to leave fossil fuels in the ground (Gathigah 2014). This is understandable in the context of the challenges ordinary Ugandans face, but it demonstrates again that the major development projects advocated by the donor community as part of peacebuilding are not likely to bring about feminist visions of peace.

Despite the commitment made by the Ugandan government,[6] and by most development agencies operational on the ground, to mainstream gender into their development programmes, women tend still to be viewed as a vulnerable group instead of economic agents. This is despite the fact that, in Northern Uganda, as in other conflict contexts, women have demonstrated resilience and coping skills and have transformed the landscape of that region's political economy. Whereas before the war, women were subsistence farmers, whilst men concentrated on commercial cash crops, women are now to a large extent the main breadwinners in the family. The war disrupted farming, and led to displacement of people in huge numbers and devastating disruption to livelihoods. Women began to sell fruit and vegetables, which were traditionally not commercialized, but were very much needed in the refugee camps; to brew beer; open canteens and kiosks; sell fish and second-hand clothing; provide the raw material for vegetable oils to private oil production companies; and even tender for road maintenance contracts. This led to several gains for women in terms of wider empowerment: 25 per cent reported an increased say in household decisions; 79 per cent voted in 2006 elections, demonstrating their participation in public life; and many testified that their role and respect in the community had increased (Sow 2012). Yet women have not really broken out of poverty.

The factors explaining the limited transformation in women's lives from these small gains in economic empowerment are interrelated. Firstly, all these activities are small scale; the vast majority of women are still mainly working to meet their practical needs and ensure the survival of their families. Northern Uganda is the country's most deprived region, with a high level of poverty, especially in rural areas. Further, the majority of women use their income to address family needs and to pay for their children's tuition fees. If they borrow finance, it is microcredit, so there is no capital to invest and expand their businesses or to tender for the larger government contracts (Sow 2012: 39). On top of this, women continue to have primary responsibility for caring for dependants, the well-documented 'double burden', thus having little time to develop their businesses.

NGOs have attempted to build on the entrepreneurial spirit of Northern Ugandan women unleashed by the war, but their efforts have generated dilemmas. Projects that focus on women's economic rights can seem to Ugandan men to single women out for special help as if women's lives are the only ones which have been devastated by the war. There is considerable evidence in Northern Uganda to suggest that the economic empowerment of women, as limited as it is, has led to 'thwarted masculinities' (El-Bushra 2012), when men can no longer act as the protectors and providers for their families, and, in turn, to a backlash, sometimes violent, against women. This provides further evidence that development projects must be attentive to gender as a structure of power, rather than think of gender as 'women's issues', if projects are going to help build peace. A further reported dilemma is whether development projects should empower only *groups* of women, in order to build communities, build capacity and operate efficiently, given the time involved for women to create and maintain groups in a context of multiple pressing demands. Both dilemmas testify to the difficulties of pursuing inclusive economic development in a neoliberal context.

There are many examples of small-scale economic empowerment projects which focus not just on development but also on capacity-building. To take an example from a different area on Uganda, women from the Slum Women's Initiative for Development utilized a UNDP Community Resilience Fund to acquire collective land in Jinja (the second largest town in the country) for planting food crops in order to secure food for their families in the face of increasing food prices, and the privatization of public lands once farmed by poor communities. Their initiative improved their positions, advanced sustainable, resilient development and also increased their empowerment through working as a group to secure the fund. Yet this sort of community-level project stands little chance of transforming women's lives or the economy as, again, there are few mechanisms on offer to 'scale up' these initiatives, despite the UNDP's efforts to incentivize 'grassroots/government collaborations' (UNDP 2013: 134).

There are also projects ongoing in Uganda to introduce gender-sensitive reparations for victims of sexual violence in conflict. Gender-sensitive reparations have transformative potential because, as outlined in the previous chapter they transfer *resources* to the survivor of violence, not merely given them a sense of justice that the perpetrator is behind bars. They can also be designed to reinforce women's social and economic rights. Both True and Ní Aoláin et al. are advocates:

'Focussing on reparations shifts our attention away from the overwhelming attention given to criminal justice and what to do with the perpetrators, toward the victims of violence and how to assist them to reclaim their lives and potentialities' (True 2014: 256). Whilst noting that the very word 'reparations' has unfortunate implications – it implies repairing or returning victims of crime to the status quo ante, which, for women in post-conflict contexts, is rarely what is desired – Ní Aoiláin et al. see reparations as an important element of the WPS agenda (Ní Aoiláin et al. 2011: 187). The International Centre for Transitional Justice (ICTJ) noted that in April 2014 the Ugandan parliament adopted a resolution that opens the door to the country's first gender-sensitive reparations fund (ICTJ 2014). It calls on the government to take robust action to remedy the plight of thousands of victims, and thus builds on the Juba Peace deal's vague commitment to 'promote redress'. The specific reference to gender in the resolution was the result of the persistent advocacy of Ugandan women's groups. They campaigned for gender-sensitive reparations that would go beyond addressing the needs of victims of sexual violence to address all conflict-related harms that have a gender dimension, such as land dispossession, lack of access to education, stigma of victimization and economic disempowerment. Through this focus on economically empowering the marginalized, the reparations have the potential to be transformative. By June 2015, however, the ICTJ was reporting that Uganda had not yet implemented its resolution, and tens of thousands of victims of the conflicts in Uganda were still suffering from the consequences of a range of violations (Otim and Kihika 2015).

The key problem for Ugandan women remains that they continue to be marginalized from the major development plans set up by the government and international development agencies at the end of the war. The PRDP did not integrate the national and international instruments available to promote gender equality, such as the Ugandan national gender policy, CEDAW or the Beijing Platform. Women are still considered in its programmes as a 'vulnerable' group, which limits the extent and the impact of the initiatives dedicated to them. Underpinning these problems is the wider macroeconomic picture of Uganda, wherein neoliberal policies increase inequalities and entrench poverty. Chapter 3 made clear that in order to transform the war economies in the aftermath of conflict, states need to have a considerable revenue base, but the tax incentives offered to foreign investors rob the Ugandan government of that resource base. Revenue lost to Uganda in 2008/9 amounted to nearly twice the country's entire health budget (Tax Justice Network-Africa and Action Aid 2012: iv). Moreover, the reforms the Ugandan government have made in order to attract investors in land have resulted in thousands of people being evicted from their property (Martin-Prével and Mohammed 2014). A quarter of the country's 34 million population lives in poverty (on less than US$1.25 a day).

It is not just women who experience hardship of course. Uganda's LGBTQ population have suffered horrific discrimination and marginalization, increasingly since 2006, when an Anti-Homosexuality Bill was adopted in parliament. The international community's response was to reduce aid to Uganda, compounding the harm done to the same marginalized groups – LGBTQ people and women – because of Uganda's reliance on aid in order to provide the basic services that ordinary people need to survive.[7]

These problems are common across post-conflict areas and act to undermine those peacebuilding initiatives which focus on the economic empowerment of women. As Eleanor O'Gorman (2014: 9) concludes in her assessment of the UNPBC's commitment to mainstreaming gender in peacebuilding: 'Many "economic empowerment" projects can be reduced to income-generating projects that do not always consider the larger picture of gender roles and needs and how economic recovery can drive empowerment, gender equality and peace.'

Tackling neoliberalism through a feminist political economy approach

What could happen in regard to empowering women economically in peacebuilding? What do feminists suggest? As I have argued, this is relatively neglected by feminists focused on the WPS agenda. Meanwhile, feminist IPE and International Development scholars who *have* focused on women's economic empowerment do not always focus on the particular challenges of post-conflict contexts specifically. Across feminist scholarship, there is arguably more focus on *identifying* the gendered harms of neoliberalism than on theorizing how it can be challenged.

Ní Aoláin et al., in their advocacy of SSJ, make a number of interconnected suggestions for a new model of development in post-conflict contexts. Firstly, they suggest that donors need to think beyond microcredit to decent-sized loans which could finance small to medium-size businesses. Secondly, the UN and NGOs could work more on the capacity-building of women, offering business leadership training, legal literacy workshops, etc. A third imperative for them is to ensure that the cultural and social pressures to conform to traditional female roles, such as domestic work and subsistence farming, are consistently resisted. Fourthly, they argue that it is important to build infrastructure but rather than the superhighways and other 'prestige projects' so beloved of donors, the focus should be more on rural roads so that women can get to market (Ní Aoláin et al. 2011).

Such recommendations could indeed be important steps towards women's economic empowerment, but they generate another dilemma for feminists. Do these measures fall into the trap of 'smart economics', the model advocated by the World Bank, described above? By encouraging entrepreneurial skills and opportunities, do they legitimate Western hegemonic notions of a market economy, where the measure of success is whether women contribute to growth? Although they do not address the risks of the World Bank's model of engendering development explicitly, Ní Aoláin et al.'s emphasis on *women's rights* to economic opportunities, rather than the benefits to the economy, implies an alternative to the World Bank's model of engendering development. The markets being advocated by these feminists are sustainable and just markets, rather than the current neoliberal global market economy. The focus of the economic policies here is around labour rights, equal access to economic opportunities and sustainable livelihoods for all. Moreover, with their concurrent emphasis on women's civil, political, social and reproductive rights, their vision is of economic development working in tandem with other aspects of the development project in ways which can perhaps avoid the impacts of the neoliberal model: cheap labour, exploitation, poverty, insecurity and human trafficking, all of which are caused or underpinned by gendered inequalities. In sum, it is not that all markets are bad, in Ní Aoláin et al.'s analysis, but the current ideologically driven idea that cutting public spending and lowering tariffs on exports and offering tax incentives for inward investment that provides no jobs – the neoliberal market detailed in earlier chapters – is not working. Similarly, it is not that inward investment is inherently bad, but it needs to be transparent, free from corruption and attentive to local political complexities, so that it can create job opportunities for all groups, and it needs to be able to be taxed at a level so that the community benefits.

In terms of how we get there from here, Ní Aoiláin et al. suggest the use of gender impact assessments (GIAs), requiring that any economic liberalization programme:

(a) consults with women about their economic needs;
(b) ensures women are represented in economic sites of transition;
(c) assesses whether plans to liberalize the economy will have negative gender outcomes;
(d) ensures that rights discourse pervades the framework of economic transition; and
(e) ensures some minimal non-negotiable provisions such as availability of food, water, shelter and healthcare throughout the liberalization process. (Ní Aoláin et al. 2011: 248)

Such GIAs would be akin to the environmental impact assessments (EIAs) which have had some success in ensuring that development projects do not destroy the environment and are sustainable (Lawrence 2003; Glasson et al. 2013). EIAs and GIAs are just a starting point, but they hold promise. GIAs have been advocated in a number of circumstances but have not yet been applied in a systematic way to post-conflict reconstruction projects. In terms of Ní Aoláin et al.'s GIA, the first two benchmarks could be extended to include other marginalized groups, such as indigenous people and the LGBTQ community, so as to be fully inclusive and attentive to the range of needs of marginalized groups. The commitment to a rights-based approach – most evidence in their fourth and fifth benchmark questions – is important and essential if such exercises are to avoid reinforcing the more instrumentalist model of engendering development found in the World Banks's 'smart economics' model. The third benchmark is also important as it gets to the heart of the neoliberal agenda: the determination to liberalize the economy, despite the evidence that it increases inequalities, vulnerabilities and insecurities particularly when applied in post-conflict contexts.

Arguably, however, Ní Aoláin et al. could have been bolder in this regard. They say little about *what to do if* if it is assessed that the plans to liberalize the economy will have negative gender outcomes. There is a sense in which underlying their argument for SSJ is an implicit assumption that the donor community just does not *realize* how bad neoliberal policies are for women. To actually make a difference, GIAs arguably require additional mechanisms which would *prevent* the donor community and post-conflict country governments from pursuing development projects and macroeconomic strategies that harm women and other marginalized groups. Assessing *whether* liberalization will have gendered effects is not enough.

GIAs could be a particularly useful tool for assessing major infrastructure projects which play a key role in post-conflict reconstruction. Before contracts are given for any reconstruction or economic project – infrastructure, extraction industry, plantation of biofuel crops, etc. – there should be a legally required GIA. This assessment should go beyond a simple checklist which considers the impact of the project on men and women in isolation from each other and as if they were homogeneous groups. Instead, it should interrogate how the project will affect gendered power relations, taking into consideration health, education, livelihoods and security. Crucially, there should be monitoring and accountability measures built in so that projects which exacerbate inequalities face penalties and are forced to change. The accountability measures would ideally be citizen-led. Democratic oversight of development projects is crucial if they are to benefit the majority of citizens instead of the few. Of course, GIAs require a certain level of expertise, but can still be conducted by way of an inclusive process, as Ní Aoláin et al. make clear. Such a GIA would have a profound impact on many of the reconstruction projects carried out as part of peacebuilding in post-conflict zones.

Indeed, this model of more democratic control is required for the macroeconomic development of post-conflict countries more generally, not just on a project-by-project basis. Parliaments and other elected bodies of the citizenry must have more say. To transform government economic planning so that it can enable feminist visions of peace requires the creation of fiscal democracy, a system in which budget processes are transparent, accountable and participatory, and in which every type of citizen has an equal voice (Bakker 2002). Andy Norton and Diane Elson (2002: 47–8) identify four important aspects of fiscal democracy: elected representatives controlling the budget; consultations between government officials and the public; shared decision-making on budget formulation and execution between government and citizens; and citizens holding statutory entitlements to public services, backed up by mechanisms of redress. Anne Marie Goetz and Robert Jenkins (2002) add an additional element of participatory auditing, to ensure that decisions are actually carried out, and that the people who were supposed to benefit actually do benefit.

Gender budget initiatives (GBIs) are another important tool, like GIAs, which can be used to challenge neoliberal models of economic development. Feminist economists have developed a range of innovative approaches in their efforts to ensure government budgets contribute to gender equality (Budlender et al. 2002; Çagatay 2003; Elson 2004), This work is less well developed in feminist scholarship on post-conflict peacebuilding, which is a missed opportunity and an area ripe for further research. Like GIAs, GBIs can be fairly limited – merely *demonstrating* that a budget does indeed exacerbate gendered inequalities – or more transformational – including additional measures to *ensure* that the budget does not exacerbate gendered inequalities. In practice, GBIs have tended to become tools by which the amount of money allocated to services for women is measured, but their intention was more radical than that. Feminist economists stress that, to be fully effective, the process has to focus on the revenue side of the budget, as well as the expenditure, and it has to address macroeconomic policy (Elson 2004: 634). Most importantly, it has to be inclusive: there is a need for budget oversight to be much more participatory. Feminists thus suggest that parliaments and civil society have to be given more powers over the budget and the macroeconomic development over post-conflict countries, rather than decisions being made between a few government officials and the donor community (Elson 2004). Not only is this democratic deficit a major injustice, but it fuels corruption, as we have seen in the examples of post-conflict reconstruction throughout this book.

The Secretary-General's 7-PAP does make reference to the need for women and civil society organizations to have oversight over infrastructure and development programmes, but it limits this in fundamentally problematic ways. Under 'Economic Recovery', the 7-PAP notes:

> The UN system will ensure that women's equal involvement as participants and beneficiaries in local-development, employment-creation, frontline service-delivery and DDR programmes in post-conflict situations.
>
> (a) Where local development and infrastructure programs are based on a participatory/community-development approach, these should require direct involvement of women and women CSOs [civil society organizations] in setting priorities, identifying beneficiaries, and monitoring implementation. (UN Secretary-General 2010: para. 50)

The clause states that it is only '*[w]here* [my italics] local development and infrastructure programs are based on a participatory/community-development approach' that women should be involved in setting priorities, identifying beneficiaries and monitoring implementation. This omits the majority of development and infrastructure projects, the very ones which tend to involve massive foreign investment with tax breaks which ensure that the majority of citizens do not benefit.

Feminists insist that for formal structures of fiscal democracy to be democratic in practice, there must be active engagement of well-informed and well-organized citizens (Elson

2004: 639). An educated and empowered civil society, including women's organizations, is crucial for sustainable peace. The focus of the WPS agenda has been primarily on empowering women to participate in peace negotiations. There is a need for more attention to the necessity of empowering women and civil society to engage with public finance and macroeconomic policy in post-conflict contexts. There are some promising examples of capacity-building projects which merit further exploration to examine the extent to which they promote women's involvement in influencing economic policy. For example, in post-conflict contexts such as Sierra Leone, South Sudan and Burundi, a range of women's civil society organizations have been able to participate in policy debates, thanks to donor funding which has provided women with resources, training and networking opportunities (Cornwall and Goetz 2005). The Afghan Women's Resource Centre attempts to foster and multiply the efforts and achievements of local women's committees in rural communities, linking them to officials at district level. It was able to support two women to become committee leaders at the district level, before being elected as MPs (Cardona et al. 2012: 51). These projects are important elements in increasing civil society and women's participation in developing economic policy.

If we adopt a methodological approach that enables us to see how small wins can be built upon in order to achieve more transformative change (see Duncanson and Woodward forthcoming), a range of possible avenues for activism and scholarship open up around GIAs and GBIs as tools to challenge the neoliberal model. Applying the insights from feminist economists into GIAs and GBIs to post-conflict contexts would be an important route to strengthening further the WPS agenda. Although GBIs exist in many post-conflict countries, including Uganda, Rwanda and Mozambique, they often conform to the more limited model described above, whereby only the expenditure side of the budget is examined, to see if money is being allocated to women. The potential for GBIs to challenge neoliberalism has not been fully exploited in post-conflict countries. The turn to include more attention to economic empowerment of women within the WPS agenda is promising, but there is a need for tools that transform the system rather than focus on ameliorating its effects on women. To realize feminist visions of peace, it is crucial that tools such as GIAs and GBIs are used to tackle neoliberal prescriptions for post-conflict reconstruction and not merely for increasing the proportion of post-conflict funding that is allocated to 'women's projects'.

Conclusion

Fifteen years on from the adoption of 1325, there are positive signs that the UN and feminist scholarship are increasingly focused on the economic empowerment of women and other marginalized groups. The previous chapter detailed the ways in which the many small gains which the focus on protection and participation had won for gender equality were undermined by the neoliberal economic policies which intensified the challenge of securing peace by exacerbating poverty, inequality and injustice whilst starving initiatives of the required resources. This chapter has detailed the feminist work which has tried to do more than identify this as a problem, which feminists have done consistently since neoliberal policies began to dominate in the 1980s, and instead has suggested ways forward. Both True's political economy approach and Ní Aoláin et al.'s SSJ focus on women's economic empowerment as the neglected but crucial element of engendering peacebuilding. I have argued, however, that there is a need to go further and to theorize how a focus on women's economic rights can be multiplied into a challenge to neoliberalism. I have suggested that GBIs and GIAs would be useful tools, and more could be done by feminists both to develop their transformatory potential and to apply them to post-conflict reconstruction contexts.

As feminist economists make clear, GBIs and GIAs will only be effective if they are participatory. Fiscal democracy is required, and it involves a strong coalition of civil society organizations from the global North and South to tackle the vested interests and the naturalized 'common-sense' that 'there is no alternative'. Suggesting that the power of civil society will make a difference might seem over-optimistic and simplistic, but it is hard to see how change can come from anywhere else. Interestingly, however, when we consider how it will take a strong civil society to challenge neoliberalism, and how a strong civil society involves the inclusion of women and other marginalized groups, we start to see how the WPS agenda on participation cannot so easily be dismissed as irrelevant, as it has been by many critical feminists. Participation in parliaments, governments, business, the security sector and, crucially, civil society is not a guarantee that neoliberalism will be challenged, but it is arguably the most promising route. Of course, the way in which the global financial system has been able to bounce back from the 2008 crash and change the narrative to imply that it was bloated states that were the problem is an indication of neoliberalism's power and resilience. Building a civil society with the power to challenge it will not be easy, but the cases explored throughout this book indicate that a crucial step in creating feminist visions of peace necessarily involves a more explicit and sustained strategy of tackling neoliberalism through a strong and economically literate civil society.

This book has argued that peacebuilding will only result in feminist visions of peace – peace as inclusive, expansive and transformative – if it challenges neoliberalism. It has deviated from some feminist and critical security scholarship in its position that peace building and neoliberalism are not inevitably linked: the 'liberal peace' is not the only possible model of peacebuilding. Of course, the challenge of decoupling UN peacebuilding from neoliberalism is immense. Current peacebuilding efforts depend on funding from IFIs and donor countries who remain wedded to neoliberal assumptions and policies. As feminist economists point out, the ability of post-conflict governments – indeed, any governments – to make their own decisions about macroeconomic policy has been severely limited by neoliberalism. Financial institutions, rather than the votes of citizens, now discipline the size of government budgets and direction of economic policy (Elson and Çagatay 2000; Bakker 2002; Elson 2004). Although neoliberal globalization has put strong limits on what can be achieved by feminist attempts to engender government budgets or build feminist capacity inside parliaments, there remains some room for manoeuvre. Through participatory GBIs and GIAs, political engagement and peaceful protest, citizens in the global North and South have the ability to challenge their governments on macroeconomic and international development policies, and can also push them to challenge the IFIs.

This book has also argued that the WPS agenda at the UN has been an important mechanism through which gains have been made for women and other marginalized groups in conflict zones. It has reviewed the criticisms of feminists, the problems of conception, implementation and ambition, and argued that those feminists highlighting problems of ambition are too harsh in their assessment of the UN, and too determinist in their assumption that peacebuilding is always inevitably part of the neoliberal project. In their approach to the topic, they are perhaps too dismissive of the importance of the small wins. Scholars from a variety of contexts have sought to theorize how small gains can add up to more transformatory change in a process of 'radical incrementalism', challenging the dichotomy of reform versus revolution (Pieterse 2008: 6–7; also see Cockburn 1989). With regard to the WPS agenda, this approach can help feminist scholars keep both the small wins of improved protection and participation pillars in our sights at the same time as the need to do more to advance the prevention pillar through a fundamental challenge to the global economy (see, e.g., Reilly).

The work which has gone on in order to improve protection of women and girls in conflict, including from sexual violence, is vitally important. The recent efforts to strengthen and engender reparations in post-conflict contexts is particularly crucial, as gender-sensitive reparations are attentive to victims' needs for economic security as well as justice. One of the key arguments of this book has been that there needs to be more attention paid to women's economic and social rights as well as civil and political rights in post-conflict contexts. Over the past 15 years, we have seen the WPS architecture start to pay more attention to the need to empower women economically. Feminist scholars of peacebuilding need to keep their eyes trained on whether this is limited to income generation projects for women, microfinance schemes and community-driven development, or whether it contains the seeds of something more transformatory, such as empowering women's organizations and other CSOs to audit government budgets and plans. As feminist economists have made clear, a well-informed and well-organized civil society that can engage with economic policy is a prerequisite for challenging the current neoliberal prescriptions for post-conflict reconstruction. Another prerequisite is a strong parliament, able to hold governments to account, engage in GBI and GIAs and challenge the imposition of neoliberal reforms on their countries. Together, these two elements of the formula for resisting neoliberalism demonstrate the importance of the participation pillar of the WPS agenda. Notwithstanding the disappointing exclusion of Syrian women from the Geneva peace talks, some progress has been made in recent years to increase women's participation in peacebuilding, as chapter 4 demonstrated. Rather than viewing small steps towards protection and participation as relatively meaningless in the context of neoliberalism, this book has suggested that, especially with the stronger WPS architecture, the small steps could and should be viewed as containing within them the seeds of neoliberalism's transformation.

Questions for discussion

1   What is the World Bank's approach to women's economic empowerment? To what extent do you think it could contribute to feminist visions of peace?

2   What are GBIs and GIAs? How could they help achieve feminist visions of peace?

3   Bearing in mind everything you have read in this book, how would you evaluate the WPS architecture at the UN?

Suggestions for further reading

Debbie Budlender 2008. 'Integrating Gender-Responsive Budgeting into the Aid Effectiveness Agenda: Ten-Country Overview Report'. United Nations Development Fund for

Women (UNIFEM). *http://www.gender-budgets.org/index.php ?option=com_joomdoc&view=documents&path=suggested -readings/integrating-gender-responsive-budgeting-into -the-aid-effectiveness-agenda-reports&Itemid=587.*
This report from one of the acknowledged experts on gender-responsive budgeting assesses the evidence from 10 countries, which include some post-conflict ones discussed in this book.

Monica Costa, Marian Sawer and Rhonda Sharp. 2013. 'Women Acting for Women'. *International Feminist Journal of Politics* 15 (3): 333–52.
This article makes interesting connections between gender-responsive budgeting and the participation of women in post-conflict parliaments, suggesting that the participation of women in the Timorese parliament made the adoption of the gender-responsive budget possible. The authors call for more research into what enables women parliamentarians to become critical actors, a call I endorse in this chapter.

Diane Elson. 2004. 'Engendering Government Budgets in the Context of Globalization(s)'. *International Feminist Journal of Politics* 6 (4): 623–42.
This article considers the strengths and weaknesses of attempts to 'engender' government budgets. It focuses on the context of globalization, rather than post-conflict contexts specifically, but is a good place to start for information about gender budget initiatives, as Elson is one of the pioneers of the field.

Fionnuala Ní Aoláin, Dina Francesca Haynes and Naomi Cahn. 2011. *On the Frontlines: Gender, War, and the Post-Conflict Process.* Oxford: Oxford University Press.
Comprehensive and persuasive, the three authors – all law professors with years of experience as women's rights advocates in conflict zones – argue for a new approach to addressing gender in post-conflict settings. Although some of the evidence they draw upon is now somewhat dated, they provide rich and detailed examples of the dilemmas introduced in this book, and a compelling argument for women's socioeconomic rights to be given as much attention as civil

and political rights, in what they term as Social Services
Justice.

Jacqui True. 2014. 'The Political Economy of Gender in UN
Peacekeeping'. In *Rethinking Peacekeeping: Gender Equality
and Collective Security*, edited by Gina Heathcote and Dianne
Otto. Basingstoke: Palgrave Macmillan.
True builds on her excellent 2012 book The Political Economy
of Violence against Women *in bringing this approach to
peace operations. A compelling call for more attention to
be paid to women's socioeconomic rights in peacebuilding
operations.*

Web resources

Association for Women Rights in Development (*http://www.
awid.org/priority-areas/economic-justice*)
*The Association for Women's Rights in Development (AWID)
is a global feminist membership organization that focuses on
economic justice. This page contains excellent analysis and
advocacy for a transformation of the economic system.*

Code Pink's Peace Economy (*http://www.codepink.org/
peaceeconomy*)
*The feminist organization's attempt to build an alternative to
the war economy – building the foundation blocks of the
peace it wishes to see in the world. The website contains ideas
for opting out of the war economy and cultivating patterns
of caring, sharing and respect.*

GSDRC's reading pack on gender-responsive budgets (*http://
www.gsdrc.org/go/professional-development-reading-packs/
gender-responsive-budgeting*)
*GSDRC (Governance and Social Development Resource
Centre) is a partnership of research institutes, think-tanks and
consultancy organizations established by the UK's Department for International Development (DFID) with expertise
in governance, social development, humanitarian and conflict
issues. The link takes you to a page which has an introduction*

to gender-responsive budgeting, links to six key readings in the field and discussion questions.

UN Women's Gender-Responsive Budgeting website (*http://www.gender-budgets.org/*)
Launched in 2001 by the United Nations Development Fund for Women (UNIFEM), now UN Women, this website aims to support efforts of governments, women's organizations, members of parliament and academics to ensure that planning and budgeting effectively respond to gender equality goals. As such, it contains a wealth of information on gender-responsive budgets, with a focus on resources, assessments and training materials for practitioners. This website is also useful because it illustrates the way that gender-responsive budgeting in practice often becomes a mechanism for tracing how much of a budget goes to 'women's issues' rather than being used to challenge neoliberal policies in a more holistic way.

Notes

Introduction

1   In peace processes, 'Track I' usually denotes official diplomacy between governments, whilst non-governmental, informal and unofficial contacts between non-state actors are referred to as 'Track 2'.

2   See, for example, George W. Bush's declaration of US foreign policy in the *New York Times* ahead of his 2002 State of the Union address: 'We seek a just peace where repression, resentment and poverty are replaced with the hope of democracy, development, free markets and free trade' (G. W. Bush 2002).

3   'In Larger Freedom' was Secretary-General Kofi Annan's five-year progress report on the implementation of the Millennium Declaration of 2000, which had been requested of him by the UN General Assembly. It called for more aid to enable developing countries to achieve the Millennium Development Goals, and asked member states to agree to establish the Peacebuilding Commission and to embrace the principle of 'Responsibility to Protect', the doctrine of collective action to counter genocide, ethnic cleansing and crimes against humanity.

Chapter 1

1   Other authors have used the conceptualization and implementation categories for the types of problem (Irvine 2013: 23; Steans

2013: 123), but I think this is to underplay the important third category.

2 Pugh et al. refer to 'combat, shadow and coping economies' (Pugh et al. 2004: 8). Peterson modifies the terms to use 'criminal' rather than 'shadow' 'to more explicitly distinguish the illicit character of that economy' (Peterson 2008: 14–15 fn. 13). She also broadens the 'coping' economy to include aspects of social reproduction that most authors ignore.

3 Many feminist and women's organizations and individuals at the UN did of course highlight the gendered nature of war and the importance of paying attention to gender in peacekeeping operations, but institutional acknowledgement and support were largely absent. Many contend that this remains the case 15 years after 1325, but my argument is that whilst examples of gender blindness remain, the picture is more accurately one of gender gaps and gender dilemmas, as the chapter will go on to argue.

4 Zainab Bangura was appointed as the UN Secretary-General's Special Representative on Sexual Violence in Conflict on 22 June 2012, as a result of UNSCR 1888 (2009), which built on 1325 and called for more attention to be paid to prosecuting and preventing sexual violence in conflict. She made this statement at the June Summit on Sexual Violence in Conflict in London. UNSCR 1888 and the London Summit will be discussed further in subsequent chapters.

5 When just one side has been primarily responsible for sexual violence, as was allegedly the case in the conflicts in El Salvador and Guatemala in the 1990s, the opposing side has an interest in raising the issue in the talks. The norm, however, has been expressed through either silence on the issue or amnesties for this human rights violation (R. Jenkins and Goetz 2010).

6 UN Action Against Sexual Violence in Conflict unites the work of 13 UN entities with the goal of ending sexual violence in conflict. It is a concerted effort by the UN system to improve coordination and accountability, amplify programming and advocacy and support national efforts to prevent sexual violence and respond effectively to the needs of survivors. See *http:// www.stoprapenow.org/about/*.

Chapter 2

1 These two aspects of freedom were included in US President Roosevelt's 1941 State of the Union address, which has now become known as the Four Freedoms speech, but were picked

up and further popularized by the United Nations, particularly in its efforts to promote the concept of Human Security.

2 The 1994 UNDP Human Development Report, 'New Dimensions of Human Security', coined the term 'Human Security' within the UN system, and at the UN Millennium Summit, then Secretary-General Kofi Annan called on the international community to advance, as the goals of the new millennium, the agendas of 'freedom from fear' and 'freedom from want' in the UN's efforts to develop better responses to old and new challenges.

3 Lederach argues that socioeconomic justice is critical to peace, identifying what he calls the 'justice gap' in peacebuilding: '[W]e have not adequately developed a peace-building framework that reduces direct violence and produces social and economic justice' (Lederach 1999: 32).

4 Meanwhile, the objectives of this policy framework have only partly been achieved. Per capita growth rates have shown a declining trend since the 1970s in developed countries. While growth rates have been rising in developing countries since the 1990s, along with a decline in income poverty, these trends are less positive if the growth rates for India and China are excluded (Kabeer 2009).

Chapter 3

1 Influential peacebuilding scholar Roland Paris, in general a defender of the liberal peace project, acknowledges that market liberalization and orthodox economic policies tend to be dangerous in post-conflict contexts. He thinks the problem is the pacing, not the policies themselves, but feminists tend to think both are problematic.

2 Microcredit and microfinance initiatives emerged in response to the failure of the formal financial system to reach the poor and marginalized, including women. They exist to lend small amounts of money (hence the 'micro'), and, although initially pioneered by NGOs, governments and commercial banks have become increasingly involved as lenders and the scale of the operations can be international. There is some evidence to suggest that such loans do empower women and enable them to be released from demeaning forms of wage labour; at the same time, there is evidence to suggest that loans can increase women's indebtedness, add to their workloads and lead to market saturation in female segments of the commodity market

(Kabeer 2009: 83–4). Moreover, in any case, coverage is patchy – it rarely reaches the poorest of the poor, and few think it alone could address adequately the underlying constraints in women's access to and control over economic and financial resources.

3   Also see the vast majority of the contributions to the edited collections Hawthorne and Winter (2002) and Hunt and Rygiel (2006).

4   Although often with the caveat in conclusion that admits that a theoretically pure position is untenable.

5   A renewed focus on the material consequences of neoliberalism would have two potential advantages. Firstly, it is detailed evidence of gendered material harm, not just exposure of civilizational discourses, that is arguably required in order to convince wider audiences (beyond feminist and critical security studies scholars) of the necessity of challenging neoliberal economic frameworks. Secondly, perhaps paradoxically, detailed evidence of exactly how and to what extent neoliberal policies have harmed women and other marginalized groups can also provide more optimism for the future than using discourse analysis to focus on the narratives by which elites ensure their dominance. A focus on the policies and their material impacts provides feminists with concrete problems to challenge, rather than somewhat uncontrollable discourses.

Chapter 4

1   I am aware, for example, that the decision to consider sexual violence under the heading of the WPS's protection agenda is to leave out other aspects of protection, and, indeed, that is one of the criticisms many feminists would make of the way that the WPS agenda has been pursued. Yet it seems to me that sexual violence in conflict has been too central to the WPS debates, and is too important a violation, to not discuss at length. For more on feminists' dilemmas about the prominence to give to sexual violence in their work, see Buss (2014).

2   Read the chair's summary here: https://www.gov.uk/govern ment/publications/chairs-summary-global-summit-to-end-sexual-violence-in-conflict/chairs-summary-global-summit-to-end-sexual-violence-in-conflict.

3   Appointed on 2 February 2010, Swedish politician Margot Wallström was the first person to hold the office of the SRSG-SVC, the new position created by UNSCR 1888 (2009). At the

end of her term in September 2012, UN Secretary-General Ban-Kimoon appointed Zainab Bangura from Sierra Leone. See http://www.un.org/sexualviolenceinconflict/about-us/about-the-srsg/.

4 It is somewhat useful to think about barriers as being things that are erected to prevent women participating, and obstacles as being those structural factors that hold women back from participating, whilst recognizing that these categories often overlap.

5 Gender budgets in most countries are tiny. My point here is not to suggest that countries in the global South 'lag behind' on gender equality, but that the resources devoted to gender equality are a tiny proportion of what is required, which is important to note when assessing whether women parliamentarians are 'making a difference'.

6 See http://www.dcaf.ch/Series-Collections/SSR-Backgrounders. For further development of the concept of SSR, see Born and Schnabel (2009); Sedra (2009); Hänggi (2011).

7 The UN Secretary-General's report of 2008 (UNGA and UNSC 2008), which sought to define principles for UN SSR, as well as potential roles for engagement, emphasized the importance of gender sensitivity. Integrating a gender perspective is highlighted as 'inherent to an inclusive and socially responsive approach to security' and 'key to developing security sector institutions that are non-discriminatory, representative of the population and capable of effectively responding to the specific security needs of diverse groups'.

Chapter 5

1 Although 'prevention' could be interpreted as a focus on tackling economic hardship, in practice it has not been interpreted that way by many actors at UN level, who tend to discuss early warning systems etc. under this heading.

2 For example, as then Secretary-General of the UN Kofi Annan argued in 2004:

> Development and security are inextricably linked. A more secure world is only possible if poor countries are given a real chance to develop. Extreme poverty and infectious diseases threaten many people directly, but they also provide a fertile breeding ground for other threats, including civil conflicts. Even people in rich countries will be more secure if their Governments help poor countries to

> defeat poverty and disease by meeting the Millennium Development Goals. (UN 2004: vii)

3   The concept of 'decent work' is central to the work of the International Labour Organization, including in countries emerging from conflict. See *http://www.ilo.org/global/topics/decent-work/lang-en/index.htm*.

4   The Juba Peace Talks began in July 2006 and resulted in a ceasefire by September 2006. A Final Peace Agreement was negotiated in 2008, but the LRA rebel leader, Joseph Kony, repeatedly failed to appear for planned signing ceremonies. Although there is no signed agreement, and the LRA took its violence to neighbouring countries, the peace talks did mark the beginning of a period of relative normalcy in Northern Uganda. There are still other ongoing armed conflicts in Uganda, however, including a rebellion led by the Allied Democratic Forces and Karimojong armed cattle-rustling and violent raids, creating displacements on a similar scale to the LRA insurgency.

5   The PRDP has been the government's main post-conflict policy framework for Northern Uganda. Its overall goal is stabilization, recovery and development through the consolidation of state authority; rebuilding and empowering communities; and revitalization of the Northern economy, peacebuilding and reconciliation.

6   Uganda introduced a policy of affirmative action for women in 1989, and its constitution is considered by women's civil society groups to be relatively gender-sensitive, although there are large gaps between rights on paper and in practice.

7   International Alert reports that Uganda was for a while the 'darling' of the donor community, because of its support to Western countries with regard to the 'war on terror' and because of its relative efficiency in accounting for aid funds (despite several corruption scandals), with aid accounting for 25 percent of Uganda's 2012–13 budget (El-Bushra et al. 2013). Recent evidence of corruption and political repression, however, and concerns over the Anti-Homosexuality Bill have raised big questions and concerns for donors. In 2012, the EU, the UK, Austria and the World Bank suspended a promised US$300 million in aid.

References

Abu-Lughod, Lila. 2002. 'Do Muslim Women Really Need Saving? Anthropological Reflections on Cultural Relativism and Its Others'. *American Anthropologist* 104 (3): 783–90.

Agence France-Presse. 2014. 'Ebola Threatening Liberia's Existence, Minister Warns'. *Guardian*, 9 October. *http://www.theguardian. com/global-development/2014/sep/10/ebola-threatening-liberia -existence*.

Al-Ali, Nadje, and Nicola Pratt. 2009. *Women and War in the Middle East: Transnational Perspectives*. London: Zed Books.

Al-Hussein, Prince Zeid Ra'ad Zeid. 2005. 'A Comprehensive Strategy to Eliminate Future Sexual Exploitation and Abuse in United Nations Peacekeeping Operations'. A/59/710. United Nations General Assembly. *http://www.un.org/ga/search/view_doc.asp? symbol=A/59/710*.

Allison, Miranda. 2007. 'Wartime Sexual Violence: Women's Human Rights and Questions of Masculinity'. *Review of International Studies* 33: 75–90.

Anderlini, Sanam Naraghi. 2000. 'Women at the Peace Table: Making a Difference'. United Nations Development Fund for Women (UNIFEM). *http://www.unwomen.org/en/digital-library/publications/2000/1/women-at-the-peace-table-making-a-difference*.

Anderlini, Sanam Naraghi. 2007. *Women Building Peace: What They Do, Why It Matters*. Boulder, CO: Lynne Rienner.

Anderlini, Sanam Naraghi. 2010. 'What the Women Say: Participation and UNSCR 1325: A Case Study Assessment'. International Civil Society Action Network and the MIT Center for

International Studies. *http://web.mit.edu/cis/pdf/WomenReport_10_2010.pdf*.

Anderlini, Sanam Naraghi, and Victoria Stanski. 2004. 'Conflict Prevention'. In *Conflict Prevention, Resolution and Reconstruction: Inclusive Security, Sustainable Peace: A Toolkit for Advocacy and Action. http://internationalalert.org/sites/default/files/library/TKConflictPrevention.pdf*.

Anthias, Floya. 1998. *Sociological Debates: Thinking about Social Divisions*. London: Greenwich University Press.

Aoi, Chiyuki, Cedric de Coning and Ramesh Thakur. 2007. *Unintended Consequences of Peacekeeping Operations*. Tokyo: United Nations University Press.

Aroussi, Sahla. 2011. '"Women, Peace and Security": Addressing Accountability for Wartime Sexual Violence'. *International Feminist Journal of Politics* 13 (4): 576–93.

Arsenijevic, Damir. 2014. 'After 22 Years of Being Bullied Bosnians Are Desperate, and Must Protest'. *Guardian*, 28 February. *http://www.theguardian.com/commentisfree/2014/feb/28/bosnia-protest-citizens-change-corruption*.

Autesserre, Séverine. 2012. 'Dangerous Tales: Dominant Narratives on the Congo and Their Unintended Consequences'. *African Affairs* 111 (443): 202–22.

Bacon, Laura. 2012. 'Building an Inclusive, Responsive National Police Service: Gender-Sensitive Reform in Liberia: 2005–2011'. No. 2013/114. WIDER Working Paper. World Institute for Development Economics Research, United Nations University. *http://hdl.handle.net/10419/93713*.

Baden, Sally, and Anne Marie Goetz. 1997. 'Who Needs [sex] When You Can Have [gender]? Conflicting Discourses on Gender at Beijing'. *Feminist Review* 56: 3–25.

Bakker, Isabella. 2002. 'Fiscal Policy, Accountability and Voice: The Example of Gender Responsive Budget Initiatives'. UNDP, Human Development Report Office Occasional Paper. *http://hdr.undp.org/en/content/fiscal-policy-accountability-and-voice*.

Ballentine, Karen, and Heiko Nitzschke. 2005. 'The Political Economy of Civil War and Conflict Transformation'. Berghof Research Center for Constructive Conflict Management, Berlin. *http://www.berghof-handbook.net/documents/publications/dialogue3_ballentine_nitzschke.pdf*.

Banfield, Jessica. 2008. 'Building a Peace Economy in Northern Uganda: Conflict-Sensitive Approaches to Recovery and Growth'. *Investing in Peace* no. 1. International Alert. *http://www.international-alert.org/sites/default/files/publications/building_a_peace_economy_in_northern_uganda.pdf*.

Barfield, Thomas. 2010. *Afghanistan: A Cultural and Political History*. Princeton: Princeton University Press.

Barnes, Karen. 2006. 'Reform or More of the Same? Gender Mainstreaming and the Changing Nature of UN Peace Operations'. *YCISS Working Paper* no. 41. *http://pi.library.yorku.ca/dspace/handle/10315/1322*.

Barsa, Michelle, and Kristin Williams. 2014. 'Syrian Women Know How to Defeat ISIS'. *Time*, 17 October. *http://time.com/author/kristin-williams/*.

Bartels, Susan, Michael VanRooyen, Jennifer Leaning, Jennifer Scott and Jocelyn Kelly. 2010. *'Now, the World is Without Me': An Investigation of Sexual Violence in Eastern Democratic Republic of Congo*. Cambridge, MA: Harvard Humanitarian Initiative; Oxford: Oxfam International.

Basini, Helen S. A. 2013. 'Gender Mainstreaming Unraveled: The Case of DDRR in Liberia'. *International Interactions* 39 (4): 535–57.

Bastick, Megan. 2008. 'Integrating Gender in Post-Conflict Security Sector Reform'. In *SIPRI Yearbook*. DCAF. *http://www.sipri.org/yearbook/2008/files/SIPRIYB0804.pdf*.

Bastick, Megan, and Kristen Valasek, eds. 2008. 'Gender and Security Sector Reform Toolkit'. DCAF, OSCE/ODIHR, UN-INSTRAW. *http://www.dcaf.ch/Publications/Gender-Security-Sector-Reform-Toolkit*.

Bateman, Milford. 2010. *Why Doesn't Microfinance Work? The Destructive Rise of Local Neoliberalism*. London: Zed Books.

Bateman, Milford, and Ha-Joon Chang. 2009. 'The Microfinance Illusion'. Unpublished manuscript, University of Cambridge. *http://www.microfinancetransparency.com/evidence/PDF/App.3%20Chang%20Bateman%20article.pdf*.

BBC. 2010. 'DR Congo Is World "Rape Capital"'. BBC, 28 April. *http://news.bbc.co.uk/1/hi/8650112.stm*.

Bell, Christine. 2004. 'Women Address the Problems of Peace Agreements'. In *Peace Work: Women, Armed Conflict and Negotiation*, edited by Radhika Coomaraswamy and Dilrukshi Foneska. New Delhi: Women Unlimited.

Bell, Christine, and Catherine O'Rourke. 2010. 'Peace Agreements or Pieces of Paper? The Impact of UNSC Resolution 1325 on Peace Processes and Their Agreements'. *International and Comparative Law Quarterly* 59 (4): 941–80.

Bell, Diane. 2002. 'Good and Evil: At Home and Abroad'. In *September 11 2001: Feminist Perspectives*, edited by Susan Hawthorne and Bronwyn Winter. Melbourne: Spinifex.

Benería, Lourdes. 2003. *Gender, Development, and Globalization: Economics as If All People Mattered*. New York: Routledge.

Benería, Lourdes, and Shelley Feldman. 1992. *Unequal Burden: Economic Crises, Persistent Poverty, and Women's Work.* Boulder, CO: Westview.

Benjamin, Medea. 2014. 'No Seat for Syrian Women at the Peace Talks'. *Huffington Post,* 22 January. *http://www.huffingtonpost.com/medea-benjamin/no-seat-for-syrian-women-_b_4645000.html.*

Berger, Susan A. 2003. 'Guatemaltecas: The Politics of Gender and Democratization'. In *Struggles for Social Rights in Latin America,* edited by Susan Eckstein and Timothy P. Wickham-Crowley. Hove: Psychology Press,

Bergeron, Suzanne. 2003. 'The Post-Washington Consensus and Economic Representations of Women in Development at the World Bank'. *International Feminist Journal of Politics* 5 (3): 397–419.

Bhattacharyya, Gargi. 2008. *Dangerous Brown Men: Exploiting Sex, Violence and Feminism in the War on Terror.* London: Zed Books.

Blackwell, Joyce. 2004. *No Peace without Freedom: Race and the Women's International League for Peace and Freedom, 1915–1975.* Carbondale, IL: Southern Illinois University Press.

Born, Hans, and Albrecht Schnabel, eds. 2009. *Security Sector Reform in Challenging Environments.* Münster: LIT Verlag.

Bowcott, Owen. 2011. 'Afghanistan Worst Place in the World for Women, but India in Top Five'. *Guardian,* 15 June. *http://www.theguardian.com/world/2011/jun/15/worst-place-women-afghanistan-india.*

Budlender, Debbie. 2008. 'Integrating Gender-Responsive Budgeting into the Aid Effectiveness Agenda: Ten-Country Overview Report'. United Nations Development Fund for Women (UNIFEM). *http://www.gender-budgets.org/index.php?option=com_joomdoc&vie=documents&path=suggested-readings/integrating-gender-responsive-budgeting-into-the-aid-effectiveness-agenda-reports&Itemid=587.*

Budlender, Debbie. 2010. 'Price of Peace: Financing for Gender Equality in Post Conflict Reconstruction'. United Nations Development Programme (UNDP). *http://www.undp.org/content/undp/en/home/librarypage/womens-empowerment/price-of-peace-financing-for-gender-equality-in-post-conflict-reconstruction.html.*

Budlender, Debbie, Diane Elson, Guy Hewitt and Tanno Mukhopadhyay. 2002. *Gender Budgets Make Cents.* London: Commonwealth Secretariat.

Bush, George W. 2001. 'Remarks by the President at Signing Ceremony for Afghan Women and Children Relief Act of 2001'. *http://2001-2009.state.gov/p/sca/rls/rm/6816.htm.*

Bush, George W. 2002. 'Securing Freedom's Triumph'. *New York Times*, 11 September. *http://www.nytimes.com/2002/09/11/opinion/11BUSH.html*.

Bush, Laura. 2001. 'Radio Address'. Edited by The White House Press Release. *http://georgewbush-whitehouse.archives.gov/news/releases/2001/11/20011117.html*.

Buss, Doris. 2014. 'Seeing Sexual Violence in Conflict and Post-Conflict Societies: The Limits of Visibility'. In *Sexual Violence in Conflict and Post-Conflict Societies: International Agendas and African Contexts*, edited by Doris Buss, Joanne Lebert, Blair Rutherford, Donna Sharkey and Obijiofor Aginam. London: Routledge.

Butler, Judith. 1990. *Gender Trouble: Feminism and the Subversion of Identity*. London: Routledge.

Butler, Judith. 2004. *Undoing Gender*. Hove: Psychology Press.

Byrne, Siobhan, and Allison McCulloch. 2012. 'Gender, Representation and Power-Sharing in Post-Conflict Institutions'. *International Peacekeeping* 19 (5): 565–80.

Çagatay, Nilüfer. 2003. 'Gender Budgets and Beyond: Feminist Fiscal Policy in the Context of Globalization'. *Gender & Development* 11 (1): 15–24.

Çagatay, Nilüfer, Diane Elson and Caren Grown. 1995. 'Gender, Adjustment and Macroeconomics. Special Issue'. *World Development* 23 (11): 1827–36.

Cardona, Ivan, Patricia Justino, Becky Mitchell and Catherine Müller. 2012. 'From the Ground Up: Women's Roles in Local Peacebuilding in Afghanistan, Liberia, Nepal, Pakistan and Sierra Leone'. Edited by Sharon Smee. Womankind Worldwide. *http://www.womankind.org.uk/wp-content/uploads/downloads/2012/09/From-The-Ground-Up-FINAL.pdf*.

Castel-Branco, Carlos Nuno. 2008. 'Aid Dependency and Development: A Question of Ownership? A Critical View'. *Maputo: IESE (Working Paper 01)*. *http://www.iese.ac.mz/lib/publication/AidDevelopmentOwnership.pdf*.

Castillejo, Claire. 2011. 'Building a State That Works for Women: Integrating Gender into Post-Conflict State Building', March, FRIDE Working Paper. *http://fride.org/download/WP107_Building_state.pdf*.

CEDAW. 2013. 'CEDAW/C/GC/30 General Recommendation No. 30 on Women in Conflict Prevention, Conflict and Post-Conflict Situations'. United Nations Convention on the Elimination of Discrimination Against Women. *http://www.ohchr.org/Documents/HRBodies/CEDAW/GComments/CEDAW.C.CG.30.pdf*.

Chant, Sylvia, and Caroline Sweetman. 2012. 'Fixing Women or Fixing the World? "Smart Economics", Efficiency Approaches, and Gender Equality in Development'. *Gender & Development* 20 (3): 517–29.

Charlesworth, Hilary. 2005. 'Not Waving but Drowning: Gender Mainstreaming and Human Rights in the United Nations'. *Harvard Human Rights Journal* 18: 1–14.

Charlesworth, Hilary. 2008. 'Are Women Peaceful? Reflections on the Role of Women in Peace-Building'. *Feminist Legal Studies* 16 (3): 347–61.

Chesterman, Simon, Michael Ignatieff and Ramesh Chandra Thakur. 2004. *Making States Work: From State Failure to State-Building*. Tokyo: United Nations International Peace Academy.

Chinkin, Christine. 2003a. 'Peace Agreements as a Means for Promoting Gender Equality and Ensuring Participation for Women'. United Nations Division for the Advancement of Women. *http://www.un.org/womenwatch/daw/egm/peace2003/reports/BPChinkin.PDF*.

Chinkin, Christine. 2003b. 'Gender, Human Rights, and Peace Agreements'. *Ohio State Journal on Dispute Resolution* 18 (3): 867–86.

Chinkin, Christine, and Hilary Charlesworth. 2006. 'Building Women into Peace: The International Legal Framework'. *Third World Quarterly* 27 (5): 937–57.

Chinkin, Christine, and Mary Kaldor. 2013. 'Gender and New Wars'. *Journal of International Affairs* 67 (1): 167–87.

Chossudovsky, Michel. 1997. *The Globalization of Poverty*. London: Zed Books.

Cloud, Dana L. 2004. 'To Veil the Threat of Terror: Afghan Women and the Clash of Civilizations in the Imagery of the US War on Terrorism'. *Quarterly Journal of Speech* 90 (3): 285–306.

Cockburn, Cynthia. 1989. 'Equal Opportunities: The Short and Long Agenda'. *Industrial Relations Journal* 20 (3): 213–25.

Cockburn, Cynthia. 1998. *The Space Between Us: Negotiating Gender and National Identity in Conflict Zones*. London: Zed Books.

Cockburn, Cynthia. 2007. *From Where We Stand: War, Women's Activism and Feminist Analysis*. London: Zed Books.

Cockburn, Cynthia. 2010. 'Gender Relations as Causal in Militarization and War'. *International Feminist Journal of Politics* 12 (2): 139–57.

Cockburn, Cynthia. 2011. 'Snagged on the Contradiction: NATO UNSC Resolution 1325, and Feminist Responses'. Unpublished manuscript. *http://www.cynthiacockburn.org/BlogNATO1325.pdf*.

Cockburn, Cynthia. 2012. *Anti-Militarism: Political and Gender Dynamics of Peace Movements*. Basingstoke: Palgrave Macmillan.

Cockburn, Cynthia. 2014. 'Plotting for a Woman-Shaped Peace: Syrian and Bosnian Women Confer'. *openDemocracy*, 24 February. *https://www.opendemocracy.net/5050/cynthia-cockburn/plotting-for-woman-shaped-peace-syrian-and-bosnian-women-confer*.

Cockburn, Cynthia, and Dubravka Zarkov. 2002a. 'Introduction'. In *The Postwar Moment: Militaries, Masculinities and International Peacekeeping*, edited by Cynthia Cockburn and Dubravka Zarkov. London: Lawrence and Wishart.

Cockburn, Cynthia, and Dubravka Zarkov. 2002b. *The Postwar Moment: Militaries, Masculinities and International Peacekeeping*. London: Lawrence and Wishart.

Cohen, Dara Kay, and Ragnhild Nordås. 2014. 'Sexual Violence in Armed Conflict: Introducing the SVAC Dataset, 1989–2009'. *Journal of Peace Research* 51 (3): 418–28.

Cohn, Carol. 1987. 'Sex and Death in the Rational World of Defence Intellectuals'. *Signs* 12 (4): 687–718.

Cohn, Carol. 2004. 'Feminist Peacemaking'. *The Women's Review of Books* 11 (5): 8–9.

Cohn, Carol. 2008. 'Mainstreaming Gender in UN Security Policy: A Path to Political Transformation?' In *Global Governance: Feminist Perspectives*, edited by Shirin Rai and Georgina Waylen. Basingstoke: Palgrave Macmillan.

Cohn, Carol. 2013. 'Women and Wars: Towards a Conceptual Framework'. In *Women and Wars*, edited by Carol Cohn. Cambridge: Polity.

Cohn, Carol, Helen Kinsella and Sheri Gibbings. 2004. 'Women, Peace and Security'. *International Feminist Journal of Politics* 6 (1): 130–40.

Cohn, Scott. 2013. 'Assad's Money Trail Is Hard to Trace'. *CNBC*, 20 November. *http://www.cnbc.com/id/101050333*.

Confortini, Catia Cecilia. 2012. *Intelligent Compassion: Feminist Critical Methodology in the Women's International League for Peace and Freedom*. New York: Oxford University Press.

Confortini, Catia Cecilia, and Soumita Basu. 2011. 'Weakest "P" in the 1325 Pod? Realizing Conflict Prevention through UN Security Council Resolution 1325'. Paper presented at the Annual Meeting of the International Studies Association Annual Conference, Montreal, Quebec, Canada.

Connell, Raewyn and Rebecca Pearse. 2015. *Gender: In World Perspective*. Third edition. Cambridge: Polity.

Cooper, Neil. 2005. 'Picking Out the Pieces of the Liberal Peaces: Representations of Conflict Economies and the Implications for Policy'. *Security Dialogue* 36 (4): 463–78.

Cooper, Neil, Mandy Turner and Michael Pugh. 2011. 'The End of History and the Last Liberal Peacebuilder: A Reply to Roland Paris'. *Review of International Studies* 37 (4): 1995–2007.

Cordell, Kirsten. 2010. 'Gender Mainstreaming in Peacekeeping Operations in Liberia 2003–2009: Best Practices Report'. Accra, Ghana: UNMIL, Office of the Gender Adviser (OGA). *http://www.resdal.org/facebook/UNMIL_Gender_Mainstreaming_in_PKO_in_Liberia-Best.pdf*.

Cornwall, Andrea, and Anne Marie Goetz. 2005. 'Democratizing Democracy: Feminist Perspectives'. *Democratisation* 12 (5): 783–800.

Corrin, Chris. 2000. 'Post-Conflict Reconstruction and Gender Analysis in Kosova'. *International Feminist Journal of Politics* 3 (1): 78–98.

Costa, Monica, Marian Sawer and Rhonda Sharp. 2013. 'Women Acting for Women'. *International Feminist Journal of Politics* 15 (3): 333–52.

Coulter, Chris. 2009. *Bush Wives and Girl Soldiers: Women's Lives through War and Peace in Sierra Leone*. Ithaca, NY: Cornell University Press.

Cox, Robert. 1981. 'Social Forces, States and World Orders: Beyond International Relations Theory'. *Millennium: Journal of International Studies* 10 (2): 126–55.

Cramer, Christopher. 2002. '"Homo Economicus" Goes to War: Methodological Individualism, Rational Choice and the Political Economy of War'. *World Development* 30 (11): 1845–64.

Cramer, Christopher. 2006. *Civil War Is Not a Stupid Thing: Accounting for Violence in Developing Countries*. London: Hurst & Company.

Cramer, Christopher. 2009. 'Trajectories of Accumulation through War and Peace'. In *The Dilemmas of Statebuilding: Confronting the Contradictions of Postwar Peace Operations*, edited by Roland Paris and Timothy D. Sisk. Abingdon: Routledge.

Crenshaw, Kimberley. 1989. 'Demarginalizing the Intersection of Race and Sex: A Black Feminist Critique of Antidiscrimination Doctrine, Feminist Theory and Antiracist Politics'. *University of Chicago Legal Forum* 140: 139–67.

Curle, Adam. 1971. *Making Peace*. London: Tavistock.

Dahlman, Carl, and Gearóid Ó Tuathail. 2005. 'Broken Bosnia: The Localized Geopolitics of Displacement and Return in Two Bosnian Places'. *Annals of the Association of American Geographers* 95 (3): 644–62.

DCAF, Megan Bastick, Ana Dangova, Beatrice Mosello and Audrey Reeves. 2011. 'Building an Inclusive, Responsive National Police Service: Gender Sensitive Reform in Liberia'. DCAF.

http://www.dcaf.ch/Publications/Gender-and-Security-Sector-Reform-Examples-from-the-Ground.

de Alwis, Malathi. 2012. 'Feminist Politics and Maternalist Agonism'. In *South Asian Feminisms*, edited by Ania Loomba and Ritty A. Lukoswe. Durham, NC: Duke University Press.

de Alwis, Malathi, Julie Mertus and Tazreena Asjjad. 2013. 'Women and Peace Processes'. In *Women and Wars*, edited by Carol Cohn. Cambridge: Polity.

De La Rey, Cheryl, and Susan McKay. 2006. 'Peacebuilding as a Gendered Process'. *Journal of Social Issues* 62 (1): 141–53.

de Langis, Theresa. 2011. 'Across Conflict Lines: Women Mediating for Peace; 12th Annual Colloquium Findings'. The Institute for Inclusive Security. *http://www.inclusivesecurity.org/wp-content/uploads/2013/05/2011-Colloquium-Report_FINAL.pdf.*

Dearden, Nick. 2014. 'Ebola Crisis: Three Things Band Aid Should Really Be Singing About'. *Guardian*, 11 November. *http://www.theguardian.com/commentisfree/2014/nov/11/ebola-africa-band-aid-three-things.*

Deleu, Marijke. 2015. 'Secure Insecurity: The Continuing Abuse of Civilians in Eastern DRC as the State Extends Its Control'. Oxfam. *https://www.oxfam.org/en/research/secure-insecurity.*

Dennis, Peter. 2005. 'A Brief History of Liberia'. The Center for Applied Linguistics. *http://ictj.org/sites/default/files/ICTJ-Liberia-Brief-History-2006-English.pdf.*

Detraz, Nicole. 2014. *Environmental Security and Gender*. London: Routledge.

Diamond, Larry, and Jack Mosbacher. 2013. 'Petroleum to the People'. *Foreign Affairs*, October. *http://www.foreignaffairs.com/articles/139647/larry-diamond-and-jack-mosbacher/petroleum-to-the-people.*

Disney, Abigail. 2008. *Pray the Devil Back to Hell*. Documentary. Fork Films. *http://www.praythedevilbacktohell.com/.*

Domingo, Pilar. 2012. 'Joint Evaluation: UN Women/UNDP Support to Women's Political Participation in Sub-Saharan Africa'. Overseas Development Institute. *http://genderevaluation.unwomen.org/en/~/documents/2013/11/20/12/59/joint-evaluation-un-womenundp-support-to-womens-political-participation-in-sub-saharan-africa.*

Domingo, Pilar, Rebecca Holmes, Alina Rocha Menocal and Nicola Jones. 2014. 'Assessment of the Evidence of Links between Gender Equality, Peacebuilding and Statebuilding: Literature Review'. Overseas Development Institute. *http://www.odi.org/publications/8087-assessment-evidence-links-between-gender-equality-peacebuilding-statebuilding-literature-review.*

Douglas, Sarah, Vanessa Farr, Felicity Hill and Wenny Kasuma. 2004. 'Getting It Right, Doing It Right: Gender and Disarmament, Demobilization and Reintegration'. United Nations Development Fund for Women (UNIFEM). *http://www.unwomen.org/ en/digital-library/publications/2010/1/getting-it-right-doing-it-right-gender-and-disarmament-demobilization-and-reintegration.*

Duffield, Mark. 2001. *Global Governance and the New Wars: The Merging of Development and Security.* London: Zed Books.

Duffield, Mark. 2007. *Development, Security and Unending War.* Cambridge: Polity.

Duffield, Mark. 2010. 'The Liberal Way of Development and the Development–Security Impasse: Exploring the Global Life-Chance Divide'. *Security Dialogue* 41 (1): 53–76.

Duncanson, Claire, and Rachel Woodward. Forthcoming. 'Regendering the Military: Theorizing Women's Military Participation'. *Security Dialogue.*

Dziewanski, Dariusz. 2012. 'Peace without Security: Violence against Women and Girls in Liberia'. Small Arms Survey. *http:// www.smallarmssurvey.org/fileadmin/docs/G-Issue-briefs/Liberia-AVA-IB3.pdf.*

Eisenstein, Zillah R. 2007. *Sexual Decoys: Gender, Race and War in Imperial Democracy.* London: Zed Books.

EITI. 2013. 'DR Congo Discloses Sobering Figures on Revenue from Natural Resources'. Extractive Industries Transparency Initiative, 21 January. *https://eiti.org/news/dr-congo-sobering-figures-on-revenue-from-natural-resources.*

El-Bushra, Judy. 2007. 'Feminism, Gender and Women's Peace Activism'. *Development and Change* 38 (1): 131–47.

El-Bushra, Judy. 2012. 'Gender in Peacebuilding: Taking Stock'. *International Alert*, June. *http://www.international-alert.org/ sites/default/files/Gender_TakingStock_EN_2012.pdf*

El-Bushra, Judy, Henri Myrttinen and Jana Naujoks. 2013. 'Renegotiating the "Ideal" Society: Gender Relations in the Wake of Conflict and Displacement in Uganda'. *http://www.international-alert.org/sites/default/files/Gender_%20RenegotiatingIdeal SocietyUganda_EN_2013_0.pdf.*

Elshtain, Jean Bethke. 1982. 'On Beautiful Souls, Just Warriors and Feminist Consciousness'. *Women's Studies International Forum* 5 (3/4): 341–8.

Elshtain, Jean Bethke. 1987. *Women and War.* Brighton: Harvester.

Elshtain, Jan Bethke. 1990. 'The Problem with Peace'. In *Women, Militarism and War*, edited by Jean Bethke Elshtain and Sheila Tobias. Savage, MD: Rowman & Littlefield.

Elson, Diane. 1991. 'Structural Adjustment: Its Effect on Women.' *http://www.popline.org/node/335968.*

Elson, Diane. 2002. 'Gender Justice, Human Rights and Neoliberal Economic Policies'. *Gendered Dimensions of Development* 37–64. United Research Institute for Social Development (UNRISD). *http://www.unrisd.org/80256B3C005BCCF9/%28httpAux Pages%29/1585F4AEF409C253C1257E2700652AA8/$file/II-Gendered%20Dimensions%20of%20Development.pdf.*

Elson, Diane. 2004. 'Engendering Government Budgets in the Context of Globalization(s)'. *International Feminist Journal of Politics* 6 (4): 623–42.

Elson, Diane, and Nilüfer Çagatay. 2000. 'The Social Content of Macroeconomic Policies'. *World Development* 28 (7): 1347–64.

Enloe, Cynthia. 1989. *Bananas, Beaches and Bases: Making Feminist Sense of International Politics.* Berkeley: University of California Press.

Enloe, Cynthia. 1993. *The Morning After: Sexual Politics at the End of the Cold War.* Berkeley: University of California Press.

Enloe, Cynthia. 2000. *Maneuvers: The International Politics of Militarizing Women's Lives.* Berkeley: University of California Press.

Enloe, Cynthia. 2002. '"Demilitarization or More of the Same?" Feminist Questions to Ask in the Postwar Moment'. In *The Postwar Moment: Militaries, Masculinities and International Peacekeeping*, edited by Cynthia Cockburn and Dubravka Zarkov. London: Lawrence and Wishart.

Enloe, Cynthia. 2007. *Globalization and Militarism: Feminists Make the Link.* Lanham, MD: Rowman and Littlefield.

Enloe, Cynthia. 2013. *Seriously!* Berkeley: University of California Press.

Enloe, Cynthia. 2014. 'Geneva Blog'. *http://www.wilpfinterna tional.org/wp-content/uploads/2014/01/Geneva-ENTIRE-Blog. pdf/www.wilpfinternational.org/cynthia-enloes-report-from-the-syrian-peace-talks/.*

Eriksson Baaz, Maria, and Maria Stern. 2013. *Sexual Violence as a Weapon of War? Perceptions, Prescriptions, Problems in the Congo and Beyond.* London: Zed Books.

Espling, Margareta. 1999. 'Women's Livelihood Strategies in Processes of Change: Cases from Urban Mozambique'. University of Gothenburg. *https://gupea.ub.gu.se/handle/2077/10923.*

Falch, Ashild. 2010. 'Women's Political Participation and Influence in Post-Conflict Burundi and Nepal'. Peace Research Institute Oslo. *http://www.peacewomen.org/assets/file/Resources/Academic/partpol_postconburundinepal_falch_2010.pdf.*

Farr, Vanessa. 2011. 'UNSCR 1325 and Women's Peace Activism in the Occupied Palestinian Territory'. *International Feminist Journal of Politics* 13 (4): 539–56.

Ferguson, Michaele L. 2005. '"W" Stands for Women: Feminism and Security Rhetoric in the Post-9/11 Bush Administration'. *Politics and Gender* 1 (1): 9–38.

Fischer, Martina, and Beatrix Schmelzle. 2005. 'Transforming War Economies: Dilemmas and Strategies'. Berghof Research Centre for Constructive Conflict Management. *http://edoc. vifapol.de/opus/volltexte/2011/2558/pdf/dialogue3_warecon_ complete.pdf*.

Ford, Tamasin. 2012. 'Liberia's Hasty Forest Sell-off Risks More Conflict'. *Guardian*, 5 July. *http://www.theguardian.com/global-development/2012/jul/05/liberia-forest-sell-off-risks-conflict*.

Ford, Tamasin, and Sonnie Morris. 2010. 'India's Female Peace-keepers Inspire Liberian Girls'. Inter Press Service, 24 October. *http://www.ipsnews.net/2010/10/indias-female-peacekeepers-inspire-liberian-girls/*.

Fox, Louise, Rui Manuel Benfica, Malcolm Ehrenpreis, Melissa S. Gaal, Hakon Nordang and Daniel Owen. 2008. 'Beating the Odds: Sustaining Inclusion in a Growing Economy: A Mozam-bique Poverty, Gender, and Social Assessment'. World Bank. *http://documents.worldbank.org/curated/en/2008/01/9788484/ beating-odds-sustaining-inclusion-mozambiques-growing-econ omy*.

Francis, Diana. 2010. *From Pacification to Peacebuilding: A Call to Global Transformation*. London: Pluto.

Fraser, Nancy. 1995. 'Recognition or Redistribution? A Critical Reading of Iris Young's Justice and the Politics of Difference'. *Journal of Political Philosophy* 3 (2): 166–80.

Friends of the Earth International. 2013. 'Land Grabs and Human Rights Violations Exposed in Liberia Ahead of Global Development Summit'. 2 January. *http://www.foei.org/press/ archive-by-year/press-2013/land-grabs-and-human-rights-violations-exposed-in-liberia-ahead-of-global-development-summit/*.

Fukuyama, Francis. 2004. *State-Building: Governance and World Order in the 21st Century*. Ithaca, NY: Cornell University Press.

Gall, Sandy. 2012. *War against the Taliban: Why It All Went Wrong in Afghanistan*. London: Bloomsbury.

Galtung, Johan. 1969. 'Violence, Peace, and Peace Research'. *Journal of Peace Research* 6 (3): 167–91.

Galtung, Johan. 1996. *Peace by Peaceful Means*. London: Sage.

Gathigah, Miriam. 2014. 'Fossil Fuels Won't Benefit Africa in Absence of Sound Environmental Policies'. Inter Press Service, 30

October. *http://www.ipsnews.net/2014/10/fossil-fuels-wont-bene fit-africa-in-absence-of-sound-environmental-policies/.*

Gibbings, Sheri Lynn. 2011. 'No Angry Women at the United Nations: Political Dreams and the Cultural Politics of United Nations Security Council Resolution 1325'. *International Feminist Journal of Politics* 13 (4): 522–38.

Giles, Wenona, and Jennifer Hyndman. 2004. *Sites of Violence: Gender and Conflict Zones.* Berkeley: University of California Press.

Giustozzi, Antonio. 2007. 'War and Peace Economies of Afghanistan's Strongmen'. *International Peacekeeping* 14 (1): 75–89.

Gizelis, Theodora-Ismene. 2009. 'Gender Empowerment and United Nations Peacebuilding'. *Journal of Peace Research* 46 (4): 505–23.

Gizelis, Theodora-Ismene, and Kristin E. Kosek. 2005. 'Why Humanitarian Interventions Succeed or Fail: The Role of Local Participation'. *Cooperation and Conflict: Journal of the Nordic International Studies Association* 40 (4): 363–83.

Glasson, John, Riki Therivel and Andrew Chadwick. 2013. *Introduction to Environmental Impact Assessment.* London: Routledge.

Global Witness. 2013a. '90% of DR Congo's Logging Revenues Lost to Tax Avoidance in 2012'. 28 October. *https://www.global-witness.org/archive/90-dr-congos-logging-revenues-lost-tax-avoidance-2012/.*

Global Witness. 2013b. 'Liberia Systematically Breaking Its Own Laws in Oil, Mineral, Forest and Land Deals Worth Billions of Dollars, New Audit Reveals'. 3 May. *https://www.globalwitness. org/archive/liberia-systematically-breaking-its-own-laws-oil-mineral-forest-and-land-deals-worth/.*

Goetz, Anne Marie. 2014. 'Stopping Sexual Violence in Conflict: Gender Politics in Foreign Policy'. *openDemocracy*, 23 October. *https://www.opendemocracy.net/5050/anne-marie-goetz/stop ping-sexual-violence-in-conflict-gender-politics-in-foreign-policy.*

Goetz, Anne Marie, and Letitia Anderson. 2008. 'Women Targeted or Affected by Armed Conflict: What Role for Military Peacekeepers?'. In *Conference Summary, Wilton Park Conference. https://www.wiltonpark.org.uk/wp-content/uploads/wp914-report.pdf.*

Goetz, Anne Marie, and Robert Jenkins. 2002. 'Accountability to Women in Development Spending: Experiments in Service-Delivery Audits at the Local Level'. Institute of Development Studies. *http://www.bridge.ids.ac.uk/global-resources/resource/ A52557.*

Goldstein, Joshua. 2001. *War and Gender: How Gender Shapes the War System and Vice Versa*. Cambridge: Cambridge University Press.

Goodhand, Jonathan. 2004. 'From War Economy to Peace Economy? Reconstruction and State Building in Afghanistan'. *Journal of International Affairs* 58 (1): 155–74.

Grady, Kate. 2010. 'Sexual Exploitation and Abuse by UN Peacekeepers: A Threat to Impartiality'. *International Peacekeeping* 17 (2): 215–28.

Greenberg, Marcia E., and Elaine Zuckerman. 2009. 'The Gender Dimensions of Post-Conflict Reconstruction: The Challenges in Development Aid'. Gender Action. *http://www.genderaction.org/images/GenderDimensionsPCR_2009.pdf*.

Haddad, Lawrence, Lynn R. Brown, Andrea Richter and Lisa Smith. 1995. 'The Gender Dimensions of Economic Adjustment Policies: Potential Interactions and Evidence to Date'. *World Development* 23 (6): 881–96.

Hänggi, Heiner. 2011.'Security Sector Reform – Concepts and Contexts'. In *Transformation: A Security Sector Reform Reader*. Pasig City: INCITEGov.

Hanlon, Joseph. 1996. *Peace without Profit: How the IMF Blocks Rebuilding in Mozambique*. Oxford: James Currey.

Hanlon, Joseph. 2000. 'Power without Responsibility: The World Bank & Mozambican Cashew Nuts'. *Review of African Political Economy* 27 (83): 29–45.

Hanlon, Joseph. 2010. 'Mozambique: "The War Ended 17 Years Ago, but We Are Still Poor"'. *Conflict, Security & Development* 10 (1): 77–102.

Hanlon, Joseph, and Teresa Smart. 2008. 'Do Bicycles Equal Development in Mozambique?' Open University. *http://oro.open.ac.uk/11519/*.

Hansen, Lene. 2006. *Security as Practice: Discourse Analysis and the Bosnian War*. Abingdon: Routledge.

Harcourt, Wendy, ed. 1994. *Feminist Perspectives on Sustainable Development*. London: Zed Books.

Harsch, Ernest. 2005. 'Women: Africa's Ignored Combatants. Gradual Progress towards a Greater Role in DDR'. *Africa Renewal* 19 (3): 17–18.

Hartsock, Nancy C. M. 1985. *Money, Sex and Power: Towards a Feminist Historical Materialism*. Reprinted edition. Boston: Northeastern University Press.

Hawkesworth, Mary E. 2006. *Globalization and Feminist Activism*. Lanham, MD: Rowman and Littlefield.

Hawley, Susan, George Soros and Raghavan Srinivasan. 2000. 'Exporting Corruption: Privatisation, Multinationals and

Bribery'. Corner House Briefing 19. *http://www.thecornerhouse .org.uk/resource/exporting-corruption-0.*

Hawthorne, Susan, and Bronwyn Winter, eds. 2002. *September 11 2001: Feminist Perspectives.* Melbourne, Spinifex.

Hickel, Jason. 2015. 'The Microfinance Delusion: Who Really Wins?' *Guardian*, 10 June. *http://www.theguardian.com/global-development-professionals-network/2015/jun/10/the-micro finance-delusion-who-really-wins.*

Higate, Paul. 2004. *Gender and Peacekeeping: Case Studies: The DRC and Sierra Leone.* Pretoria: Institute of Security Studies.

Higate, Paul. 2007. 'Peacekeepers, Masculinities and Sexual Exploitation'. *Men and Masculinities* 10 (1): 99–119.

Higate, Paul, and Marsha Henry. 2004. 'Engendering (In)security in Peace Support Operations'. *Security Dialogue* 35 (4): 481–98.

Hipkins, Dominic. 2003. 'Bosnia Sex Trade Shames UN'. *Scotland on Sunday*, 9 February. *http://www.scotsman.com/world/Bosnia-sex-trade-shames-UN.2400797.jp.*

Hirschkind, Charles, and Saba Mahmood. 2002. 'Feminism, the Taliban, and Politics of Counter-Insurgency'. *Anthropological Quarterly* 75 (2): 339–54.

Holvikivi, Aiko. 2014. 'Women and War – Gendered Engagements'. *Journal of Intervention and Statebuilding* 8 (2–3): 250–61.

hooks, bell. 1984. *Feminist Theory from Margin to Center.* Boston: South End Press.

hooks, bell. 1989. *Talking Back: Thinking Black, Thinking Feminist.* Boston: South End Press.

Hooper, Charlotte. 2001. *Manly States: Masculinities, International Relations, and Gender Politics.* New York: Columbia University Press.

Howden, Daniel. 2014. 'Football-Mad President Plays on While Burundi Fears the Return of Civil War'. *Guardian*, 6 April. *http:// www.theguardian.com/world/2014/apr/06/football-mad-presi dent-burundi.*

Hudson, Heidi. 2012a. 'A Bridge Too Far? The Gender Consequences of Linking Security and Development in SSR Discourse and Practice'. In *Back to the Roots: Security Sector Reform and Development*, edited by Albrecht Schnabel and Vanessa Farr. Geneva: DCAF. *http://www.isn.ethz.ch/Digital-Library/Publica tions/Detail/?lng=en&id=153074.*

Hudson, Heidi. 2012b. 'A Double-Edged Sword of Peace? Reflections on the Tension between Representation and Protection in Gendering Liberal Peacebuilding'. *International Peacekeeping* 19 (4): 443–60.

Hudson, Natalie Florea. 2009. *Gender, Human Security and the United Nations: Security Language as a Political Framework for Women*. New York: Routledge.

Hudson, Valerie, Bonnie Ballif-Spanvill, Mary Caprioli and Chad Emmett. 2012. *Sex and World Peace*. New York: Columbia University Press.

Hughes, Melanie M. 2009. 'Armed Conflict, International Linkages, and Women's Parliamentary Representation in Developing Nations'. *Social Problems* 56 (1): 174–204.

Hughes, Melanie M., and Aili Mari Tripp. 2015. 'Civil War and Trajectories of Change in Women's Political Representation in Africa, 1985–2010'. *Social Forces* 93 (4): 1513–40.

Hunt, Krista. 2002. 'The Strategic Co-optation of Women's Rights'. *International Feminist Journal of Politics* 4 (1): 116–21.

Hunt, Krista, and Kim Rygiel, eds. 2006. *(En)gendering the War on Terror: War Stories and Camouflaged Politics*. London: Ashgate.

ICTJ. 2014. '"My Healing Has Begun": Uganda Votes to Provide Gender-Sensitive Reparations Fund'. International Centre for Transitional Justice. *https://www.ictj.org/news/uganda-gender-sensitive-reparations-fund*.

IFAD. 2010. 'Rural Poverty in Bosnia and Herzegovina'. Rural Poverty Portal, International Fund for Agricultural Development. *http://www.ruralpovertyportal.org/country/home/tags/bosnia_and_herzegovina*.

IMF. 2008. 'Liberia: Poverty Reduction Strategy Paper'. IMF Country Report No 08/219. International Monetary Fund. *https://www.imf.org/external/pubs/ft/scr/2008/cr08219.pdf*.

Inman, Phillip. 2012. 'Bashar Al-Assad Has Amassed Fortune of up to £950m, Analysts Estimate'. *Guardian*, 19 July. *http://www.theguardian.com/world/2012/jul/19/bashar-al-assad-950m-fortune*.

Irvine, Jill A. 2013. 'Leveraging Change: Women's Organizations and the Implementation of UNSCR 1325 in the Balkans'. *International Feminist Journal of Politics* 15 (1): 20–38.

Jabbra, Nancy W. 2006. 'Women, Words and War: Explaining 9/11 and Justifying US Military Action in Afghanistan and Iraq'. *Journal of International Women's Studies* 8 (1): 236–55.

Jacob, Margarete. 2008. 'Engendering Security Sector Reform: Sierra Leone and Liberia Compared'. In *Engendering Security Sector Reform: A Workshop Report*, edited by Margarete Jacob, Daniel Bendix and Ruth Stanley. Free University of Berlin. *https://statebuildingmonitor.files.wordpress.com/2012/01/engendering-security-sector-reform-margarete-jacob-daniel-bendix-ruth-stanley.pdf*.

Jacobson, Ruth. 2013. 'Women "after" Wars'. In *Women and Wars*, edited by Carol Cohn. Cambridge: Polity Press.

Jarstad, Anna K., and Timothy Sisk. 2008. *From War to Democracy: Dilemmas of Peacebuilding*. New York: Cambridge University Press.

Jenkins, Robert, and Anne Marie Goetz. 2010. 'Addressing Sexual Violence in Internationally Mediated Peace Negotiations'. *International Peacekeeping* 17 (2): 261–77.

Jenkins, Simon. 2011. 'Vanity, Machismo and Greed Have Blinded Us to the Folly of Afghanistan'. *Guardian*, 6 October. *http://www.theguardian.com/commentisfree/2011/oct/06/afghanistan-folly-expense*.

Jennings, Kathleen. 2010. 'Unintended Consequences of Intimacy: Political Economies of Peacekeeping and Sex Tourism'. *International Peacekeeping* 17 (2): 229–43.

Jennings, Kathleen, and Vesna Nikolić-Ristanović. 2009. 'UN Peacekeeping Economies and Local Sex Industries: Connections and Implications'. Social Science Research Network. *http://papers.ssrn.com/sol3/papers.cfm?abstract_id=1488842*.

Jones, David E. 1997. *Women Warriors: A History*. Washington, DC: Brassey's.

Justino, Patricia, Ivan Cardona, Rebecca Mitchell and Catherine Müller. 2012. 'Quantifying the Impact of Women's Participation in Post-Conflict Economic Recovery'. HiCN Working Paper 131, Households in Conflict Network. *http://www.hicn.org/wordpress/wp-content/uploads/2012/06/HiCN-WP-131.pdf*.

Kabeer, Naila. 2009. 'Women's Control over Economic Resources and Access to Financial Resources, Including Microfinance: 2009 World Survey on the Role of Women in Development'. United Nations Division for the Advancement of Women. *http://www.un.org/womenwatch/daw/public/WorldSurvey2009.pdf*.

Kaldor, Mary. 1999. *New and Old Wars: Organized Violence in a Global Era*. Cambridge: Polity.

Kaldor, Mary. 2012. *New and Old Wars: Organized Violence in a Global Era*. Third edition. Cambridge: Polity.

Kandiyoti, Deniz. 2007a. 'Between the Hammer and the Anvil: Post-Conflict Reconstruction, Islam and Women's Rights'. *Third World Quarterly* 28 (3): 503–17.

Kandiyoti, Deniz. 2007b. 'Old Dilemmas or New Challenges? The Politics of Gender and Reconstruction in Afghanistan'. *Development and Change* 38 (2): 169–99.

Kanetake, Machiko. 2010. 'Whose Zero Tolerance Counts? Reassessing a Zero Tolerance Policy against Sexual Exploitation and Abuse by UN Peacekeepers'. *International Peacekeeping* 17 (2): 200–14.

Karim, Lamia. 2011. *Microfinance and Its Discontents: Women in Debt in Bangladesh*. Minneapolis: University of Minnesota Press.

Keen, David. 2012. *Useful Enemies: When Waging Wars Is More Important Than Winning Them*. New Haven, CT: Yale University Press.

Kennedy-Pipe, Caroline. 2000. 'Women and the Military'. *Journal of Strategic Studies* 23 (4): 32–50.

Khalili, Laleh. 2011. 'Gendered Practices of Counterinsurgency'. *Review of International Studies* 37: 1471–91.

Klein, Naomi. 2008. *Shock Doctrine: The Rise of Disaster Capitalism*. London: Penguin.

Konneh, Amara. 2014. 'Ebola Isn't Just a Health Crisis – It's a Social and Economic One Too'. *Guardian*, 10 October. *http:// www.theguardian.com/commentisfree/2014/oct/10/ebola-liberia-catastrophe-generation-poverty*.

Krause, Jana, and Cynthia Enloe. 2015. 'A Wealth of Expertise and Lived Experience: Conversations between International Women Peace Activists at the "Women Lead To Peace Summit" Preceding the Geneva II Peace Talks on Syria, January 2014'. *International Feminist Journal of Politics* 17 (2): 328–38.

Kühn, Florian P. 2008. 'Aid, Opium, and the State of Rents in Afghanistan: Competition, Cooperation, or Cohabitation?' *Journal of Intervention and Statebuilding* 2 (3): 309–27.

Kühn, Florian P., and Mandy Turner. 2012. 'Introduction: Peacebuilding, Peace Operations and Regime Change Wars'. *International Peacekeeping* 19 (4): 393–5.

Lawrence, David P. 2003. *Environmental Impact Assessment*. New York: John Wiley & Sons, Inc.

Le Billon, Philippe. 2001. 'Angola's Political Economy of War: The Role of Oil and Diamonds, 1975–2000'. *African Affairs* 100 (398): 55–80.

Leatherman, Janie. 2011. *Sexual Violence and Armed Conflict*. Cambridge: Polity.

Lederach, John Paul. 1998. *Building Peace: Sustainable Reconciliation in Divided Societies*. Washington, DC: United States Institute of Peace Press.

Lederach, John Paul. 1999. 'The Challenge of the 21st Century: Justpeace'. In *People Building Peace: 35 Inspiring Stories from Around the World*. Utrecht: European Centre for Conflict Prevention.

Liddington, Jill. 2005. *The Road to Greenham Common: Feminism and Anti-Militarism in Britain since 1820*. Syracuse, NY: Syracuse University Press.

Ling, L. H. M. 2002. 'The Fish and the Turtle: Multiple Worlds as Method'. In *Millennial Reflections on International Studies*, edited by Frank P. Harvey and Michael Brecher. Ann Arbor: University of Michigan Press.

Lovenduski, Joni, and Pippa Norris. 2003. 'Westminster Women: The Politics of Presence'. *Political Studies* 51 (1): 84–102.

McCall, Leslie. 2005. 'The Complexity of Intersectionality'. *Signs* 30 (3): 1771–800.

Mackay, Angela. 2005. 'Mainstreaming Gender in UN Peacekeeping Training'. In *Gender, Conflict and Peacekeeping*, edited by Dyan Mazurana, Angela Raven-Roberts and Jane Parpart. Lanham, MD: Rowman and Littlefield.

MacKenzie, Megan. 2009. 'Securitization and Desecuritization: Female Soldiers and the Reconstruction of Women in Post-Conflict Sierra Leone'. *Security Studies* 18 (2): 241–61.

MacKenzie, Megan. 2012. *Female Soldiers in Sierra Leone: Sex, Security and Post-Conflict Development*. New York: New York University Press.

McLeod, Laura, Rachel Johnson, Sheila Meintjes, Alice Brown and Valerie Oosterveld. 2014. 'Gendering Processes of Institutional Design: Activists at the Negotiating Table'. *International Feminist Journal of Politics* 16 (2): 354–69.

Marchand, Marianne H., and Anne Sisson Runyan. 2011. *Gender and Global Restructuring: Sightings, Sites and Resistances*. Abingdon: Routledge.

Marten, Kimberly Zisk. 2004. *Enforcing the Peace: Learning from the Imperial Past*. New York: Columbia University Press.

Martin, Sarah. 2005. 'Must Boys Be Boys? Ending Sexual Exploitation and Abuse in UN PK Missions'. Refugees International. *http://refugeesinternational.org/policy/in-depth-report/must-boys-be-boys-ending-sexual-exploitation-abuse-un-peacekeeping-missions*.

Martin-Prével, Alice. 2014a. 'The World Bank's Bad Business in the Democratic Republic of the Congo (DRC)'. Oakland Institute. *http://www.oaklandinstitute.org/world-banks-bad-business-democratic-republic-congo-drc*.

Martin-Prével, Alice. 2014b. 'Willful Blindness: How the World Bank's Country Rankings Impoverish Smallholder Farmers'. Oakland Institute. *http://ourlandourbusiness.org/wp-content/uploads/2014/03/Brief_Eng_Final.pdf*.

Martin-Prével, Alice, and Faris Mohammed. 2014. 'The world bank's bad business in Uganda'. Oakland Institute. *http://ourlandandourbusiness.org/wp-content/uploads/2014/10/Uganda_factsheet_hirez.pdf*

Mazurana, Dyan. 2005. 'Gender and the Causes and Consequences of Armed Conflict'. In *Gender, Conflict and Peacekeeping*, edited by Dyan Mazurana, Angela Raven-Roberts and Jane Parpart. Lanham, MD: Rowman and Littlefield.

Mazurana, Dyan, and Linda Eckerborn Cole. 2013. 'Women, Girls and Disarmament, Demobilization and Reintegration'. In *Women and Wars*, edited by Carol Cohn. Cambridge: Polity.

Mazurana, Dyan, Angela Raven-Roberts and Jane Parpart. 2005. *Gender, Conflict and Peacekeeping*. Lanham, MD: Rowman and Littlefield.

Meger, Sara. 2010. 'Rape of the Congo: Understanding Sexual Violence in the Conflict in the Democratic Republic of Congo'. *Journal of Contemporary African Studies* 28 (2): 119–35.

Meintjes, Sheila, Anu Pillay and Meredeth Turshen. 2001. *The Aftermath: Women in Post-Conflict Transformation*. London: Zed Books.

Mendelson, Sarah Elizabeth. 2005. 'Barracks and Brothels: Peace-keepers and Human Trafficking in the Balkans. Center for Strategic and International Studies. *http://csis.org/files/media/csis/pubs/0502_barracksbrothels.pdf*.

Michel, Sonya, and Seth Koven. 1993. *Mothers of a New World: Maternalist Politics and the Origins of Welfare States*. London: Routledge.

Miller, Laura. 1997. 'Do Soldiers Hate Peacekeeping?' *Armed Forces and Society* 23 (3): 415–49.

Miller, Laura, and Charles Moskos. 1995. 'Humanitarians or Warriors? Race, Gender and Combat Status in Operation Restore Hope'. *Armed Forces and Society* 21: 615–37.

Mobekk, Eirin. 2010. 'Gender, Women and Security Sector Reform'. *International Peacekeeping* 17 (2): 278–91.

Moran, Mary H. 2010. 'Gender, Militarism, and Peace-Building: Projects of the Postconflict Moment'. *Annual Review of Anthropology* 39: 261–74.

Moser, Caroline O. N., and Fiona Clark. 2001. *Victims, Perpetrators or Actors? Gender, Armed Conflict, and Political Violence*. London: Zed Books.

Mpoumou, Doris. 2004. 'Women's Participation in Peace Negotiations: Discourse in the Democratic Republic of the Congo'. In *The Implementation of Quotas: African Experiences*, edited by Julie Ballington. Stockholm. The International Institute for Democracy and Electoral Assistance. *http://www.idea.int/africa/upload/women_drc.pdf*.

Munro, Jean. 2000. 'Gender and Peacebuilding'. Peacebuilding and Reconstruction Programme Initiative. International Development Research Centre. *http://idl-bnc.idrc.ca/dspace/bitstream/10625/27182/1/114720.pdf*.

Myrttinen, Henri. 2009. 'Poster Boys No More: Gender and Security Sector Reform in Timor-Leste'. DCAF. *http://dspace.cigilibrary.org/jspui/handle/123456789/27845*.

Nafziger, E. Wayne, and Juha Auvinen. 2002. 'Economic Development, Inequality, War, and State Violence'. *World Development* 30 (2): 153–63.

Nagel, Joane. 1998. 'Masculinity and Nationalism: Gender and Sexuality in the Making of Nations'. *Ethnic and Racial Studies* 21 (2): 242–69.

Nallu, Preethi. 2015. 'Rape Is Being Used to Terrorise the Population, says DRC gynaecologist'. *Guardian*, 22 May. *http://www.theguardian.com/world/2015/may/22/rape-congo-doctor-denis-mukwege*.

Nanourou, Serge, and Abigail Wilson. 2014. 'Analysis of the Status of Women in Burundi's Political and Electoral Processes'. International Foundation for Electoral Systems. *https://www.ifes.org/sites/default/files/burundi_gender_analysis.pdf*.

Narayan, Deepa, and Talat Shah. 2000. 'Gender Inequity, Poverty, and Social Capital'. Policy Research Report on Gender Development, Working Paper Series. World Bank.

Nayak, M. 2006. 'Orientalism and "Saving" US State Identity after 9/11'. *International Feminist Journal of Politics* 8 (1): 42–61.

Nesiah, Vasuki. 2013. 'Feminism as Counter-Terrorism: The Seduction of Power'. In *Gender, National Security and Counter-Terrorism: Human Rights Perspectives*, edited by Margaret L. Satterthwaite and Jayne C. Huckerby. London: Routledge.

Ní Aoláin, Fionnuala, Dina Francesca Haynes and Naomi Cahn. 2011. *On the Frontlines: Gender, War, and the Post-Conflict Process*. Oxford: Oxford University Press.

Nordås, Ragnhild, and Siri C. A. Rustad. 2013. 'Sexual Exploitation and Abuse by Peacekeepers: Understanding Variation'. *International Interactions* 39 (4): 511–34.

Norton, Andy, and Diane Elson. 2002. *What's Behind the Budget? Politics, Rights and Accountability in the Budget Process*. London: Overseas Development Institute.

Nussbaum, Martha C. 1999. *Sex and Social Justice*. Oxford: Oxford University Press.

O'Carroll, Lisa. 2014. 'Head of WHO Warns against Complacency in the Fight against Ebola'. *Guardian*, 10 December. *http://www.theguardian.com/world/2014/dec/10/who-warns-against-complacency-in-fight-against-ebola*.

O'Gorman, Eleanor. 2014. 'Independent Thematic Review on Gender for the UN Peacebuilding Support Office (PBSO) Final Report'. United Nations Peacebuiding Support Office. *http://www.un.org/en/peacebuilding/pbso/pdf/Final%20Report_Thematic%20Review%20on%20Gender%20&%20Peacebuilding.pdf*.

OHCHR. 2013. 'Access to Justice and Reparations for Victims of Sexual Violence in the Democratic Republic of the Congo'. United Nations Office of the High Commissioner for Human Rights. *http://www.ohchr.org/EN/NewsEvents/Pages/Accessto justiceinDRC.aspx.*

Olonisakin, Funmi, Karen Barnes and Eka Ikpe. 2011. *Women, Peace and Security: Translating Policy into Practice.* Abingdon: Routledge.

Olsson, Louise, and Theodora-Ismene Gizelis. 2013. 'An Introduction to UNSCR 1325'. *International Interactions* 39: 425–34.

Olsson, Louise, Inger Skjelsbaek, Elise Fredrikke Barth, and Karen Hostens. 2004. *Gender Aspects of Conflict Interventions: Intended and Unintended Consequences.* Oslo: International Peace Research Institute (PRIO).

Orford, Anne. 1997. 'Locating the International: Military and Monetary Interventions after the Cold War'. *Harvard International Law Journal* 38: 443–85.

Orford, Anne. 1999. 'Muscular Humanitarianism: Reading the Narratives of the New Interventionism'. *European Journal of International Law* 10 (4): 679–711.

Orford, Anne. 2003. *Reading Humanitarian Intervention: Human Rights and the Use of Force in International Law.* Cambridge: Cambridge University Press.

Ormhaug, Christin, Patrick Meier and Helga Hernes. 2009. 'Armed Conflict Deaths Disaggregated by Gender'. International Peace Research Institute. *http://file.prio.no/Publication_files/Prio/Armed%20Conflict%20Deaths%20Disaggregated%20by%20Gender.pdf.*

Otim, Michael, and Kasande Sarah Kihika. 2015. 'On the Path to Vindicate Victims' Rights in Uganda: Reflections on the Transitional Justice Process since Juba'. ICTJ Briefing, June. *https://www.ictj.org/sites/default/files/ICTJ-Briefing-Uganda-TJProcess-2015_0.pdf*

Otto, Dianne. 2006. 'A Sign of Weakness: Disrupting Gender Certainties in the Implementation of Security Council Resolution 1325'. *Michigan Journal of Gender and Law* 13: 113–76.

Otto, Dianne. 2009. 'The Exile of Inclusion: Reflections on Gender Issues in International Law over the Last Decade'. *Melbourne Journal of International Law* 10 (1): 11–26.

Pankhurst, Donna. 2000. 'Women, Gender and Peacebuilding'. Working Paper 5, Centre for Conflict Resolution, Department of Peace Studies, University of Bradford. *http://www.ceipaz.org/images/contenido/CCR5.pdf.*

Pankhurst, Donna. 2007. *Gendered Peace: Women's Struggles for Post-War Justice and Reconciliation.* Abingdon: Routledge.

Pankhurst, Donna. 2008. 'The Gendered Impact of Peace'. In *Whose Peace? Critical Perspectives on the Political Economy of Peacebuilding*, edited by Michael Pugh, Neil Cooper and Mandy Turner. Basingstoke: Palgrave Macmillan.

Paris, Roland. 2004. *At War's End: Building Peace after Civil Conflict*. Cambridge: Cambridge University Press.

Paris, Roland. 2010. 'Saving Liberal Peacebuilding'. *Review of International Studies* 36 (2): 337–65.

Paris, Roland, and Timothy D. Sisk. 2009. *The Dilemmas of Statebuilding: Confronting the Contradictions of Postwar Peace Operations*. Abingdon: Routledge.

Parmar, Sharanjeet, and Guy Mushiata. 2012. 'Judgment Denied: The Failure to Fulfill Court-Ordered Reparations for Victims of Serious Crimes in the Democratic Republic of Congo'. International Centre for Transitional Justice. *https://www.ictj.org/sites/default/files/ICTJ-Briefing-DRC-Reparations-2012-ENG.pdf*.

Paxton, Pamela M. Marie, and Melanie M. M. Hughes. 2007. *Women, Politics, and Power: A Global Perspective*. London: Sage Publications.

People's Health Movement. 2014. 'Ebola Epidemic Exposes the Pathology of the Global Economic and Political System'. *http://www.phmovement.org/en/node/9611*.

Peterman, Amber, Tia Palermo and Caryn Bredenkamp. 2011. 'Estimates and Determinants of Sexual Violence against Women in the Democratic Republic of Congo'. *American Journal of Public Health* 101 (6): 1060–7.

Peterson, V. Spike. 1992. *Gendered States: Feminist (Re)visions of International Relations Theory*. Boulder, CO: Westview Press.

Peterson, V. Spike. 2007. 'Thinking through Intersectionality and War'. *Race, Gender & Class* 14 (3–4): 10–27.

Peterson, V. Spike. 2008. '"New Wars" and Gendered Economies'. *Feminist Review* 88 (1): 7–20.

Peterson, V. Spike. 2012. 'Rethinking Theory: Inequalities, Informalization and Feminist Quandaries'. *International Feminist Journal of Politics* 14 (1): 5–35.

Peterson, V. Spike, and Anne Sisson Runyan. 2010. *Global Gender Issues: In the New Millennium*. Third edition. Boulder, CO: Westview Press.

Pettman, Jan Jindy. 1996. *Worlding Women: A Feminist International Politics*. New York: Routledge.

Pieterse, Edgar. 2008. *City Futures*. London: Zed Books.

Pinnington, Rosie. 2014. 'What's in It for Us? Gender Issues in Uganda's Oil and Gas Sector'. International Alert. *http://www.international-alert.org/sites/default/files/Uganda_GenderOil Gas_EN_2014.pdf*.

Plümper, Thomas, and Eric Neumayer. 2006. 'The Unequal Burden of War: The Effect of Armed Conflict on the Gender Gap in Life Expectancy'. *International Organization* 60 (3): 723–54.

Porter, Elisabeth. 2007. *Peacebuilding: Women in International Perspective*. Abingdon: Routledge.

Potter, Antonia. 2005. 'We the Women: Why Conflict Mediation Is Not Just A Job for Men'. Reliefweb. *http://reliefweb.int/node/22264*.

Pratt, Nicola. 2013. 'Reconceptualizing Gender, Reinscribing Racial–Sexual Boundaries in International Security: The Case of UN Security Council Resolution 1325 on "Women, Peace and Security"'. *International Studies Quarterly* 57 (4): 772–83.

Pratt, Nicola, and Sophie Richter-Devroe. 2011. 'Critically Examining UNSCR 1325 on Women, Peace and Security'. *International Feminist Journal of Politics* 13 (4): 489–503.

Puechguirbal, Nadine. 2005. 'Gender and Peace Building in Africa: Analysis of Some Structural Obstacles'. In *Gender and Peace Building in Africa*, edited by Dina Rodríguez and Edith Natukunda-Togboa. University for Peace. *http://womin.org.za/images/the-alternatives/women-organising-resisting-and-defying/University%20for%20Peace%20-%20Gender%20and%20Peace%20Building%20in%20Africa.pdf*.

Puechguirbal, Nadine. 2010a. 'Discourses on Gender, Patriarchy and Resolution 1325: A Textual Analysis of UN Documents'. *International Peacekeeping* 17 (2): 172–87.

Puechguirbal, Nadine. 2010b. 'Peacekeeping, Peacebuilding and Post-Conflict Reconstruction'. In *Gender Matters in Global Politics: A Feminist Introduction to International Relations*, edited by Laura J. Shepherd. Abingdon: Routledge.

Pugh, Michael. 2005. 'The Political Economy of Peacebuilding: A Critical Theory Perspective'. *International Journal of Peace Studies* 10 (2): 23–42.

Pugh, Michael. 2006. 'Post-War Economies and the New York Dissensus'. *Conflict, Security & Development* 6 (3): 269–89.

Pugh, Michael, Neil Cooper, and Jonathan Goodhand. 2004. *War Economies in a Regional Context: Challenges of Transformation*. Boulder, CO: Lynne Rienner.

Pugh, Michael, Neil Cooper, and Mandy Turner. 2008. *Whose Peace? Critical Perspectives on the Political Economy of Peacebuilding*. Basingstoke: Palgrave Macmillan.

Pupavac, Vanessa. 2005. 'Empowering Women? An Assessment of International Gender Policies in Bosnia'. *International Peacekeeping* 12 (3): 391–405.

Ramsbotham, Oliver, Tom Woodhouse and Hugh Miall. 2011. *Contemporary Conflict Resolution*. Third edition. Cambridge: Polity.

Rashid, Ahmed. 2002. *Taliban: Islam, Oil and the New Great Game in Central Asia*. London: I. B. Tauris.

Rashid, Ahmed. 2009. *Descent into Chaos: The World's Most Unstable Region and the Threat to Global Security*. London: Penguin.

Raven-Roberts, Angela. 2013. 'Women and the Political Economy of War'. In *Women and Wars*, edited by Carol Cohn. Cambridge: Polity.

Razack, Sherene. 2004. *Dark Threats and White Knights: The Somalia Affair, Peacekeeping and the New Imperialism*. Toronto: University of Toronto Press.

Rees, Madeleine. 2002. 'International Intervention in Bosnia-Herzegovina: The Cost of Ignoring Gender'. In *The Postwar Moment: Militaries, Masculinities and International Peacekeeping*, edited by Cynthia Cockburn and Dubravka Zarkov. London: Lawrence and Wishart.

Rees, Madeleine. 2014. 'Syrian Women Demand to Take Part in the Peace Talks in Geneva'. *openDemocracy*, 12 January. *https://www.opendemocracy.net/5050/madeleine-rees/syrian-women-demand-to-take-part-in-peace-talks-in-geneva*.

Rehn, Elizabeth, and Ellen Johnson Sirleaf. 2002. 'Women, War, Peace: The Independent Experts' Assessment of the Impact of Armed Conflict on Women and Women's Role in Peacebuilding'. United Nations Development Fund for Women (UNIFEM). *http://www.unwomen.org/en/digital-library/publications/2002/1/women-war-peace-the-independent-experts-assessment-on-the-impact-of-armed-conflict-on-women-and-women-s-role-in-peace-building-progress-of-the-world-s-women-2002-vol-1*.

Reilly, Niamh. 2007. 'Seeking Gender Justice in Post-Conflict Transitions: Towards a Transformative Human Rights Approach'. *International Journal of Law in Context* 3 (2): 155–72.

Richmond, Oliver. 2006. 'The Problem of Peace: Understanding the "Liberal Peace"'. *Conflict, Security & Development* 6 (3): 291–314.

Richmond, Oliver. 2010. *Peacebuilding: Critical Developments and Approaches*. Palgrave Advances in Peacebuilding. Basingstoke: Palgrave Macmillan.

Richter-Devroe, Sophie. 2009. '"Here, It's Not about Conflict Resolution – We Can Only Resist": Palestinian Women's Activism in Conflict Resolution and Non-Violent Resistance'. In *Women and War in the Middle East: Transnational Perspectives*, edited by Nadje Al-Ali and Nicola Pratt. London: Zed Books.

Richter-Montpetit, Melanie. 2007. 'Empire, Desire and Violence: A Queer Transnational Feminist Reading of the Prisoner "Abuse" in Abu Ghraib and the Question of "Gender Equality"'. *International Feminist Journal of Politics* 9 (1): 38–59.

Risen, James. 2010. 'US Identifies Vast Mineral Riches in Afghanistan'. *New York Times*, 14 June. *http://www.nytimes.com/2010/06/14/world/asia/14minerals.html*.

Roberts, Adrienne, and Susanne Soederberg. 2012. 'Gender Equality as Smart Economics? A critique of the 2012 World Development Report'. *Third World Quarterly* 33 (5): 949–68.

Robinson, Fiona. 1999. *Globalizing Care: Ethics, Feminist Theory and International Relations*. Boulder, CO: Westview Press.

Roodman, David. 2012. *Due Diligence: An Impertinent Inquiry into Microfinance*. Washington, DC: Center for Global Development.

Rubio-Marín, Ruth, ed. 2006. *What Happened to the Women? Gender and Reparations for Human Rights Violations*. Brooklyn, NY: Social Science Research Council. *http://www.ssrc.org/workspace/images/crm/new_publication_3/%7Bd6d99c02-ea4a-de11-afac-001cc477ec70%7D.pdf*.

Rubio-Marín, Ruth. 2012. 'Reparations for Conflict-Related Sexual and Reproductive Violence: A Decalogue'. *William & Mary Journal of Women and the Law* 19 (1): 69–104.

Ruddick, Sara. 1983. 'Pacifying the Forces: Drafting Women in the Interests of Peace'. *Signs* 8 (3): 471–89.

Ruddick, Sara. 1989a. *Maternal Thinking: Towards a Politics of Peace*. New York: Ballantine Books.

Ruddick, Sara. 1989b. 'Mothers and Men's Wars'. In *Rocking the Ship of State: Towards a Feminist Peace Politics*, edited by Adrienne Harris and Ynestra King. Boulder, CO: Westview Press.

Russo, Ann. 2006. 'The Feminist Majority Foundation's Campaign to Stop Gender Apartheid'. *International Feminist Journal of Politics* 8 (4): 557–80.

Saferworld. 2015. 'Reviving Conflict Prevention in 1325'. *http://www.saferworld.org.uk/resources/view-resource/890-reviving-conflict-prevention-in-1325*.

Salahub, Jennifer Erin. 2011. 'African Women on the Thin Blue Line: Gender-Sensitive Police Reform in Liberia and Southern Sudan'. The North–South Institute. *http://www.nsi-ins.ca/publications/gender-police-reform-africa/*.

Schia, Niels Nagelhus, and Benjamin de Carvalho. 2009. '"Nobody Gets Justice Here!": Addressing Sexual and Gender-Based Violence and the Rule of Law in Liberia'. Security in Practice 5. *http://reliefweb.int/report/liberia/nobody-gets-justice-here-addressing-sexual-and-gender-based-violence-and-rule-law*.

Sedra, Mark, 2009. 'The Future of Security Sector Reform'. Waterloo, Canada: Centre for International Governance Innovation (CIGI). *https://www.cigionline.org/publications/2010/11/future-security-sector-reform*.

Segal, David R., and Ronald B. Tiggle. 1997. 'Attitudes of Citizen-Soldiers toward Military Missions in the Post-Cold War World'. *Armed Forces & Society* 23 (3): 373–90.

Sheldon, Kathleen E. 2002. *Pounders of Grain: A History of Women, Work, and Politics in Mozambique*. London: Heinemann Educational Books.

Shepherd, Ben. 2013. 'Oil in Uganda'. International Lessons for Success. Chatham House. February. *http://www.chathamhouse. org/publications/papers/view/188959*.

Shepherd, Laura J. 2008. *Gender, Violence and Security: Discourse as Practice*. London: Zed Books.

Sivakumaran, Sandesh. 2010. 'Lost in Translation: UN Responses to Sexual Violence against Men and Boys in Situations of Armed Conflict'. *International Review of the Red Cross* 92 (877): 259–77.

Sjoberg, Laura. 2014. *Gender, War, and Conflict*. Cambridge: Polity.

Sørensen, Birgitte. 1998. *Women and Post-Conflict Reconstruction: Issues and Sources*. Darby, PA: Diane Publishing.

Sow, Ndeye. 2012. 'Women's Political Participation and Economic Empowerment in Post-Conflict Countries: Lessons from the Great Lakes Region in Africa'. London: International Alert. *http://www. international-alert.org/resources/publications/womens-political-participation-and-economic-empowerment-post-conflict*.

Sparr, Pamela. 1994. *Mortgaging Women's Lives: Feminist Critiques of Structural Adjustment*. Basingstoke: Palgrave Macmillan.

Spivak, Gayatri Chakravorty. 1988. 'Can the Subaltern Speak?'. In *Marxism and the Interpretation of Culture*, edited by Cary Nelson and Lawrence Grossberg. Urbana: University of Illinois Press.

Standing, Guy. 1989. 'Global Feminization through Flexible Labor'. *World Development* 17 (7): 1077–95.

Steans, Jill. 2013. *Gender and International Relations*. Third edition. Cambridge: Polity.

Stearns, Jason. 2011. *Dancing in the Glory of Monsters: The Collapse of the Congo and the Great War of Africa*. New York: PublicAffairs.

Stern, Maria, and Joakim Öjendal. 2010. 'Mapping the Security–Development Nexus: Conflict, Complexity, Cacophony, Convergence?' *Security Dialogue* 41 (1): 5–29.

Suhrke, Astri. 2011. *When More Is Less: The International Project in Afghanistan*. London: Hurst.

Swaine, Aisling. 2009. 'Assessing the Potential of National Action Plans to Advance Implementation of UNSCR 1325'. *Yearbook of International Humanitarian Law* 12: 403–33.

Sylvester, Christine. 1987. 'Some Dangers in Merging Feminist and Peace Projects'. *Alternatives* 12 (4): 493–509.

Sylvester, Christine. 1994. *Feminist Theory and International Relations in a Postmodern Era*. Cambridge: Cambridge University Press.

Sylvester, Christine. 1994. 'Empathetic Cooperation: A Feminist Method for IR'. *Millennium* 23 (2): 315–34.

Sylvester, Christine. 2002. *Feminist International Relations: An Unfinished Journey*. Cambridge: Cambridge University Press.

Tate, Tony. 2004. 'How to Fight, How to Kill: Child Soldiers in Liberia'. Human Rights Watch. *http://dspace.cigilibrary.org/ jspui/handle/123456789/18290*.

Tax Justice Network-Africa and Action Aid. 2012. 'Tax Competition in East Africa: A Race to the Bottom? Tax Incentives and Revenue Losses in Uganda'. *http://www.actionaid.org/sites/files/ actionaid/uganda_report1.pdf*.

Tertsakian, Carina. 2014. 'Burundi's Crackdown on Dissent Must Not Go Unnoticed'. *Guardian*, 28 August. *http://www.theguard ian.com/global-development/poverty-matters/2014/aug/28/ burundi-dissent-pierre-claver-mbonimpa*.

Theidon, Kimberly. 2009. 'Reconstructing Masculinities: The Disarmament, Demobilization, and Reintegration of Former Combatants in Colombia'. *Human Rights Quarterly* 31 (1): 1–34.

Thobani, Sunera. 2007. 'White Wars: Western Feminisms and the "War on Terror"'. *Feminist Theory* 8 (2): 169–85.

Tickner, J. Ann. 1992. *Gender in International Relations: Feminist Perspectives on Achieving Global Security*. New York: Columbia University Press.

Tickner, J. Ann. 1995. 'Introducing Feminist Perspectives into Peace and World Security Courses'. *Women's Studies Quarterly* 28 (3/4): 48–57.

Tickner, J. Ann. 1999. 'Why Women Can't Run the World: International Politics According to Francis Fukuyama'. *International Studies Review* 1 (3): 3–12.

Tickner, J. Ann. 2001. *Gendering World Politics: Issues and Approaches in the Post-Cold War Era*. New York: Columbia University Press.

Tickner, J. Ann. 2002. 'Feminist Perspectives on 9/11'. *International Studies Perspectives* 3: 333–50.

Trenholm, Jill E., Pia Olsson and Beth Maina Ahlberg. 2011. 'Battles on Women's Bodies: War, Rape and Traumatization in Eastern Democratic Republic of Congo'. *Global Public Health* 6 (2): 139–52.

Tripp, Aili Mari, Isabel Casimiro, Joy Kwesiga and Alice Mungwa. 2009. *African Women's Movements: Transforming Political Landscapes*. New York: Cambridge University Press.

Tripp, Aili Mari, Myra Marx Ferree and Christina Ewig. 2013. *Gender, Violence, and Human Security: Critical Feminist Perspectives*. New York: New York University Press.

True, Jacqui. 2012. *The Political Economy of Violence against Women*. Oxford University Press.

True, Jacqui. 2013. 'Women, Peace and Security in Post-Conflict and Peacebuilding Contexts'. Norwegian Peacebuilding Resource Centre, Policy Brief, March. *http://peacebuilding.no/var/ezflow_site/storage/original/application/350cb287327f86cdf2369b23c9 8a17da.pdf*.

True, Jacqui. 2014. 'The Political Economy of Gender in UN Peacekeeping'. In *Rethinking Peacekeeping, Gender Equality and Collective Security*, edited by Gina Heathcote and Dianne Otto. Basingstoke: Palgrave Macmillan.

Tryggestad, Torunn L. 2009. 'Trick or Treat? The UN and Implementation of Security Council Resolution 1325 on Women, Peace, and Security'. *Global Governance: A Review of Multilateralism and International Organizations* 15 (4): 539–57.

Turner, Mandy, and Michael Pugh. 2006. 'Towards a New Agenda for Transforming War Economies'. *Conflict, Security & Development* 6 (3): 471–9.

Turshen, Meredeth. 2015. 'Women, War and Peace in Africa: A Reflection on the Past 20 Years'. 2 March. *http://www.unrisd.org/UNRISD/website/newsview.nsf/%28httpNews%29/1DD7A E33859C2825C1257DF6004DEA51?OpenDocument*.

Turshen, Meredeth, and Clotilde Twagiramariya. 2001. *What Women Do in Wartime: Gender and Conflict in Africa*. London: Zed Books.

UN. 1992. 'A/47/277 An Agenda for Peace'. United Nations Secretary-General. *http://www.un-documents.net/a47-277.htm*.

UN. 1997. 'Women, Gender Equality and Climate Change'. United Nations Women Watch: Information and Resources on Gender Equality and Empowerment of Women. *http://www.un.org/womenwatch/feature/climate_change/*.

UN. 2004. 'A More Secure World: Our Shared Responsibility. Report of the High-Level Panel on Threats, Challenges and Change'. *http://www.un.org/en/peacebuilding/pdf/historical/hlp_more_secure_world.pdf*.

UN. 2013. 'Women and Natural Resources Unlocking Peacebuilding Potential'. United Nations Environment Programme, United Nations Entity for Gender Equality and the Empowerment of Women, United Nations Peacebuilding Support Office and United Nations Development Programme. *http://www.undp.org/content/dam/undp/library/crisis%20prevention/WomenNatural ResourcesPBreport2013.pdf*.

UN. 2014a. 'Background Information on Sexual Violence Used as a Tool of War'. United Nations Outreach Programme on the Rwanda Genocide and the United Nations. *http://www.un.org/en/preventgenocide/rwanda/about/bgsexualviolence.shtml.*

UN. 2014b. 'Guidance Note of the Secretary-General: Reparations for Conflict-Related Sexual Violence'. *http://www.ohchr.org/Documents/Press/GuidanceNoteReparationsJune-2014.pdf.*

UN. 2015. 'Statement by Kyung-Wha Kang, Assistant Secretary-General for Humanitarian Affairs and Deputy Emergency Relief Coordinator'. United Nations Office for the Coordination of Humanitarian Affairs. *https://docs.unocha.org/sites/dms/Documents/OCHA%20POC%20STATEMENT%20TO%20SEC%20CO%2030Jan2015%20CAD.pdf.*

UN Millennium Project. 2005. 'Investing in Development: A Practical Plan to Meet the Millennium Development Goals'. United Nations Development Programme. *http://www.unmillenniumproject.org/documents/MainReportComplete-lowres.pdf.*

UN Secretary-General. 2010. '7-Point Action Plan'. United Nations Secretary-General. *http://www.un.org/en/peacebuilding/pbso/pdf/seven_point_action_plan.pdf.*

UN Secretary-General. 2014. 'Report of the Secretary-General on Women Peace and Security'. S/2014/693. United Nations. *http://www.securitycouncilreport.org/atf/cf/%7B65BFCF9B-6D27-4E9C-8CD3-CF6E4FF96FF9%7D/s_2014_693.pdf.*

UN Women. 2011. 'Progress of the World's Women: In Pursuit of Justice'. *http://www.unwomen.org/en/digital-library/publications/2011/7/progress-of-the-world-s-women-in-pursuit-of-justice.*

UN Women. 2012a. 'Reparations, Development and Gender'. UN Women and UNDP. *http://www.unwomen.org/~/media/headquarters/attachments/sections/library/publications/2012/10/wpssourcebook-06a-reparationsdevelopmentgender-en.pdf.*

UN Women. 2012b. 'Women's Participation in Peace Negotiations: Connections between Presence and Influence'. *http://www.unwomen.org/~/media/headquarters/attachments/sections/library/publications/2012/10/wpssourcebook-03a-womenpeacenegotiations-en.pdf.*

UN Women. 2012c. 'Addressing Conflict-Related Sexual Violence: An Analytical Inventory of Peacekeeping Practice'. *http://www.unwomen.org/~/media/headquarters/attachments/sections/library/publications/2012/10/wpssourcebook-04d-addressing-sexualviolence-en.pdf.*

UN Women. 2012d. 'Gender-Sensitive Police Reform in Post-Conflict Countries'. *http://www.unwomen.org/~/media/head*

quarters/attachments/sections/library/publications/2012/10/wps
sourcebook-04b-gendersensitivepolicereform-en.pdf.

UN Women. 2014. 'Liberian Women Prosper with Newfound Skills'. 9 January. *http://www.unwomen.org/en/news/stories/ 2014/1/liberia-economic-empowerment-for-peace.*

UN Women. 2015. 'Women Take the Reins to Build Peace in Colombia'. 28 May. *http://www.unwomen.org/en/news/stories/ 2015/5/women-build-peace-in-colombia.*

UNDP. 1994. *UN Human Development Report: New Dimensions of Human Security.* New York: Oxford University Press. *http://hdr.undp.org/en/content/human-development-report-1994.*

UNDP. 2008. 'Empowered and Equal: Gender Equality Strategy 2008–11'. *http://www.jposc.org/content/JPOs/Workshops/Bang kok/Gender-Equality-Strategy-2008-2011.pdf.*

UNDP. 2013. 'Powerful Synergies: Gender Equality, Economic Development and Environmental Sustainability'. *http://www. undp.org/content/dam/undp/library/gender/f_PowerfulSynergies 2013_Web.pdf.*

UNDP. 2014a. 'DR Congo: Legal Clinics Help Victims of Sexual Violence'. *http://www.undp.org/content/undp/en/home/ourwork/ ourstories/RDC-lutte-contre-violences-sexuelles.html.*

UNDP. 2014b. 'Fighting Sexual Violence in the Democratic Republic of Congo'. *http://www.undp.org/content/undp/en/home/ ourwork/ourstories/fighting-sexual-violence-in-the-democratic-republic-of-congo.html.*

UNDP/BCPR. 2011. 'Women's Leadership, Voice, Economic Recovery and Access to Justice: UNDP in Action in Post-Conflict Countries 2010–2011'. United Nations Development Programme/ Bureau for Crisis Prevention and Recovery. *http://www.undp.org/ content/dam/undp/library/crisis%20prevention/undp-cpr-wom ens-lead-voice-econ-recover-access-justice-action-postconflict-countries-2011-05.pdf.*

UNGA. 2005. 'In Larger Freedom: Towards Development, Security and Human Rights for All, Report of the Secretary-General'. United Nations General Assembly. UN Doc. A/59/2005 (21 March). *http://www.un.org/en/events/pastevents/in_larger_free dom.shtml.*

UNGA and UNSC. 2008. 'Report of the Secretary-General: Securing Peace and Development: The Role of the United Nations in Supporting Security Sector Reform'. A/62/659–S/2008/39. United Nations General Assembly and United Nations Security Council. *http://www.unog.ch/80256EDD006B8954/%28httpAssets%29/ 904B9EE812B7591FC12573F400322816/$file/Joint+Seminar_ A-62-659_S-2008-39.pdf.*

UNGA and UNSC. 2013. 'Peacebuilding Commission, Seventh Session, Organizational Committee'. PBC/7/OC/3. United Nations General Assembly and Security Council. *http://www. un.org/en/peacebuilding/pdf/oc/Declaration%2026%20Sept %2013.pdf*.

UNHCR. 2015. 'More Than Four Million Syrians Have Now Fled War and Persecution'. 9 July. United Nations High Commioner for Refugees. *http://www.unhcr.org/cgi-bin/texis/vtx/search?page= search&docid=559d648a9&query=syria%20july%202015 %20worst%20refugee%20crisis*.

UNICEF. 1989. *Children on the Frontline*. Third edition. New York: UNICEF.

UNICEF. 2011. 'Child Poverty and Disparities in Mozambique 2010'. *http://www.open.ac.uk/technology/mozambique/sites/www. open.ac.uk.technology.mozambique/files/pics/d130873.pdf*.

UNSC. 2000. 'United Nations Security Council Resolution 1325'. United Nations Security Council. *http://www.un.org/ga/search/ view_doc.asp?symbol=S/RES/1325(2000)*.

UNSC. 2005. 'United Nations Security Council Resolution 1645'. United Nations Security Council. *http://www.securitycouncilre port.org/atf/cf/%7B65BFCF9B-6D27-4E9C-8CD3-CF6E4FF 96FF9%7D/PBC%20SRES%201645.pdf*.

UNSC. 2007. 'Statement by the President of the Security Council'. S/PRST/ 2007/3. United Nations Security Council. *http://www. securitycouncilreport.org/atf/cf/%7B65BFCF9B-6D27-4E9C- 8CD3-CF6E4FF96FF9%7D/Arms%20SPRST%202007%203. pdf*.

UNSC. 2013. 'Resolution 2122'. United Nations Security Council. *http://www.un.org/en/ga/search/view_doc.asp?symbol=S/RES/ 2122%282013%29*.

UNSC. 2015. 'Conflict-Related Sexual Violence: Report of the Secretary-General, S/2015/203'. United Nations Security Council. *http://www.securitycouncilreport.org/atf/cf/%7B65BF CF9B-6D27-4E9C-8CD3-CF6E4FF96FF9%7D/s_2015_203. pdf*.

Vayrynen, Tarja. 2004. 'Gender and UN Peace Operations: The Confines of Modernity'. *International Peacekeeping* 11 (1): 125–42.

Vayrynen, Tarja 2010. 'Gender and Peacebuilding'. In *Palgrave Advances in Peacebuilding*, edited by Oliver Richmond, 137–53. Basingstoke: Palgrave Macmillan.

Virtanen, Pekka, and Dag Ehrenpreis. 2007. 'Growth, Poverty and Inequality in Mozambique'. Country Study 10. International Policy Centre for Inclusive Growth. *https://ideas.repec.org/p/ipc/ cstudy/10.html*.

Vlachová, Marie, and Lea Biason. 2005. *Women in an Insecure World: Violence against Women: Facts, Figures and Analysis*. Geneva: Centre for the Democratic Control of Armed Forces (DCAF).

Volpp, Leti. 2001. 'Feminism versus Multiculturalism'. *Columbia Law Review* 101 (5): 1181–218.

Walsh, Martha. 1997. *Post-Conflict Bosnia and Herzegovina: Integrating Women's Special Situation and Gender Perspectives in Skills Training and Employment Promotion Programmes*. Training Policies and System Branch, International Labour Office. *http://ilo-mirror.library.cornell.edu/public/english/employment/skills/training/publ/pub12.htm*.

Watkins, Kevin. 2013. 'Equity in Extractives: Stewarding Africa's Natural Resources for All'. Africa Progress Panel. *http://www.africaprogresspanel.org/publications/policy-papers/africa-progress-report-2013/*.

Waylen, Georgina. 2007. *Engendering Transitions: Women's Mobilization, Institutions, and Gender Outcomes*. Oxford: Oxford University Press.

Waylen, Georgina 2014. 'Women and Constitutional Reform: Is a Seat at the Table Enough?' Development Progress, 29 May. *http://www.developmentprogress.org/blog/2014/05/29/women-and-constitutional-reform-seat-table-enough*.

Weber, Cynthia. 1994. 'Good Girls, Little Girls, and Bad Girls: Male Paranoia in Robert Keohane's Critique of Feminist International Relations'. *Millennium – Journal of International Studies* 23 (2): 337–49.

Welland, Julia. 2015. 'Liberal Warriors and the Violent Colonial Logics of "Partnering and Advising"'. *International Feminist Journal of Politics* 17 (2): 289–307.

Whitworth, Sandra. 2004. *Men, Militarism and UN Peacekeeping: A Gendered Analysis*. Boulder, CO: Lynne Rienner.

Willett, Susan. 2010. 'Introduction: Security Council Resolution 1325: Assessing the Impact on Women, Peace and Security'. *International Peacekeeping* 17 (2): 142–58.

Williams, Kristin. 2014. '10 Ways Syrian Women Are Building Peace and Democracy'. The Institute for Inclusive Security, 21 February. *http://www.inclusivesecurity.org/10-ways-syrian-women-building-peace-democracy/*.

WILPF. 2014. 'Gender, Economic, Social and Ecological Justice for Sustainable Development: A Feminist Declaration for Post 2015'. Women's International League for Peace and Freedom. *http://www.wilpfinternational.org/wp-content/uploads/2014/03/Feminists-Post-2015-Declaration.pdf*.

World Bank. 2003a. 'Breaking the Conflict Trap: Civil War and Development Policy'. World Bank Policy Research Report.

http://www-wds.worldbank.org/servlet/WDSContentServer/WDSP/IB/2003/06/30/000094946_0306190405396/additional/310436360_200500070100031.pdf.

World Bank. 2003b. 'Afghanistan – Transitional Support Strategy'. *http://documents.worldbank.org/curated/en/2003/02/2156908/afghanistan-transitional-support-strategy.*

World Bank. 2004. 'Afghanistan – Mining as a Source of Growth'. *http://documents.worldbank.org/curated/en/2004/03/3055454/afghanistan-mining-source-growth.*

World Bank. 2005. 'The Investment Climate in Afghanistan: Exploiting Opportunities in an Uncertain Environment'. *http://www.trade.gov/static/afghanistan_investmentclimate.pdf.*

World Bank. 2012. 'World Development Report 2012: Gender Equality and Development.' Open Knowledge Repository. *https://openknowledge.worldbank.org/handle/10986/4391.*

World Bank. 2014. 'Afghanistan: Country Snapshot'. *http://documents.worldbank.org/curated/en/2014/03/19424006/afghanistan-country-snapshot.*

World Bank. 2015. 'Burundi Overview'. January. *http://www.worldbank.org/en/country/burundi/overview.*

Young, Brigitte, Isabella Bakker and Diane Elson, eds. 2011. *Questioning Financial Governance from a Feminist Perspective.* London: Routledge.

Youngs, Gillian. 2006. 'Feminist International Relations in the Age of the War on Terror: Ideologies, Religions and Conflict'. *International Feminist Journal of Politics* 8 (1): 3–18.

Yuval-Davis, Nira. 2006. 'Intersectionality and Feminist Politics'. *European Journal of Women's Studies* 13 (3): 193–209.

Zarkov, Dubravka. 2007. *The Body of War: Media, Ethnicity, and Gender in the Break-up of Yugoslavia.* Durham, NC: Duke University Press.

Zine, Jasmin. 2006. 'Between Orientalism and Fundamentalism: Muslim Women and Feminist Engagement'. In *(En)gendering the War on Terror: War Stories and Camouflaged Politics*, edited by Krista Hunt and Kim Rygiel. London: Ashgate.

Index